To Jen

To an all round
great guy.

Paul Mells

i

Copyright © 2018 by Paul Mellor

ISBN 978-0692160596

You're Almost There

Sights, Sounds, and Exhilaration
of Running a Marathon in All 50 States

Paul Mellor

To Ben and Max

~ a father's love is always there ~

Acknowledgements

There's a big difference between running a marathon and writing about running a marathon. In the former, once you're done, you're done. In the latter, once you're done, your work is only beginning. The project needs to be revised and revised some more.

A special 'thank you' to Pegeen Singley, who took those beautifully typed written pages and marked them with her red pen. She even added a coffee stain on page 112. The talented writer and artist spent countless hours on this project. I am forever grateful to my dear friend.

To my brothers, Duke, Tom, and Don, and to my sisters Joan and Jackie, thank you for helping me qualify for Boston. One couldn't ask for better siblings.

To my parents, Don and Helen Mellor, truly, the best parents anyone could ever ask for. Thank you for all your love and support, for always believing in me, and for putting the map on the kitchen wall.

Thank you to all the spectators across America who clapped their hands and shouted, "You're Almost There."

Table of Contents

Table of Contents

Table of Contents

"I dare you to train for a marathon, and not have it change your life."

Susan Sidoriak
-marathoner-

If I hadn't seen it I would have starved. For over 20 years it was with me for every breakfast, lunch, and dinner. As long as the Scotch Tape was holding it, it wasn't going anywhere.

The map on the kitchen wall opened my eyes to a world outside my window. Every day, at every meal, I would look to that map to learn about geography and about our 50 states. I studied the eight states that border Missouri. I studied the four states that border each other. I studied the state that borders only one state. I'd quiz my sister as to which city is farther west, Reno, Nevada, or Los Angeles, California. I was glad my parents enjoyed the map too. One summer, they loaded all five of their kids into a station wagon, proving to my sister that Reno really is farther west.

It's hard to fathom taking five young kids cross country in a station wagon, but we had such a good time we traveled again the next summer. Years later, after the sixth child was born, a motor home replaced the station wagon and we went out again. After our trips, the map on the wall began to come to life. Places that once didn't mean anything brought memories, such as the town of Staunton, Iowa, where every house is painted white. I watched the beautiful sunrise outside of Gallup, New Mexico. It was as if the sun were sitting atop Interstate 40. I had always wondered why Montana was called Big Sky Country. After our trips I knew why.

My mother highlighted the map with routes we had taken. Several states fell victim to a blue, yellow, or red marker depending upon the year in which we traveled. There was a blue line going through Colorado Springs, Colorado. I have the pictures from the Air Force Academy to prove it as I sit on my Dad's shoulders. There was a

yellow line going through the Grand Canyon in Arizona. This was where my brother retrieved a toy I had dropped near a cliff. There was a red line going through Browning, Montana. That's where we had a flat tire on the road to Glacier National Park. The tiny state of Rhode Island was filled with a mixture of reds, blues, and yellows because that's where all those trips began.

Friends would see the map and ask what all those lines meant. I'd tell them about the trips, while pointing to Sheridan, Wyoming, explaining how my sister's nose wouldn't stop bleeding. Not because I hit her, but because of the thin air.

I'd point to the Black Hills of South Dakota, describing how my brothers and I posed as Washington, Jefferson, Roosevelt, and Lincoln beneath Mount Rushmore. I'd tell them about campgrounds we stayed at in Burley, Idaho; Moorhead, Minnesota; and Kamloops, British Columbia. I'd amaze them by reeling off state capitals, one right after another: Columbus, Columbia, Salem, Cheyenne, Bismarck and Boise. I knew them all. I might not have been a whiz in Physics or French, but I knew Phoenix and Frankfurt, Montpelier

and Madison, and Juneau and Jackson. When *Jeopardy* came on television and the category was *U.S. States*, I'd wager everything. We never lost the house.

After spending two years at a junior college, I decided to transfer to a school in another state. I chose North Carolina. Why? I had never been there. Living away from home brought new responsibilities and decisions I had to make. I took a big chance going so far from home without first visiting the campus or community. It never occurred to me I'd be homesick and want to pack up and leave. After graduating from college, I didn't plan on going back to my hometown to live. I wanted to experience life in a place that was new to me in a different part of the country. My brothers and sisters felt the same. Today, my parents' six children live in six states.

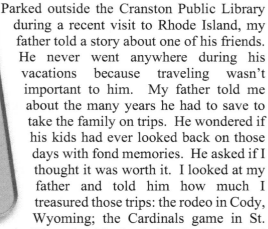

Parked outside the Cranston Public Library during a recent visit to Rhode Island, my father told a story about one of his friends. He never went anywhere during his vacations because traveling wasn't important to him. My father told me about the many years he had to save to take the family on trips. He wondered if his kids had ever looked back on those days with fond memories. He asked if I thought it was worth it. I looked at my father and told him how much I treasured those trips: the rodeo in Cody, Wyoming; the Cardinals game in St. Louis; Disneyland in Anaheim. I told my Dad how those trips opened my eyes to so many places and to so many people. I do not believe I would have ventured off to a faraway school, sold books one summer in the Midwest, or made my home in Virginia without so many wonderful years of traveling.

As we rode home from the library that day, I thought about how all those trips helped shaped my life, and thought back to that map on the kitchen wall.

My parents put something in me I couldn't shake. They gave me an appreciation and a love for my country. After college, I worked for AAA and continued to get the geography questions correct on *Jeopardy*. Decades later, there's a map on *my* kitchen wall. I still yearn to travel and I continue to study the states that border Missouri. Unfortunately, I've never owned a station wagon. Instead, I bought a pair of running shoes.

When I moved to North Carolina to attend college, my years of lacing up ice skates were over. There was no hockey team. After years of lacing up cleats, my years of playing baseball were numbered. I was cut from the team. However, across from my dorm, the lights to the track were always on. No one could prevent me from running.

There was freedom in running. I could do it anytime and anywhere I wished. If I didn't like the all familiar route of the track, I could run down dirt roads or across fields. The more I ran, the more I was building endurance, but running the marathon distance of 26 miles was out of the question.

Just off the campus of Western Carolina University in Cullowhee, I ran a 10-mile route. It was tough. I ran up the mountain by the Jackson County Airport and down the other side. When I got home, I flopped on the floor exhausted. To run 26 miles I'd have to go another 16 miles. How in the world can people run that far?

To me, the marathon was all about Boston. It was the only marathon I had heard of. From that city's bus station, my childhood friend, Tom Kenney, and I would walk the several blocks to Fenway Park. The Prudential Building, where the marathon ended, was on the way. On the ground floor, I studied pictures of the grueling race and those who partook in it. I looked at tired and struggling bodies. I saw people who were on the verge of exhaustion and saw expressions from those who looked like they had bit off more than they could chew. It didn't help that I already knew about that Greek runner, who in 490 BC, died from running that far.

I come from a family of athletes. My father, Don Mellor, played semi-pro hockey in the 1940's. My brother, Tom, was an Olympic Silver Medalist and played in the National Hockey League. Another brother, Don, is a professional rock climber and has authored several books. My older brother, Duke, the best conditioned of all, skates on frozen water and dives under waters that aren't. But none of us were known as runners. We were more like adventurers.

One adventure I had was when I was 14 years old. My brother, Don and I rode our bicycles to the highest point in Rhode Island. The roundtrip to Jerimoth Hill, elevation 812 feet, was about 50 miles. Three blocks from home, I vomited near Joe Piacitelli's house. I don't think he saw me. He would have mentioned it at school.

A year later, I joined Don and a few of his friends on another 50-mile trip. We walked from our home in Cranston, Rhode Island to Boston's Fenway Park. It took us 16 hours. We sat in the right field stands behind Reggie Jackson of the Oakland A's. Don't ask me who won. I do recall, when he met us at the Providence bus station later that night, my father said we didn't look too good.

The running bug hit our family in 1979. From my parent's beautiful lakefront cabin in Bridgton, you could see across Highland Lake to a race course that was part of the largest road race in Maine. The annual *4 on the 4th* brought hundreds of runners to Bridgton each July. Thank goodness, our founding fathers didn't declare independence on the 29th.

Highland Lake and the summer memories
in Bridgton, Maine

My brother may have the silver medal, but my mother, Helen, has all the gold. She has participated in almost all the races and has earned her share of age division awards. Standing with her before the start, she'd poke me to ask if that old coot over there was in her 70's. I don't know, Mom, but I'll do my best to trip her up.

The four miles was a piece of cake for my mother. She walked five miles every day. I'm surprised my father was never arrested when he'd pull off to the side of the road to let his 75-year-old wife walk home from breakfast. My mother insisted.

Go Mom!

1962 in California ...

... 30 years later in Maine

Brothers, sisters, cousins, nephews, and nieces all came to Maine to run the race. In family photos you'll see many of us wearing shirts of the same type. We were now runners.

It's been said a marathon is like a mini Mount Everest that comes to a town near you.

In 1987 I moved to Richmond, VA.

My adventure was about to begin.

What Was I Thinking
in
RICHMOND, VIRGINIA

Richmond Newspapers Marathon / VA

Sunday, October 18, 1987
Age 28

2

The invitation appeared in the newspaper. It requested my presence, with other like-minded individuals, to take part in a fun and exciting event to test our mental and physical strength.

If those like-minded individuals reacted as I did after reading the invitation, the party would have been cancelled. I threw it away. When the invite appeared again and again over the following four weeks, I started to think I was being targeted. Each week I dismissed it, until finally I gave in. Maybe there was something to this bash. I let them know I was coming.

If it weren't for the event sponsor, I doubt I would have succumbed. Those ads kept coming for a reason. The 26.2 mile footrace was named the Richmond Newspaper's Marathon. The day after the party I cancelled my subscription.

The newspaper made no mention of the aches and pains I would endure. It made no mention of the blisters I would bear, the fatigue I would feel, and the misery I would meet. I do remember there might have been a line or two about the importance of training. So much for details.

I trained for this event, but it wasn't consistent. I was running one day a week, working my way up to 18 miles. Sunday through Friday was my Sabbath. With the rest, the last thing I wanted to do was over train. I made sure I was going to be well-rested come Sunday, October 18th, 1987.

I was excited to stand in downtown Richmond with over 500 competitors. I felt great and looked forward to my 26-mile city tour. Covering the distance a week earlier, I was confident I could do it again, even without the three-cylinder, 40 miles to the gallon, Geo Metro. I was ready to run.

An October noon start in the Commonwealth of Virginia proved the race was centered around non-runners. Midday south of the Mason-Dixon Line was not the best time to begin running 26.2 miles.

Separation between Church and State? How about separation between Church and Sportsman? Closed streets on a Sunday morning would have caused too much havoc for Richmond churchgoers. Plus, with the sun at its highest, it was an ideal time for spectators to step outdoors to cheer. It would be one of the few marathons in which no runner had to set their alarm clock.

Dashing off from downtown, we traversed through the urban campus of Virginia Commonwealth University and into the Fan District of this historic city. Many residents had parties on their porches or on their balconies. They were eating and drinking and yelling their support as the runners swept by. While deep in the pack, I called out to a group on a balcony to ask if I was going the right way. They assured me I was.

The course moved down the Boulevard and past the war memorial tower of the Carillon. On the left was the Byrd Park running trail where I ran those 18 one-mile loops. So far, the training was paying off. I felt great.

The course moved across the narrow and picturesque Boulevard Bridge. Fortunately, the orange cones were properly placed and we stayed off the sidewalk. A recent article told me about a runner falling through a broken slab, yet catching himself as his feet dangled over the James River. Years later, the bridge closed for major renovations, but on this day, we crossed safely while avoiding the 20-cent toll. However, as we continued running, I had a feeling the marathon was going to make us pay a much higher price.

Turning right onto Forest Hill Avenue, we were on our way to following the rapids of the mighty James. A couple of miles later, we crossed the river by way of the Huguenot Bridge.

Back on the north side of the river, General Lee was waiting. The steep climb, adjacent to the Country Club of Virginia, was nicknamed "Lee's Revenge." Legend has it a Northern marathoner gave it its name because it was the South's way of retaliating for the beating it received during the Civil War. However, if they wanted to punish Northern runners, why not make them pay a higher race

4

fee and make the course flat? As it was, the hill also punished native Virginians. But then, this was the city, to keep Northerners at bay, Southerners burned to the ground.

"Lee's Revenge" burned my energy to the ground. I was near the 18-mile mark and I was hurting. Maybe I should have done a few more laps at Byrd Park.

I was far from my groove while running on Grove with the finish, about six miles away, in front of me. So why did the course turn right? It was a turn I didn't want to make, but I had no choice.

We entered the multimillion dollar neighborhood of Windsor Farms. The area was home to best-selling murder mystery author, Patricia Cornwell. I felt I was up for a part in her latest novel. I was ready to drop dead.

The sun had been beating down on me all day. It was affecting me more than I wanted to admit. Oh yeah, maybe running one or two days a week had something to do with it too. It was amazing. I was surrounded by hundreds of people at the start. Where were they now? It's not like they ran in the opposite direction. We all followed the same course. Could they all be in front of me? Come to think of it, I had seen the back of a lot of shirts today.

Every now and then I'd hear footsteps behind me. The steps would get louder and louder. They were closing in on me. "Hang in there," I'd hear. Afterwards, the footsteps would get softer and softer, and soon I'd be by myself again.

A few miles from the finish, while running on Monument Avenue, I looked up to the statues of Civil War Generals Stonewall Jackson, Robert E. Lee, and Jeb Stuart, envying them that they were atop a horse. Oh, how I wanted to sit.

It was well past 5 p.m. and I was all alone. The race had officially closed. The trucks going by, stacked with mile markers, confirmed it. The course I thought I knew so well confused me. I wasn't sure which way to go, but fortunately, my guardian angels did.

5

Two guys, who ran the half marathon earlier in the day, understood my pain. They ran up to me saying, "We're going to help you get to the finish." They encouraged me and made sure I stayed on course the rest of the way. At the rotary around the Robert E. Lee Monument, they told me the course followed the street, as I was prepared to go straight and over the grass.

Street lights were coming on when I moved past the Jefferson Hotel, and by the runner lying in the street clutching his sprained ankle. Well, at least I wasn't going to finish last. My new friends told me how most people could never cover the distance I had already run. They stayed positive and said, "You're almost there. We're going to turn right, then make a left." I was determined to press on even though my legs ached incredibly. When I came back into downtown, my buddies pointed out the finishing area. "You can stop now," they said. I would not have known. The banner was no longer there, neither were the spectators. The people responsible for awarding finishing certificates had left as well. The thought of leaving seemed like a good idea. I got in my car and drove home.

I watched highlights of the race on the 11 o'clock news. It was as if I were viewing a different race from the one I had participated in. The camera showed a throng of people cheering Walt Adams, as well as those who followed him. The finishing area was splashed in bright sunshine, looking nothing like the scene when I arrived at 5:30 p.m. However, I am forever grateful for my two guardian angels who were there for me. Without them, I seriously doubt I would have finished.

With a sigh of relief, I collapsed into my bed. I felt proud of my accomplishment and lucky to have found my two unnamed heroes who wouldn't let me quit.

Virginia

Robert E. Lee Monument

The Carillon - WWI Memorial

Beautiful Richmond, Virginia

7

A Monumental Run
in
WASHINGTON, D.C.

Marine Corps Marathon / DC

Sunday, November 8, 1987
Age 29

8

I n a town known for its influence and persuasion, Washington, D.C. changed my point of view too. But it wasn't done through the halls of Congress, nor through the powers of a President. In fact, I wasn't even approached by a lobbyist. No, it was something bigger than that. Can you say, "Marines Corps?" Good job Soldier. Now get back in line.

The Marine Corps Marathon opened my eyes to the enormity of the "World of Marathoning." There was the pre-race pasta dinner, the transportation to the starting area, and the medal awarded to finishers. By the way, did I mention the thousands and thousands and thousands and thousands of participants? Over 12,000 runners from around the globe converged on the streets of Washington. This was no ordinary neighborhood run. This was exciting, and I was right in the middle of it.

It had been only three weeks since I vowed I would never run another marathon, but the thrill of running in Washington, D.C. overshadowed the aches and pains I suffered in Richmond. Plus, I was feeling much better now, and the course map indicated there would be no "Lee's Revenge," a steep hill I could do without.

It was a short bus ride from the Pentagon parking lot to the start at the Iwo Jima Memorial. It was awe inspiring to see this famed monument of soldiers raising the American Flag. I had seen pictures of it, but it meant more to me to see it up close. My battle was a lot less significant.

The area was filled with runners and non-runners alike. I saw young and old, husbands and wives, and friends and family hovering by their athlete in waiting. Some of the runners were eating bananas or drinking water or having their pictures taken. Others were stretching in the grass or loosening up by the road or ducking behind the bushes, as runners have been known to do. In the distance, I saw the Lincoln Memorial, the Washington Monument, and the Capitol building. I was moments away from beginning a journey that would give me a closer look at them all. Tour bus not necessary.

9

I had never heard of this marathon, until after I ran the marathon in Richmond. I was surprised when I learned about the number of entrants and that the course would go past monuments, memorials, and museums. The streets belonged to us and we were welcomed, by not only the President, but by thousands of enthusiastic fans along the route.

The race information packet, given to me the night before, included a letter from President Reagan welcoming the runners to the 12th running of this event. The letter concluded with, *"Nancy joins me in sending our best wishes to all the participants in this magnificent race. God bless and keep you all."* If Ronald Reagan had left town during the day, it was most likely by helicopter. The streets outside his residence were mobbed with people in shorts, singlets, and smiles.

I stopped two miles into the run. I had no choice. The off ramp to another road created a bottleneck. The traffic jam quickly broke and I was on my way again.

After crossing the Key Bridge, we ran through Georgetown, past the Watergate Hotel, and Kennedy Center. We got a better look at the Lincoln Memorial, and then headed down Constitution to the Capitol. On the left I'd be seeing The White House, the Justice Department, and the National Archives, where the original copy of the Bill of Rights and Declaration of Independence is housed.

This marathon was a "We the People" event because it was open to anyone who had a desire to compete. It did not discriminate. I saw authentic runners who had artificial limbs and blind runners who had a clear vision to endure. Their sighted guide had to be quick to maintain the pace. I saw black and white, men and women, and heard many languages.

We all had reasons to come to Washington. Was it to lose weight? Was it to win or just to finish? Regardless, we all put one foot in front of the other, doing it over and over again about 42,000 times. Collectively, we reached for 270,000 cups, and drank over 21,000 gallons of water and sports drink. We were all in this together.

10

We ran past the American and Natural History Museums. We passed the Capitol and looked up the long steps to the Supreme Court building. We turned onto Independence on our way by the Air and Space Museum, Hirshhorn Museum and Sculpture Garden, and by the red castle of the Smithsonian.

The streets were lined with people. Many were cheering, others were playing politics with a sense of humor. As I ran down Independence, I saw a tall gentleman, attired in a judge's robe, puffing on a gigantic makeshift marijuana cigarette. He'd take a puff and then offer a smoke to the runners. Evidently, he knew nothing about the "runner's high" we were already experiencing. What he did know about was the front pages of the newspaper.

Judge Douglas Ginsburg, appointed by President Reagan to serve on the Supreme Court, failed to get confirmation. Questions were raised about his past marijuana use.

From Independence, the course turned left toward Haines Point across from the Jefferson Memorial. The monuments and the beautiful architectural buildings were behind us. There were fewer spectators, fewer historical sites, and a lot more physical pain.

Surrounded by trees, grass, and alongside the Potomac River, I watched planes landing at nearby National Airport, now known as Reagan National Airport. I was anxiously awaiting my final approach too.

The route was out and back before we would cross the bridge returning to Arlington, Virginia, for the final two-mile push to the finish. The runners going the other way looked a lot better than the way I looked. I'm sure they felt a little better too.

I was running slowly and was passed by many runners, including a tiny, slender woman running with tremendous ease. It was as if she were floating across the paved trail. Unlike my first marathon, I was never alone and far from finishing last. I continued to struggle but kept going. The encouraging words from volunteers and fans, along with music from *Rocky* and *Chariots of Fire*, were motivational.

11

Although I was hurting, I felt much better than I had in Richmond. It was exciting to realize I would finish before mile markers were picked up or street lights turned on. Of course, the early morning start was a big help.

I was running a marathon and feeling especially proud of myself, and then it happened. My confidence was shattered. I couldn't believe what was happening. A runner wearing a tuxedo passed. He was jovial and kept a steady pace. With only a mile to go, he shot past me. It's one thing to get beat by an elite runner or even a runner who trained more, but from a guy wearing a tuxedo? That's just plain embarrassing.

The sign read, "26." It was the first time I had seen a 26-mile marker in my short marathon career. I had only 385 yards to go. I visualized running down a football field, and running down another one and another one after that, when suddenly, Washington's version of "Lee's Revenge" occurred. I call it "Grant's Payback." The hill, just about 100 yards from the finish, was like Mount Everest. At least that's what it looked and felt like after running over 26 miles.

At the top of the hill, I turned making my way to the finish with the Iwo Jima Memorial on my left. I kept my head up and paralleled through the ropes, straight on to the end. I did it. I finished another marathon and flopped on the grass to rest my tired legs.

I shaved an hour off from my first marathon. I watched runner after runner following my footsteps. I felt like a real marathoner and vowed it would not be my last.

12

Let's see, I thought, I ran a marathon in Virginia and now one in the District of Columbia. I wonder if every state holds one of these crazy events. Oh well, it was just a thought.

Iwo Jima Memorial

Semper Fidelis

Cleaning the Streets
in
BALTIMORE, MARYLAND

Tour Baltimore Marathon / MD

Sunday, September 28, 1988
Age 29

S hoelaces were triple knotted, excitement was doubled over, and the mission was singular: Maintain a steady pace. The beginning miles were easy. I was seldom passed, wasn't winded, and even bypassed several water stops. Confidently, I shifted into a higher gear, passing even more people. I was one of the first to arrive. Then came the hard part: Get out of my car to run 26 miles, 385 yards.

If running a marathon is a glutton for punishment, what would you call awakening at 3:30 in the morning to drive 135 miles in the rain to run a marathon? I call it a long day.

The start began at the finish. I waited in my car at Patterson Park for the transfer via the rubber wheel trolley to Johns Hopkins University. It was comforting to see cars pulling up to the park with drivers getting out in shorts and T-shirts. I knew then I was in the right place. With the start and finish in separate parts of the city, I also knew I was about to get a great look at the city of Baltimore. The name gave it away too. This was the first annual Tour Baltimore Marathon.

Having moved the previous year from North Carolina to Richmond, I was anticipating frequent visits to Baltimore. A citywide revitalization was taking place, most notably, to the waterfront, bringing millions of visitors to downtown. A once dilapidated area, the Inner Harbor is a magnet for shoppers, strollers, and seals, with the latter being housed at the National Aquarium. In a few years, a flock of Orioles would nest nearby. After years playing at Memorial Stadium on 33rd Street, the Baltimore Orioles moved downtown to a state-of-the-art ballpark. Oriole Park at Camden Yards had become the envy of the league. Proving birds of a non-feather flock together, the football Ravens would later move into their splendid new stadium next door.

Yes, Baltimore was on its way back. Meanwhile, I was on my way to the starting line. Less than 100 runners took to the street outside the stadium at Johns Hopkins. The fan base was a lot less than the gathering who come to see the nationally ranked Johns Hopkins lacrosse games. Known as the fastest game on foot, lacrosse would take a back seat on this Sunday morning to the longest race on foot.

The tour didn't fool around. After a downhill first mile, the course shot upward for the next eight miles. Surely, you have 26 flat miles somewhere in this city, I thought. After conquering one long hill, I turned a corner and started up another.

Beginning at mile 9, the downhill running lasted for 3 miles. At mile 13, it was up and down for 10 miles. After looking at the race elevation chart, it made sense why the race began at the famed university known for its health care. The chart resembled an EKG Monitor from a healthy heart. A few more hills and my EKG would have resembled a finish line.

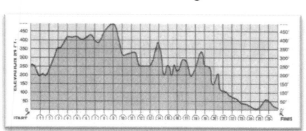

For a small race, we had excellent support. There were plenty of volunteers with cups of water at the end of their extended arms. I was amazed at the police presence. Officers at several intersections kept cars at bay allowing us to pass. I gave a wave and a quick "thanks" to all.

I was feeling strong when I passed the Baltimore Zoo and Towson University (formerly known as Towson State). The feeling remained as I continued through several neighborhoods. During one stretch, while running alone, a young boy shouted at me from his front steps. From the other side of the road, came "Hey Mister, Hey Mister." It was a great moment when I heard him call out to me. I felt like a true athlete on the playing field when I picked up the voice from the stands. However, I questioned whether to acknowledge him. What would other Baltimoreans have done? Would Johnny Unitas have looked up in the stands if he were dropping back to throw a pass or would Frank Robinson have stepped out of the batter's box to tip his helmet to a crazed fan? Probably not, but I did it anyway. I turned my head giving him my full attention. I showed that even though I was competing, I hear your voice. "Hey Mister, Hey Mister. Everybody has passed you." Thanks kid. Get back inside your house, you brat.

The clouds did not disappoint. It began to rain and rained hard. I was soaked, but not sapped. I continued running. Through the miles and through the streets of Baltimore, the course took us northward before making a southern swing through downtown and into Patterson Park.

With just a few miles to go, I discovered a runner's worst nightmare. My shoes were falling apart. The rubber foam was pulling away from my sole. I couldn't believe my eyes. How could this be happening? The strange part was my shoes felt okay, but they certainly didn't look okay. In all my years of lacing up and hitting the streets, I had never experienced this, nor had I heard of anyone going through something like this. I had heard of runners who injured themselves, which knocked them out of races, but not from equipment failure. Other athletes suffer through that, but not runners.

Race car drivers deal with flat tires, busted gaskets, or engines that just quit running. Baseball players break their bats, hockey players break their sticks, and tennis players break their strings. So, how in the world did I break my shoes? With every step I was losing foam. I turned away from the Inner Harbor on my way to the park, hoping and praying my shoes would hold out. Not only were my shoes coming apart, but they were squeaking. That's all I needed. Plus, the noise they were emitting was drawing attention to me. I didn't need this.

Wait a minute! It wasn't foam. It was SUDS! My shoes weren't failing me. It was just my mind. It all started to make sense. I had washed my shoes days earlier. It was the first time I had done this, and apparently, the washing machine didn't rinse very well. The Maryland Monsoon was making up for it. I was so happy, yet still a little embarrassed. I was leaving a trail of white suds all over downtown Baltimore. My shoes continued to squeak, but the Baltimore streets were never cleaner.

Approaching Patterson Park, I was cutting it close to breaking a sub four-hour marathon. I could see the finish, but the twists and turns of the path weren't going to bring me to the line in time. When I did cross the finish line the clock read 4:00:34. A runner "comforted" me by saying, "You just missed it. That's a real bummer." I thought, you don't have a little brother living at the 16-mile mark, do you?

The date was September 28th, 1988. I had made tremendous progress from my first marathon 11 months earlier. I was beginning to get accustomed to the marathon distance. It wouldn't be long before I believed I would break the four-hour barrier.

I was soaked when I walked back to my car by the curb at Patterson. I changed my shirt, buckled up, and headed home. I was tired. An hour into the drive I had to pull off the interstate to rest. I arrived home in the late afternoon.

In the runner's packet, given to me before the event, was not only my official marathon T-shirt, but a bumper sticker. I debated putting it on my car. I never was into bumper stickers, but I decided to make an exception. It meant I was determined, strong, and committed to my sport. The sticker read, Real Runners Run the Tour Baltimore Marathon. I could live with that. Although for me, it should have read, Real Runners Don't Wash Their Shoes.

Marathon #3 in the books

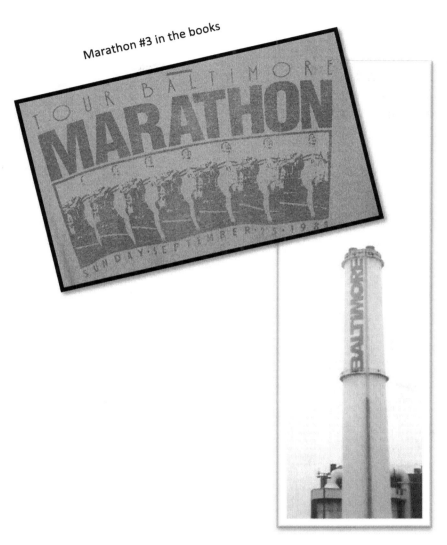

Can't ignore BALTIMORE

Misery
in
PITTSBURGH, PENNSYLVANIA

Pittsburgh Marathon / PA

Sunday, May 7, 1989
Age 30

Pittsburgh, Pennsylvania, a once smoke-filled steel community, was now a shimmering metropolis of skyscrapers, shops, and a spirit alive and well. In fact, in 1985, *Places Rated Almanac* had ranked the city as "America's Most Livable City."

On May 7th, 1989, I got my first look at Pittsburgh. By the end of the day I didn't want to look at it ever again. It rained, it snowed, and it sleeted. Of the 2,300 runners who finished the race, over 300 were treated for medical problems, 14 were sent to hospitals, and frankly, I didn't feel so great myself. Reporters David Templeton and Joe Sterling of the *Pittsburgh Press* summed it up best when they wrote,

It was not a good day to run 26 miles, not that many are, but in terms of suitability of weather conditions for the fifth Pittsburgh Marathon, consider that it was not a particularly good day to drive 26 miles. Just to drive it, you needed your intermittent wipers, your non-intermittent wipers (dual speed), your defroster, your heater, your rear window defogger, your all-season tires, maybe your glove compartment containing actual gloves and of course, special dispensation from Pittsburgh's barrier police. To run it in shorts and a T-shirt all you needed was to be just a little nuts.

It was fitting the race began at the Pittsburgh Zoo. They never should have let us out.

My host in Pittsburgh was my friend, Jim Duff. He had recently moved back to his hometown and invited me to his house. The night before the race, he gave me a tour of Pittsburgh. He took me to the best spot to look down upon the city, above the cog rail atop Mt. Washington. The skyline was difficult to see, as well as the rivers Alleghany, Ohio, and Monongahela. It was rainy, foggy, and there was a cold wind whipping across our faces. I looked at Jim and said, "Tell me it's not going to be like this tomorrow." He never answered. He didn't need to. The next morning, when I was stretching to prepare for the race, the answer became clear. Snow was falling outside the picture window. What is going on here? It's

21

May, for Pete's sake. The snow had subsided when Jim dropped me off at the zoo, but it would jump back into the race later.

The event was big in Pittsburgh. The four-year marathon had steady growth and the city had a reputation for outstanding fan support. This day would be no different. The race would get excellent media coverage too. I looked up at the news photographer documenting the start, as his leg hung comfortably out the helicopter door. He must have been strapped down. The video came out great.

I was into my second year of marathon running and I was already running with some of the best. Up ahead was Olympian Margaret Groos, who had run in Seoul the previous year. On this day she would win the women's division with a time of 2:31. I almost finished at 2:31 too, but that's 31 minutes after 2 p.m.

The course was marked by green feet painted on the streets. According to marathon officials, there were 534 green feet. I saw them all. During the day, those green feet had white snow, wet rain, and ice falling on them. All that precipitation was making me feel green too. The running tights I had packed in my carrying bag weren't meant to run the race in, but with sloppy weather conditions, it was the shorts, along with the short sleeve shirt, that stayed folded. The long sleeve Pittsburgh Marathon shirt received the night before remained on active duty.

Like many runners, I don't like to wear the trophy shirt until I've earned it. On this pitiful day in Pittsburgh I made an exception. I should have also worn gloves. For the entire race my hands were numb. They were numb when I ran by the Heinz building, numb when I ran by Three Rivers Stadium, and numb when I ran across the bridges of the three rivers. At the 11-mile mark it really got tough. Near Forbes Avenue it started to snow. I was running close to the old site of the Pirates ballpark, yet I was a long way from home. I would have hitchhiked to the finish, but my hand was so frozen I couldn't extend my thumb. I strongly considered packing it in, while thinking, what's the point? My body was trembling, yet I still had 15 miles to go. I didn't need to see any more green feet, but it was no use. I had to go on. There were no buses waiting to pick

22

me up, and I didn't have change to make a phone call. I had to go on. I had no choice. Plus, I told Jim to look for me at the finish line around noon. I couldn't afford to stop.

My run was labored, but I never stopped taking in my city tour. I ran through the neighborhoods of Oakland, Shadyside, Point Breeze, Homewood, and East Liberty. There were bands, balloons, and batons along the course that helped inspire me. It was incredible to see all those people venture out on such a miserable day.

When I signed up to run, I looked forward to finishing at Point State Park, the crossroads to the three rivers. I remembered seeing it on television when Phil Donahue had broadcast one of his talk shows there years earlier. The day was beautiful, with an abundance of sunshine, when Phil tossed his microphone into the crowd. I told myself I wanted to be there one day and to stand by the edge of those waters and look out toward the stadium. Now, running on Liberty Avenue with about six miles to go, I wanted to see that park more than ever. Thankfully, the rest of the way was slightly downhill, but what bothered me most was that stuff falling from the sky.

I was about 100 yards from the finish when I saw Jim standing by the snow fence. What a trooper! I was nine minutes late. Moments later, I crossed the line and received my finisher's medal. I caught up with Jim and we headed back. I was sick to my stomach. Back at his house, I felt better once I showered and ate. I declined his offer to spend the night and began my six-hour trek back to Richmond. It was the last time I saw Jim Duff. He accepted a position as an insurance executive in Charlotte, North Carolina. It was a better position and you can't beat the weather.

Yes, the weather. It's what comes to mind when I see the word, *Pittsburgh*. They are synonymous for me now. May 7th, 1989, set a record for the lowest mean temperature; the midpoint between the day's high and low, according to meteorologist Dave Sisk. With a low of 34° and a high of 45°, the mean was 40°. The high for the day was reached at 9 p.m. at a time when Pittsburgh was in my rearview mirror. That temperature tied a record that was set in 1958, the year I was born. Race Director Larry Kuzmanko said, "It was

23

bitter cold, nasty weather. But we had nothing to do with it. It's just indicative of Pittsburgh." A 15 mph wind, making it feel like 15°, was the result of Canadian air hovering over Pennsylvania.

There's a lot of Pittsburgh I had wanted to see. I would have liked to have attended a Pirate's game. The weather wasn't the only thing that kept them out of their park. They were on the road that weekend. I would have liked to have visited Heinz and toured some of the city's universities, but I was too sick to even think about it during my 26-mile ordeal. I would have liked to have stood at the banks of the Allegheny, Ohio, and Monongahela Rivers at Point State Park, but once I finished, I was finished. The area looked nothing like it had when the *Donahue* show was there many years before. Umbrellas replaced sunglasses.

Pittsburgh has been known to battle back from adversity. The weather battled back too. Forecasters predicted the high for the next day to be near 60°.

A medal of honor in the toy department of life

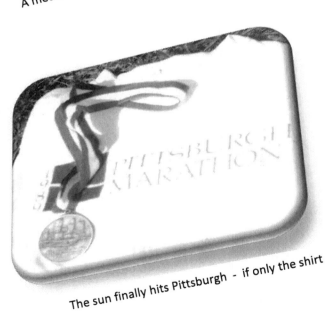

The sun finally hits Pittsburgh - if only the shirt

On Track
in
GREENSBORO, NORTH CAROLINA

Greensboro Marathon / NC

Sunday, November 12, 1989
Age 31

With less than a quarter of a mile to go, history was about to be rewritten. Unfortunately, the media didn't show and those standing by the finish didn't care. But for me, Sunday, November 17th, 1989, was a breakthrough. On that day, I finally broke the four-hour marathon. I was elated. Could the four-minute mile be next?

I had come close to breaking four hours before, but on this day, there wasn't going to be a doubt. With my finishing time of 3:25:45, I could have completed a sub four while walking the last few miles. From the looks of my number and shirt, I could sense this race was going to be different. My number was even, yet odd; 36C. Maybe that had something to do with why I *busted* out to a fast time.

The shirt, made from the same material used in building houses, was a Tyvek jacket. Its new home would be in the closet away from the typical marathon cotton T-shirts and would be worn only on wet or windy days. It would become apparent why it would not be worn on this day. Greensboro was a welcome relief from my last marathon six months earlier in Pittsburgh. The sunshine and blue skies was southern hospitality at its best. I was ready to run.

At the start line in front of Grimsley High School, over 100 runners were ready too. Many of those could have graduated from Grimsley. Over 90% of the participants hailed from the Tar Heel State.

The speedwork I had done in my training runs paid dividends in Greensboro. I spent a lot of weekend mornings on the track, which helped me run much faster through my neighborhood. The Greensboro Marathon was similar to those runs. The course also finished on a track. It was as close to a training run as I could have

27

hoped. The only difference was I didn't have to stop for traffic. In that sense, marathons are easier than training runs because you don't have to deal with distractions. Police hold traffic when you come to busy intersections, no one's dog is chasing you, you're not slowed by motorists asking directions, you don't feel compelled to retrieve a homeowner's newspaper, you know exactly where the other runners are going, and you're given drinks and fruit along the way. Training runs don't do any of that.

In a marathon the roads are yours. You know you're going to be encouraged and cheered along the way from people who don't know you, but who are curious about all the hoopla taking place in front of their home. Providing your training runs were put in, the marathon is the fun part. In this race, however, at the 10-mile mark a feeling came over me you never want to have during a race. It was a need to use the bathroom. Marathoners, typically, don't want to discuss this topic, but it needs to be dealt with before it gets flushed away.

USA Today did a feature on wacky 50 state hobbies. There are those whose goals are to climb the highest peak in every state, visit every state capitol building, play a round of golf in every state, and one person who actually had a goal to urinate outdoors in every state. That's one accomplishment 50 state marathoners have done, but don't talk about much.

It's important to note, in running 26 miles your feet will strike the ground about 42,000 times, give or take a step or two. Thus, gravity has a tendency to win out when the principle of "what goes in must come out" applies. In the chaotic minutes leading up to a race, you'll see runners, male and female, dashing off in different directions in search of a secluded place to lay their scent. If you ever want to find a lost dog, save your money on a reward and just hold a 10K in front of your house.

The organizers of the Greensboro race were smart. They had the marathon begin in front of a school with plenty of restrooms available. The only problem was this event was not a 100-yard dash that was going to be over soon. Marathoners are competing for hours and hours while taking in fluids along the way. Those high school facilities weren't going to be seen again for a long, long time. I continued to run after my 10-mile feeling, and fortunately, mind over matter won out.

The entire race mirrored my training runs. The course was a double-loop through beautiful neighborhoods of Greensboro. Runners were probably no more than seven miles from the finish line at any given point in the race. The many turns, which may have slowed elite runners, was perfect for me. Each street brought new scenery, new homes to look at, and more welcome distractions to keep my mind off the distance I still had ahead of me.

There were other factors that led to my fast time as well. The weather was ideal. The 100 or so runners didn't slow me as the throng of runners had in Washington two years earlier. I also slept well the night before, unlike prior to the Baltimore run. My attire, except for the race number pinned on my shirt, looked like all my training runs. On this day I wore my Marine Corps Marathon shirt, blue shorts, white socks, and Asics running shoes. To take my game to another level, the shirt would have to be replaced with a singlet.

Singlets are the official garb for the runner. They're lightweight while exposing your shoulders. I've always believed they were made for the lead pack; the racers, the ones who looked like they could win. I wasn't ready for singlets. It just wouldn't seem right to see a singlet wearer walking. The same is true for cyclists. You never see a cyclist who's wearing a colorful shirt walk the bike up the hill. If you're going to wear bicycle shorts and a colorful shirt, you have to stay on the bike.

Some runners in Greensboro weren't wearing shirts. My unofficial polling reports it was only in the male division. This is an incentive not to draft, although drafting wouldn't help marathon runners. Once you're out on the course, it's just you and your running shoes. No one is going to help you. A caddie, a coach, or a car isn't going to get you to the finish ... legally anyway.

That's what makes running so pure. You need no fancy equipment like those used by hockey or football players, no fancy machines like those used by cyclists or race car drivers, and you need no fancy uniform like those used by ballplayers, fencers, or equestrian riders. Plus, using a bat, a sword, or a horse will result in immediate disqualification. It's just running; pure and simple. It's a sport you can participate in for many, many years.

Unfortunately, the same can't be said for the Greensboro Marathon. The race is no longer held, but the memory, like the *Tyvek* jacket, lives on.

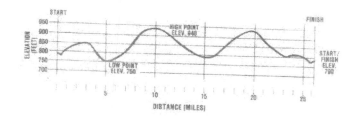

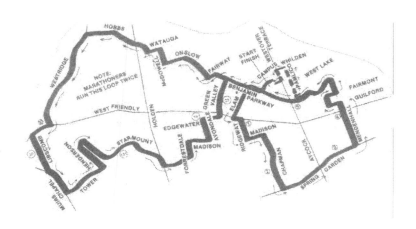

Decades later, the Tyvek jacket still holding up

The Balloons
in
LAS VEGAS, NEVADA

Las Vegas Marathon / NV

Saturday, February 3, 1990
Age 31

I prefer the window seat. I can see the mountains and the rivers, and spy on the miniature cars and trucks maneuvering down the road. On clear nights, I try to guess which city lies below as I'm speeding along at 600 mph from above. Is that Kansas City? Maybe it's Topeka or Wichita. I'm not really sure. Some cities are harder to distinguish from 35,000 feet. Other cities are much easier.

Over Chicago, Lake Michigan gives the impression half the city is going through a power outage. Over New York, the nighttime accentuates Central Park, surrounded by the glow of neighboring buildings. Then there's Las Vegas. Surrounded by all that desert darkness is that strip of sheen. Those desert lights are blinking and flashing and giving the impression they are in constant motion. The Las Vegas illumination is the longest running show in town.

Once I arrived at McCarron Airport, I was warmly greeted by actress Suzanne Somers, as well as my sister, Joan. One of the greetings came from a giant television monitor. As much as I regard Ms. Somers, it was great getting a hug from my sister.

Married to an Air Force Lieutenant stationed at Nellis Air Force Base, Joan, Jack, and children Shelby and John lived in neighboring Henderson. Their house sits in the fastest growing city in the country. It had been over a year since I had seen my older sister. After graduating from Utah State University and marrying Jack, the Air Force life had taken them to many places. They've lived in cities and towns, such as Alomogordo, Amarillo, San Antonio, Tucson, and Bentwaters, England. Their time in the Las Vegas area was running out. What better time for a visit. And yes, there was a marathon going on that weekend too.

The size of my luggage indicated I was a novice in air travel. It was appropriate when Joan commented, "Are you staying a month?" The suitcase was much too big for my two-day visit. I wore a suit and tie, brought several pairs of underwear, two pair of pants, and a few shirts. Plus, I'd add another shirt from the marathon. I brought shoes, an extra pair of shorts, and several pairs of socks. This was my first flight for a marathon. I didn't want to

33

leave anything out. In future trips I'd carry less and less. Over the years, I was able to bring very little on my marathon treks with the entire luggage fitting underneath the seat in front of me. In Las Vegas I wanted to be prepared for anything. Maybe it was just as well I brought a large suitcase. I certainly packed a lot in during my Vegas stay.

I arrived in Las Vegas at the best time: Night. Joan gave me a nice tour of the Strip and we stopped at the new Mirage Hotel and ate an ice cream cone. In the lobby, were two white Bengal tigers that were part of the Siegfried and Roy act. The performers would put the Mirage on the map with their sold-out shows. Thirteen years later, on October 3rd, 2003, the show would suffer a dark day after a tiger would attack Roy Horn on his 59th birthday. Tonight though, the city was anything but dark.

What started out in 1941, when the El Rancho Vegas wanted to draw customers by their flashy neon lights, had grown to be a *watt* of copycats. Each hotel and casino trying to outdo the next has their own light show. Las Vegas is not only a haven for gamblers, but also for moths. The lights are going all night long.

The Las Vegas Marathon stayed away from those lights. The race began in the town of Jean, Nevada, closer to the California border than it was to Las Vegas. There wasn't a lot to see in Jean, and I was convinced the town must have been named after its only resident. If Jean had come out of her home on February 3rd, 1990, she would have seen a lot of activity. Over a thousand runners converged on State Road 604 to run the race.

The runners came from all over the country and beyond. Not surprisingly, neighboring California led the way with 339, followed by 90 from Nevada, 59 from Utah, and the 2 that came from Brazil doubled the number that came from Virginia. Runners from 40 states and 5 countries, involved with copious occupations, came to compete. Twenty scientists, 5 social workers and 3 security guards strapped on their running shoes. Fifteen computer programmers, 12 contractors, and 5 casino workers competed. Twenty-three retired folk, 10 realtors, and 2 railroad workers ran. Nine electricians

34

exercised, 3 librarians laced up, and 7 postal employees pounded the pavement. But on this Saturday morning, none of that mattered. We all had the same job: run 26 miles, 385 yards to Sunset Park. The first one there wins. Good luck.

It was chilly when Joan dropped me off in Jean for the 7:30 a.m. start. I wore shorts, a short sleeve shirt, and white gloves. I was ready to run. I felt I was well trained for this event. My training mileage had increased as I was doing more speed work. I had the confidence because two-and-a-half months earlier I ran a 3:28 at Greensboro. I believed I had become a bona fide marathon runner. My goal was not just to finish, but to run the distance in a time that would qualify me to run the Boston Marathon ten weeks later. At age 31, I needed to run a 3:15 or less.

The Las Vegas course was considered one of the fastest in the country. It was a straight line for 23 miles before turning right for the final three miles to the finish. The start was at an elevation of 2,900 feet. The first nine miles were slightly uphill. It was downhill the rest of the way on a course that ran parallel to I-15, the main thoroughfare to Los Angeles. I covered the first mile in 7 minutes and 10 seconds. I averaged the next 22 miles at 7:20 per mile. I felt strong and knocked off mile after mile with ease. My training was paying off and the balloons were a welcome sight.

Yes, balloons. The greatest sight a runner sees is the mile marker. It provides information as to the miles covered and the miles to be discovered. Coming to a mile marker is a small success, knowing you've crossed one more off the list. Some marathons don't place a lot of emphasis on markers. Some marathons don't even have mile markers. The Las Vegas Marathon had the best markers I had ever seen. Each mile was represented by a cluster of helium balloons. Those beautiful, brightly colored balloons lit up the desert sky like brilliant rainbows. It wasn't as if I were running a marathon, but running from one set of balloons to another. The marathon was broken down to an attainable goal. Shortly after I passed one set of balloons, I could see the next set up ahead. The passing of balloons and miles went by quickly. I said "hello" to Joan less than 90 minutes into the race while she stood at the 13.1 mark. She would meet me at the finish. Seventeen miles, 18 miles, 19, 20, and 21 I kept my steady pace.

At the 23-mile mark the straight line ended, and sadly, so did the balloons as the course veered right. The remaining three miles seemed as if they were half a world away. Not only couldn't I see a balloon, I couldn't see the finish. I had lost sight of my goal. Strangely, once I turned the corner, I hit the "wall" that hits marathoners late in the race. My legs ached terribly and I was very dehydrated, even though I never passed up water at aid stations. I came to mile 23 in 2 hours, 54 minutes. Mile 24 would have to be patient. At the next aid station, I stopped and gulped down one sports drink after another. I also sat on the curb watching the parade of runners go by. I continued to drink and rub my legs. One runner tried to persuade me to run with him, but I could barely move. I motioned to him to go like a driver signaling a car to cut in front.

I was running so well with the Boston Marathon qualification time clearly within my grasp, but the marathon seemed as if it was three miles too long. With time continuing to slip away, my original goal changed. I would be glad just to finish the race. I sat for several minutes, and then I would stand to begin running, but walking won out. With less than a half mile to go, I started running and headed to the finish. Seconds from crossing the line, a runner almost tripped me while sprinting to the finish. I was a bit annoyed. A month later, I received the results and hometowns of all the runners. "Hey, Steven, I know who you are and where you live."

Jack, Joan, and the kids met me at Sunset Park. I was found flopped on the grass while holding my Pepsi and pizza. I asked myself, what went wrong? Did I train too much? Did I go out too fast? Was I affected by the long travel and altitude? Possibly "yes" to all those questions, but I think the real answer was the absence of the balloons. It was mentally too much for me to bear. I clearly lost sight of my goal, and in doing so, almost lost sight of the race.

Running a marathon is a difficult task. It's vital that not only your legs be strong, but also your mind. Every runner must be mentally tough, especially when the rest of your body is calling out for you to stop. I'm proud I finished in a respectable time, but not proud of my last three miles. At mile 23, I put myself within reach to qualify for Boston. My time of 3:37:04 was too slow. Coincidently, as I ran down Sunset Road and by the home of entertainer Wayne Newton, I saw the finish banner up ahead. The runners would run through an archway signaling the end of the race.

It was so unfair. The arch was covered with balloons.

In Vegas, qualifying for Boston wasn't in the cards

Smelling Salt
in
NEWPORT, RHODE ISLAND

Rhode Island Marathon / RI

Sunday, November 4, 1990
Age 32

Weekends in the fall attract thousands to Rogers High School. Its top ranked football team had a history of producing top athletes. Through hard work and dedication, the football program had won numerous state titles. However, the mob outside Rogers on this November day came to see another sport. How big was this event? Well, if you look over there you'll see a few politicians. "Hey, isn't that Senator Pell?"

Competitors from all over New England converged outside the high school, but the Senator was interested in only those who lived in Little Rhody. Rhode Islanders would go to the polls in two days.

The Senator had good intentions, as well as Claudine Schneider, who was running against him. But marathon runners don't want to hear any political speech when their toes are on the starting line. Political speech or any speech, it doesn't matter, we want to run. Sometimes the race director feels compelled to thank all those who made the event possible. The accolades go out to Johnson's Plumbing, Thompson's Auto Supply, and to the local pizzeria for their valuable support. As runners, we're extremely grateful for their sponsorship, but thanking them seconds before the start is useless. We're just plain not listening. Our feet are anxiously trying to catch up to our minds, which are already racing.

Whatever Senator Claiborne Pell said worked. He was reelected to his sixth term.

The Rhode Island Marathon was homecoming for me. I spent 21 years living in the Ocean State before attending college in the South. This day was special. My parents were there, my sister and brother and his wife were there too. And yes, did I mention my 20-year-old nephew David? He was there also.

David laced up to run his first marathon. Poor soul. He didn't know what he was getting himself into. Surely, the marathon would tear him apart. He did, however, quit running 3 hours and 11 seconds into the race. He had no choice. The miles had run out. Five months later, David ran the Boston Marathon in three hours and four minutes. He decided it would be his last marathon.

David was always a great athlete. In Little League, David's team came close to going to Williamsport for the national championship. In high school, he was a star football player. During his college years, he competed in the annual race to the top of the Empire State Building. All he did that day was climb the 1,860 steps faster than most. He placed ninth.

David became a star in another arena. Following the career path of his mother, who in 2004 was chosen National Teacher of the Year, David became a top-notch educator at Rhode Island's North Smithfield High School. I've always admired my nephew. On this day in Newport, I was following him in his footsteps, but then I was several miles behind.

Rhode Island had always been known as "vacationland." Newport had a lot to do that. The city had many lovely "cottages" that brought the likes of The Vanderbilt's, The Duke's, and other comfortable cronies to town. Many of those Newport mansions would be along the marathon route. Unfortunately, no one came out of the house to cheer.

Newport was also known for its popular Jazz Festival, the America's Cup races, and the National Tennis Hall of Fame. It was the perfect place to visit. It was the perfect place to run.

After a one-mile loop around the high school, the course made another loop back to the school, this one for six miles before heading out toward Middletown.

It was windy when I hit Ocean Drive. The kites at Brenton Point Park were high in the sky and not even a broken string would bring them down. I'd see those kites 23 miles later when the course came back to Brenton. Hopefully, the winds wouldn't take me down.

My pace had fallen off since the Las Vegas Marathon, as well as the marathon I ran 15 days later in Maryland. It would be another three years when I would better my time in the desert. Rhode Island was a bit of a struggle. The wind, the warmth, and the marathon wall had its effect on me. My pace slowed greatly when I reached 19 miles. Knowing I was going to be awhile, I was hoping my family was going to be patient.

There's always this excitement at the beginning of the race. I felt strong when I stood with my father, well behind the starting line, 20 minutes before the gun. Unlike a 50-yard dash or 5K race, the time it takes to complete a marathon is hard to gauge. I wasn't sure of my time, but I was quite sure I'd finish before David.

My parents came to many of my games in school. They cheered me when I stepped into the batter's box, crossed their fingers when a ground ball was hit to me at second base, and stood when a forward rushed up ice to shoot a puck at me in goal. This sporting event was different. Between the hugs at the start and finish, they never see you. The wider the gap between those hugs indicates how well you did. All they know is you covered the distance and you've accomplished something that 98% of the population hasn't done.

If my parents were to see me run, they would have had to follow me on Ridge Road, Harrison Avenue, Ochre Point, Memorial Boulevard, Hanging Rock Road, and many other streets and avenues in between. If they were on a boat they could have seen me all day.

The course stayed close to the waters of Narragansett Bay and the Atlantic Ocean as the racers made their way around Newport. Chasing down mile nine toward Easton's Beach, it was as if I was entering a sodium factory. I turned the corner at Ochre Point on Annandale and the smell smacked me right in the face. Yes, this was Rhode Island; the land with over 400 miles of coastline.

Near mile 11, on the other side of Easton's Beach, was a restaurant, where nine years later, I'd be smelling salt there too. It would be the site for my sister's wedding rehearsal dinner. It was apparent Jackie and Stuart would go the distance. As for me, I had another 15 miles to go. A few miles later, I was running side by side with

41

David, but only for a split second. We were running in opposite directions on Hanging Rock Road. Appropriately, he looked like a rock, while I was hanging on.

On Ruggles Avenue I was less than a mile from the finish. Unfortunately, the course veered left instead of right. I had six more miles to run. I saw more of Ocean Drive on this go-around than the last. My slower pace had a lot to do with it.

At the 24-mile mark I passed Hammersmith Farm. Over 30 years earlier, the site attracted a large gathering when another Jackie got married. The couple would later move into The White House.

On Harrison Avenue I said to the struggling runner beside me, "We have two miles to go. We've gone this distance hundreds of times with ease. We can do it now." The traffic going the other way was backed up on Harrison. This was no time to look defeated. I raised my head and raised my energy. I looked straight ahead and passed too many cars to count. I finished the 1990 Delta Dental Rhode Island Marathon in 3:57:36. I was happy I finished and relieved my family was still there.

The winner of the race was 42-year-old Bobby Doyle. He first won the event in 1976. On this day he claimed his 7th Newport title. Wow, a 7-time winner. Claiborne Pell couldn't even do that.

One more step to go ... maybe two

David, the 3:11:03 marathoner, with his grandfather

Magnificent Miles
in
CHICAGO, ILLINOIS

Chicago Marathon / IL

Sunday, October 27, 1991
Age 32

The Willis Tower, the Water Tower, Oprah, O'Hare, DePaul, Da Bears, and The L.

It's a city that's a must for any sports lover, museum lover, food lover, and anyone else who wants to see tall buildings, short plays, and a wide variety of interesting stuff. It's home to the Blues, the White Sox, and the green beer. In short, Chicago is red hot. It was my first trip to "The Windy City" and I was blown away with the anticipation.

In a city close to three million people, I was proud to know two of its residents. Cousin Rob Falciglia, an insurance underwriter, lived in nearby Lisle, and my very own sister Jackie, an aspiring actress, lived in the hustle and bustle of the city. Both had left their home state of Rhode Island to move to Chicago. Rob moved years earlier, whereas Jackie was a recent transplant. Rob met me at the airport and we immediately headed to downtown. After he skillfully parallel parked, we walked the short distance to Jackie's apartment.

The youngest of six children, Jackie, 25, was a recent graduate of the University of Rhode Island. She's a talented singer, comedian, and actress who decided if she were ever going to pursue her dream, now was the time. She already had friends in Chicago and knew the city was a great theatre town. While holding down a steady day job, she "acted up" on nights and weekends.

Looking to the left from her 6th floor window, I could see the Willis Tower (formerly known as Sears Tower), and the rest of the city's skyline. Looking down, I could see into other apartments. Before I could finish the sentence beginning with "Look, I can see ..." another sentence came booming from across the room. "Get your head back inside the window." Am I really to blame? With millions of people covering this metropolitan area, it's hard not to look into someone else's apartment. People are everywhere. They're walking, jogging, riding in cars, in buses, on trains, and eating in restaurants.

In Chicago, a person could spend years eating in a different restaurant each night. In fact, right outside of Jackie's building were several eateries within walking distance. We opted for Chinese.

It didn't take me long to realize Chicago would be a great place to live. I was happy for my sister in her new city and wished I had made a similar move when I was just out of college. What's not to love? I imagined taking the train to Wrigley Field for an afternoon game, then taking a train to Comiskey Park for a night game. Did Jackie have any idea how lucky she was? I envisioned working downtown, riding the rails, and making Chicago my kind of town. However, I do remember reading many years ago there were more rats in Chicago than people, but who's counting? The rats must have been hiding when I showed up. Of course, a few more minutes peering out the window could have alarmed Jackie's neighbors one was near.

It was a great reunion I had with my cousin and sister. We stayed up late talking and laughing about a lot of things, including the new comedy show, *Seinfeld*, that recently premiered. Rob even spent the night. Earlier in the evening, Jackie prepared a birthday cake for me. She promised it wouldn't ruin me for the upcoming race. The diet might not have been balanced, but at least the numbers were. In a few days I would turn 33.

The next night we all went to the marathon pasta dinner held at the Chicago Hilton and Towers. Little did we know, but two years later, the hotel would be the site of a fight scene in the blockbuster movie, *The Fugitive,* starring Harrison Ford. On this night, the only fighting going on in the full ballroom was over the mashed potatoes. The crowd didn't even boo when a Chicago Cub got up to speak. Fittingly, catcher Joe Girardi was well received.

On Sunday morning, with overcast skies and short periods of rain, I stood in the middle of the street near Daley Plaza waiting for the start. Anxiously, I shuffled back and forth until a photographer tapped me on the shoulder to stop. He was preparing to snap a low picture of the runners' feet in waiting. The poor guy. Over 2,500 runners all around him and I was the only one whose feet were moving. It's a good thing he snapped and got out of there because moments later those 5,000 other feet began moving as well. The race had begun.

Like any big city, I found myself in bumper-to-bumper traffic. It was comforting to know I wouldn't be running alone on the downtown streets. With so many runners converging on the streets of Chicago, organizers of the event had a dual start. A street over on Dearborn, a thousand other runners were anticipating their beginning as well. Hopefully, none of them were shuffling back and forth lest they also have to deal with the wrath of my new photographer friend. Shortly after the one-mile mark, my overall place ranking got hammered. The other runners blended into our path and I found myself farther down in the pack.

The course gave the throng a nice tour of the city, including the 1,454 foot tall Willis Tower. Upon its completion in 1974, Chicagoans could claim to have the tallest building in the world. That would change 23 years later when the Petronas twin towers in Malaysia were built. However, controversy remained as the height of the Malaysian towers included the antennas. The antennas atop the Willis Tower are not included in calculating the building's height, because they are not considered part of the building. Thankfully, the sport of marathoning strives to avoid such controversy.

A marathon is 26 miles and 385 yards, no more, no less. A lot of non-runners have trouble understanding that. I'm often asked, "How long was that marathon in Wyoming?" However, there are moments while enduring the pain and suffering, I have felt some marathons were measured a bit longer. Chicago, I'm sure, was 26.2.

I felt comfortable in the early miles. There was good reason. The sights, the sounds, and the side-stepping by runners made the race enjoyable. We passed Merchandise Mart, one of the largest office buildings in the world covering two city blocks. Just how big is that building? Well, if the hallways were to be connected in a straight line, it could be used for a 10K race with a little room left over.

The course took us into another world as we entered Chinatown. On both sides of the street, enthusiastic people cheered. Some people were dressed in colorful costumes, while others played music. It was a wonderful welcome. But in a moment's time we were gone.

Looking to my right, near the 10-mile mark, I could see Comiskey Park. I would have loved to have run alongside the park, but the busy Dan Ryan Expressway and the marathon course were preventing me from getting any closer. There was a consolation prize. Four miles later, I'd be running by the front gates of Soldier Field, but not before I'd be seeing a familiar face. There was Rob wishing me well near the 14-mile mark.

After running past the home of the Bears, I came across the home of the elephants, the dinosaurs, and the mummies. At the Field Museum they're always in complete harmony. On my left was the magnificent skyline of Chicago. On my right was the peacefulness of Lake Michigan. At the 20-mile mark, my view of the sand and the city changed places. I saw Rob again. He and Jackie were cheering me on. Rob had spent part of the morning helping Jackie move her belongings out of her old apartment and into her new. As much as I dislike packing and lifting, I was glad the Chicago Marathon gave me a legitimate excuse to cop out of moving day. I hoped Jackie understood.

The crowds were getting thicker as I ran down Lake Shore Drive. I could hear music coming from Grant Park and I was anxious to finish. My legs were tiring faster than the miles were ending. I made a quick turn at Roosevelt and powered my way to the finish. I cracked the four-hour mark by seven minutes, an hour after Rob's college buddy, Mark Clark, of Boston, cracked the three-hour mark.

Surrounded by sweaty bodies, I, Paul Mellor, located the "reunion area" with the makeshift post with the printed letter *M*, and waited for the arrival of Jackie and Rob. As Jackie walked up to me, a runner very close to us was throwing up. Fortunately, the sickly runner wasn't a Matthews or a Montgomery or a McCarthy. If he were, Rob would never have let us back into his car.

Wrigley Building

Chicago River

Homecoming
in
GREENVILLE, SOUTH CAROLINA

Upstate Marathon / SC

Sunday, December 29, 1991
Age 33

Sitting in a Cobb County coffee shop, while reading the classifieds in the Atlanta Journal-Constitution, was when I made the decision. Choosing to live in Atlanta was going to be expensive. I needed to try another city. I'd heard good things about Greenville. I'll go there.

Three hours later, I was lying on my new couch in my new apartment in Greenville, South Carolina. My post college life was officially beginning. Now what would I do? The next day, I secured a job with the Kirby Company selling vacuum cleaners door-to-door. For the next 13 months, I would knock on a lot of doors, and in doing so, would acquire a tremendous amount of business experience. In the school of hard knocks, little did I know I would be at the top of my class.

Although I worked six days a week, I still found time to exercise. I was on a bowling team, a softball team, and played hockey on Sunday. I also watched top young athletes play baseball at the new Municipal Stadium, home of the Southern League's Double-A Greenville Braves. After a year or two, the best ones moved on to Richmond. So did I.

Six years later I came back. I drove down Augusta Terrace and by my old apartment. Except for the car parked in front, everything looked the same. I drove past McAllister Mall, where I once shook Vice President Bush's hand during a campaign swing. I drove past Greenville Technical College, where I once waited for hours to hear President Reagan speak. I drove past the bowling alley, where on two occasions I bowled a 200 game. To fill the vacuum of time, I drove past the Kirby Company on Airport Road. The next day I took another tour of the city, but this time it was on foot for the 2nd Annual Upstate Marathon. I would be on the streets for almost four hours, covering over 26 miles. The good news? I wouldn't be knocking on any doors.

At the prerace pasta dinner held at the downtown Hyatt, I reintroduced myself to Ed Barreto. I had met him when he ran the Richmond Marathon and had heard a lot about his accomplishments. Not only had he run a marathon in every state, but during a 52-week period, Ed ran 84 marathons. I stood behind his wife in the buffet line and told her about my dream to run a marathon in every state. When I mentioned my goal was to run at least three a year, she said, "That's the best way to do it." Ed had developed knee problems. In fact, when I saw him in Richmond, he was shuffling very slowly before hitting the one-mile mark. To his credit, he had run a 26-mile race the day before.

Another well-known marathoner was at the dinner too. South Carolina native Bob Schlau was the keynote speaker. He was one of the best runners to have come out of the Palmetto State. That dreaded day in Pittsburgh two years earlier, when I was shivering at the 11-mile mark, 41-year-old Bob Schlau had already finished. His 2:22 mark earned him 8th place. I had always known Bob was a great runner. After hearing him speak, and visiting with him afterwards, I learned Bob is a great person as well.

It was cold and rainy on Sunday morning, December 29th, 1991. I squeezed every remaining minute in the comfortable Hyatt lobby before the marathon started right outside its doors. As we left Main Street the rain stayed behind. Hours later, the sun appeared and the day seemed perfect. December was the best month to run 26 miles in South Carolina. It's no wonder Greenville was ranked one of America's sweatiest cities. Summer months in this part of the south can do that for you. It would have been even worse had this course been used for a summer marathon. The course took us on busy roads that surrounded the city. There wasn't a lot of shade to hide under, but on this day, it didn't matter.

We ran on Augusta Drive, just a couple of miles from my old place. We turned right on Washington Avenue and then picked up Highway 253 on our way north of the city. At Bob Jones University we turned right, an appropriate direction for the Christian university. The school became a political hot topic years later when candidate George W. Bush chose to speak there. South Carolinians didn't seem to care. They helped elect him president. If runners had missed Bob Jones, they had another chance to see it. The course made a six-mile loop back to the school before going onto North Avenue for the remaining miles.

Near the university on Pleasantburg Drive, the traffic was busy and I was feeling the effects of running a marathon. A volunteer lifted my spirits. She cheered, "Paul, you're doing great." It's a tremendous feeling when you hear your name called. She was like my personal cheerleader. How could I let her down? She was holding a clipboard with the names of all the runners. She looked down seeing who number 53 was and called my name. Either that or she remembered me from knocking on her door trying to sell her an $850 vacuum cleaner. I didn't know her, but she made a big difference. As runners, we seldom have a chance to stop and thank people for their support. Usually, we're too focused to look and wave, but we hear them and appreciate their efforts. So, to the lady calling my name on the corner of Pleasantburg and Wade Hampton Boulevard, I say, "thank you."

I was hurting with just a couple of miles from the finish. Each step made me long for the end, but I continued down the steep hill on Richland. Those downhills can be worse than those uphills. I was hot and tired, and desperately wanted to see the finishing banner to come into view in Cleveland Park, but I would have to wait. I was running a steady pace, which means for me, I was running steady. I never stopped, yet my second half had been drastically slower. Glancing down to my left wrist, I saw I still had an opportunity to break four hours. Three out of the last four marathons I had run, I finished in the 3-hour 50-minute-plus range. Greenville was looking right on target.

Soon, I was in familiar territory. I could see the baseball field, where on many summer nights I had sprinted home. Why couldn't I do it now? I could see the finish in Cleveland Park, but I was being teased at the end. The route took us near the finish and through a trail in the park. Off to my right I saw runners finishing up. I was so close.

As I ran through the trail, I heard the sound of monkeys. Fortunately, my Greenville days told me I wasn't hallucinating or going nuts. Nearby was the Greenville Zoo and the animals were making their presence known. It wasn't as if a volunteer was calling my name, but the sound of the monkeys made me smile. Not too many people out for a Sunday jog could hear what I was hearing on this day in Greenville. It was the perfect ending to my long run.

My old college friend, David Sawyer, accompanied me to Greenville. A photography buff, David was by the finish waiting for me to return. A week later, he mailed to me the pictures he had taken. I had just crossed the finish line in 3:58:34 when he snapped the perfect picture. A volunteer was putting a medal around my neck, while another volunteer was tearing off the bottom portion of my race bib. Surrounded by these helpful souls, I looked weary and beat. I also looked relieved. I had good reason. It was homecoming in Greenville, South Carolina.

Welcome Home

With Sharon Mordorski, first woman to run a marathon in every state

Reel Him In
in
JACKSONVILLE, FLORIDA

Jacksonville Marathon / FL

Saturday, January 9, 1993
Age 32

What kind of welcome was this? Wasn't Florida known for its warmth and sunshine? Wasn't this the state where free orange juice was given to you upon entering the state at welcome centers? Yes, I knew that. I also knew about another Florida trait. It can get some nasty rain storms. I was welcomed with a beauty when I came through. On top of that, I didn't even get any orange juice.

The skies opened its arms as soon as I saw the welcome sign into one of the country's fastest growing cities. After I made out the sign reading *Jacksonville*, it was hard to make anything else out. The rain was pounding the windshield and the wipers were doing their best to keep up. I'm just grateful the windshield didn't break. Would the people at Enterprise Rent-A-Car believed me if it had?

My destination was 1st Place Sports at Baymeadows Road to pick up my packet to run the Jacksonville Marathon the next day. Good luck was on my side. I found the store and the sun was out. Things were looking up. But when I got into my car to drive away, I realized I had left my bib number back at the store. Quickly, I ran back and nonchalantly grabbed it off the water cooler. I clutched that #97 tightly and headed back out the door.

At the Holiday Inn, my life was staring right back at me. I was walking down the hallway to the marathon pasta dinner when I passed a meeting room. I recognized the timing lights and paused outside the door. A Toastmasters contest was going on. My two loves were in the same building. Which way do I go? Do I want to stay for Toastmasters or go to the marathon dinner? Shortly after moving to Richmond, I joined a Toastmasters club. The organization was founded to help people improve their communication skills. I was the past President of the Richmond Toastmasters Club and competed in several contests.

Toastmasters was a big part of my life. I worked hours writing and rehearsing speeches. I also spent hours running. My two interests were speaking and marathons. On this night my two worlds collided. After a short stay, I continued walking down the hallway to the pasta dinner. Soon, my thoughts were strictly on running.

Every visit I had made to Florida had been hot. It didn't matter which month I was there. There's a reason why it's known as The Sunshine State. I felt a little apprehensive about running 26 miles, 385 yards in Florida. I do not run well in heat, and I was hoping I wouldn't have to deal with much of it. It helped that the event was in January and the start began at 8 a.m. However, the scene at Bolles School on marathon morning gave me some concern. When I saw the swim team doing laps in the outdoor pool, things didn't seem right. Granted, every coastal state on the Atlantic has its January Polar Bear swimmers, but the guys I saw weren't getting out of the water. Where's that rain when I need it?

Since I started my marathon journey in October 1987, this was my longest layoff. My last marathon was in 1991. Now, it was January 1993, more than a year without running a marathon. A week earlier I ran a 5K race. My time was faster than anyone else on the course. Unfortunately, I took a wrong turn through the maze of neighborhoods in the Richmond suburb. Thankfully, the other 75 runners followed me. I was declared the winner in the longest 5K race any of us had ever run.

For Jacksonville, I felt strong and fast. My goal was a 7-minute, 10-second pace. I was ready for it. Instead of wearing my usual training shoes designed for support, I opted for the racing flat designed for speed. The shoes are extremely light weight and you just feel faster once they're on your feet. With my red shorts, red and white singlet and my red and white number, I was ready for action. So what if my shoes were green. Let the race begin.

Jacksonville was considered a fast course. It had received high marks from the running community where you could bang out a good time. There was another reason I chose Jacksonville. It was the closest Florida city to my home that held a marathon. The route was away from the ocean, but close to the waters of the St. Johns River, famous for its northward flow. However, the runners would be flowing south on Scott Mill Road. After a loop through the town of Mandarin, it would be back on Scott Mill again to begin the trip back north.

My major concern was not my feet, but my mouth. A year earlier, I had upper and lower jaw surgery correcting an open bite. Braces had recently come off my teeth, and I was running with retainers in my mouth. The doctor assured me the jarring wouldn't affect my teeth. It was the first time I was running with the retainers, and it took a little getting used to. But it wasn't long before the retainers got out of my mind and stayed fixed in my mouth.

I was comfortably clicking off the miles as I headed toward Mandarin. At the 10-mile mark, I felt as strong and as fresh as I did at the start. I was surprised at how well I was feeling. Was this right? Shouldn't I have been hurting a little? I was running a marathon. I've hurt in every 26-miler I've run. When was the hurt going to get me? Well, maybe I should have plugged that retainer into my mind after all because my pace began to slow.

At the halfway point, I noticed a strain in my legs I hadn't felt three miles earlier. People were starting to pass me. In the background, I overheard a runner lending support to his partner. He was giving him positive affirmations. They obviously worked. I heard him say, "Okay, get this runner up ahead. Reel him in." Afterward, he'd say, "Good. Now, let's reel in the next guy." I heard the "reel in" line about five times and suddenly, the next "reel in" was referring to me. "Okay, let's reel him in." Seconds later they did. The two of them passed me never to be seen again. I thought, you son of a gun. How dare you?

My thoughts drifted away from them and on to Harriet Beecher Stowe. Her house was no Uncle Tom's Cabin, but a nice corner lot in Mandarin. Aren't marathons great, I thought. How else would I have seen the home of one of this country's famed writers?

Boy, I wasn't feeling as strong on Scott Mill Road as I had the last time I was there. I could see now why rivers have difficulty flowing north. I was feeling their pain. Still, I kept moving, even though my strides were shortening.

Race organizers have a plan where a race will start and where it will end. Those are the first things discussed. It's filling in the remaining miles they wrestle over. Jacksonville was a nice course, but at the 24-mile mark the course veered into a neighborhood. I was getting comfortable running on San Jose Boulevard. I knew the finish was just up the road, but race officials had to find some more land to make the 26.2 miles finish on the track.

A race photographer was snapping pictures of the runners, as they were making their way out of Jose Circle, past the 25-mile mark. Knowing the picture was about to be taken, I pulled back my shoulders and swung my arms. But now as I study the picture, it looks anything but. My feet are dragging, as the runner behind me looks like he's in great form. Yes, he reeled me in too.

I turned left on the campus of the private school and ran around the soccer field, then made my way to the track for the ¾ mile run to the finish. My legs were in a lot of pain. I moved to an open area to lie down, but it wasn't easy. I slowly bent down and then dropped to the ground. The swimming pool looked inviting, but I probably would have drowned if I had jumped in. With my back on the soft green grass, I looked up to the warm Florida sun and felt proud of my strong run. My official time was 3:25:35, a pace of 7:51 per mile. It was my fastest marathon. I finished 131 out of 554, which means I did okay, but more importantly, it meant 423 runners weren't able to reel me in.

Still hanging on after 25 miles

That Big, Bad Lake
in
LAKE GENEVA, WISCONSIN

Lake Geneva Marathon / WI

Saturday, May 7, 1994
Age 35

I guess it could have been worse. They could have had us run around Lake Michigan or Lake Superior. You have to be careful when the race circles a lake. There are a lot of big lakes in Wisconsin. The town of Lake Geneva has a big one. However, if you know the word *lake* is in the name of the town, you should have an idea of what you're getting yourself into.

Considered one of the great blue lakes of the world, Geneva Lake has been attracting tourists for over 100 years. Its close proximity to Milwaukee and Chicago had brought the rich and the wealthy to its shores. In fact, here's something to chew on, pedal over, and hang out to dry with: Lake Geneva summer residents have included the Wrigley's, the Schwinn's, and the Maytag's. Too bad none of them were marathoners. If so, they would have arrived in the spring. Springtime in Lake Geneva attracts runners.

Ninety percent of the 127 runners in the Lake Geneva Marathon resided in Illinois or Wisconsin. The locals should have been grateful. If runners from around the country knew the beauty that was in this southern Wisconsin area, the town would have overflowed. I made the right decision to come to Lake Geneva, even if I did have to run around that big, bad lake.

My journey to Wisconsin began three days before the race when I arrived in Chicago. My sister, Jackie, graciously offered me a room in her apartment. I had visited her three years earlier when I came to run the Chicago Marathon. Since that time, she had moved into a larger place. My visit back in 1991 served me well for this trip. I had a better understanding of Chicago and I was able to find my way around. After a train ride from O'Hare Airport, I walked to Jackie's apartment. Knowing she was going to be at work, she left her key with a neighbor for me to pick up. I opened the door, dropped off my bags, and headed out.

I walked about 20 minutes until I got to the corner of Addison and Clark. I was in heaven. I walked up to the ticket window and traded a ten and a five for a box seat ticket directly behind the visiting dugout. It was a beautiful Wednesday afternoon and I was going to watch my first game at Wrigley Field.

May 4th, 1994, was about to become a memorable day in Chicago Cubs history. The home team had started the season winless while playing in the friendly confines of Wrigley. They lost 12 home games in a row. Since they couldn't win with their pitching, fielding, or hitting, they decided to bring out their secret weapon. On this day they brought out the goat.

Back in 1945, a barkeep was prevented from bringing his goat to the 4th game of the World Series. The man protested and even presented the goat's ticket at the gate, but it was no use. Legend has it this lifelong Cub fan placed a curse on the team that they wouldn't win another championship, because his goat was mistreated. The curse lived. Now, almost 50 years later, the Cubs let the goat in. My hunch tells me it wasn't the same goat, but it's the thought that counts. Before the game, the goat was led onto the field to erase the curse. The gesture must have helped. Chicago beat Cincinnati 5-2.

After the game, I walked away from the noisy crowds to the quietness of Jackie's neighborhood. She welcomed me and our reunion began. On Friday, we picked up a rental car and headed to Wisconsin. The traffic was heavy as I maneuvered my way out of the city. When I saw a yellow taxi cab with *NYC* printed on it, I was surprised to see the cab so far from home, but Jackie informed me movies are made very often in Chicago. Whatever that movie was, they weren't going to fool me. I knew which city I was in. Now, all I had to do was find the roads to get out of there. My co-pilot was on her toes. It wasn't long until we had Chicago in our rearview mirror. We headed north past Evanston, Winnetka, and Northbrook. We passed the amusement park, Six Flags Great America, and got closer and closer to Wisconsin.

It wouldn't be the first time Jackie and I had been to Wisconsin together. We made the trip 18 years earlier in a motor home with our parents. Our brothers and sister were either married or had other commitments, but traveling didn't stop our parents. Jackie and I were eager to go, riding in our motor home from Rhode Island to British Columbia. We got along much better on this trip.

The Lake Geneva Marathon shirt was clearly the best I had ever gotten. Of course, it would never be worn during a race, unless the race was to be run during the winter at Lake Geneva. The thick sweatshirt had a beautiful design on it with no advertisements on the back. So far, two for two, the pasta dinner and the shirt were tops. The forecast for the following day was preparing to break the perfect streak. The skies, like the shirt, were going to be gray.

The next morning, Jackie and I headed down to the lake for the start. I felt badly for her. We had checked out of the hotel, stores weren't opened, and it began to rain. At least I knew what I was going to be doing, but how about her? Jackie assured me she didn't mind and she would fill the time with activities. As the race director offered last minute instructions to all the runners, Jackie was standing off to the side, hovering under a small tree. Being the comedian she is, she started making funny faces at me. I tried hard not to laugh, but it was difficult to do. Didn't she know this was serious business? The race director was talking.

At 8:00 a.m., with Jackie standing under the tree, I ran off. I was hoping she'd still be there when I got done. I knew it was going to be a difficult run. The race brochure described the course as demanding, with unbelievable hills, and with a final run on an ancient Indian path. At least we didn't have to swim. It wasn't long before we left the town of Lake Geneva and entered the Villages of Fontana and Williams Bay. The beautiful scenic lake gave way to a beautiful pastoral setting. We ran by farmland, as I soon realized the run around the lake was taking a wide turn. We certainly weren't hugging the nine-mile lake.

I don't mind the smell of cow manure. I can deal with it if I'm riding in a car with the windows down, knowing I won't be able to smell the odor a few hundred feet down the road. The problem with this was that I wasn't in a car and I was smelling a lot of cow manure. Each turn of the road, the smell never went away, but neither did the cows. I started thinking, could this be the place where Mr. Wrigley invented gum, not to chew, but to block his nostrils? Could this be the place where Mr. Schwinn invented the bicycle, so he could get away from the smell a little quicker. Could this be the place where Mr. Maytag invented the washing machine after too many wayward steps? Finally, the smell from the end of the cows had gone away. I was now at the end of the lake. Still, I had a long way to go. I was running all alone. I was confident that most of my comrades were in front of me.

The course took an even wider turn the last half of the race than it had earlier. I was running farther and farther from the lake. I hoped Jackie was having fun. My fun was about to run out. I started missing the cows. I was a long way from farmland, running on a busy road. I doubted motorists knew a race was going on in their town. I looked like a solo runner out for a leisurely jog. But if I were, I wouldn't have chosen this stretch. I hoped the drivers understood that. Hey, it's not my fault I'm running on the edge of your highway. This was the way I was instructed to go. I was doing everything I could to put one foot in front of the other.

This must be the place where the unbelievable hill is, I thought. I have found it. Now, how can I lose it?

Slowly but surely, the course pointed back in the direction of the lake. I picked up the narrow Indian trail and zigged and zagged behind the heels of Carl Tolleson of Green Bay. I finished two seconds behind him at 3:57:52. I also finished smack-dab in the middle of the pack.

The first person I saw was Jackie. She enthusiastically greeted me with a big hug, as the smoke from the bratwurst filled the air. We sat at a picnic table, as I rested and tasted what this state is known for. A few minutes later, we walked to an ice cream shop and traded stories on how we spent the last four hours. Jackie said she got breakfast, and then walked to the library to catch up on some reading. She said the time went by quickly. I told her all about the sights and the sounds I encountered. But as we walked to the car clutching our giant ice cream cones, I thought better of telling her about the smells.

All smiles after the Lake Geneva Marathon

Harmony of Heartbeats
in
NEW YORK, NEW YORK

New York City Marathon / NY

Saturday, November 6, 1994
Age 36

Experts say it takes six months to prepare yourself to run 26.2 miles. The same can be said for registering for the New York City Marathon. Over 26,000 people had their entries rejected because they were sent in too late. They might have been fast runners, but they weren't fast enough. They couldn't even beat a guy with a broken foot. Like a college hopeful dashing out to the mailbox anticipating getting the acceptance letter, I let out a howl when the acceptance came in from New York. The opening line said it all, *Congratulations!! You're in the 25th Anniversary New York City Marathon.*

The instructions were clear. The registration was to be postmarked no earlier than midnight, May 15th, with a self-addressed postage paid envelope. That day in May loomed large. I was determined to get to the post office to drop that envelope in the slot. I didn't foresee doing it with a cast on my foot.

I was a weekend warrior playing in an "over 30" baseball league. I was standing on second base when the ball scooted past the catcher to the backstop. Suddenly, I put my head down and raced for third. Since my left side of my leg was a little sore, I slid into the bag leading with my right leg. My first thought was, I shouldn't have done that. At least I was safe. I returned to shortstop the last half of the inning, relieved a ball wasn't hit to me. I knew something was wrong. The cast stayed on for six weeks. Still, I had plenty of time to get ready for the November marathon in New York.

I jumped in the cab after the six-hour train ride to New York's Penn Station. It was my first time in the city as an adult and the pace was quick. The cabbie never slowed as I witnessed pedestrians jumping back on the curb. I was at the hotel within minutes. Traveling with my friend, Mike Ryan, we spent the first day touring the city. That evening, we walked out to the observation deck of the Empire State Building. The night was clear and the streets were busy. In a couple of days the runners would be taking over.

The next day, Mike met up with his New York friend, Denise. We had planned to have dinner at Tavern on the Green; the site of the marathon pasta dinner. That plan was quickly nixed. The line

69

stretched out the door and partway down Central Park West. The wait was too long. We took the subway downtown and dined at an Italian restaurant. After dinner, I left Mike and Denise and walked back to my hotel near Rockefeller Center. The next morning, attired in my running garb, I walked to Bryant Park and stood in the long line waiting for the buses to take us to the start.

The buses let us out on Fort Wadsworth on Staten Island. The field was packed with runners. The staging area was set up like an Army compound. Tents and toilets were set up, including the world's longest urinal, which I was proud to visit. The staging area was a great place to get acquainted with other runners. Printed on our bib numbers was our name, hometown, and age. It beat any bar scene for meeting people. The long wait at the staging area made me antsy. It was chilly and misty, and the start of the marathon was still a couple of hours away. We were all anxious to get going.

The race had three starting lines. The Blue Start, which would begin atop the Verrazano-Narrows Bridge; the Green Start, which would start on the lower level of the bridge; and the Red Start, for women starting on the upper level in the left-hand lane.

When the call came forth, I followed my fellow Blues and made my way to the start. I watched many runners discard their warm-up clothes and toss them in trees. It resembled Halloween night, but instead of toilet paper, the branches were decked in shirts and sweatpants. Organizers encouraged it. The clothing would be donated to New Yorkers in need.

My feet never moved when the starting gun was fired by Mayor Rudy Giuliani. It took a few more minutes before the mass in front started shuffling.

On my left was the New York skyline. I saw the Twin Towers and the Empire State Building, and the rest of the skyscrapers in this city of over seven million people. On my right, I saw quite a few runners who obviously never saw the world's longest urinal. They stood on the edge of the mile-long bridge raising the water levels to the river below. I was glad to get off the bridge.

The first few miles were maddening; wall-to-wall people of bodies in motion. They represented over 100 countries and 50 states. Waiting for the start, I stood next to a runner from Japan. Behind him was a competitor from France and next to him a runner from Ireland. The guy to my left was from New Jersey. The area was certainly a melting pot with thousands of runners representing different backgrounds, different religions, and different languages, but all with one mission. Our purpose was to get to Central Park as fast as we could. We came off the Verrazano Bridge and into Brooklyn. At the four-mile mark, we were joined by thousands of runners on our left. The Green Line turned into Blue. The New York City Marathon was getting crowded.

Most marathons have their aid stations on one side of the street. New York had them on both sides and down the center too. They did their best to make sure every one of the 30,000-plus runners had an opportunity to drink.

I ran straight down 4th Avenue in Brooklyn and watched the spectators cheering. We continued on Lafayette and Bedford and the applauding didn't stop. At the 13-mile mark, we crossed the Pulaski Bridge into Queens. For the next two miles, the spectators in this borough did what they were doing in Brooklyn. I saw people sitting by their upstairs window looking down on us. There were people in front of markets, gas stations, and brownstones cheering and clapping as the parade of runners went by. Coming off the Queensboro Bridge into Manhattan at the 16th mile, the sidewalks were packed with enthusiastic people. They made you feel like you were an Olympic champion. They gave me a rush that put more energy into my running.

On Fifth Avenue, balloons formed an arch over the street. Clusters of yellow, black, green, and blue balloons welcomed us into their neighborhood. All along the course marathon banners hung from posts. The city embraced each of us.

Sixteen, 17, 18 miles into the race, there was never much elbow room amongst the runners. It was bumper-to-bumper the entire way. Needless to say, I was surprised when a runner was coming my way. Was he going back for water? I had no choice. I pushed him aside like a fly when he approached me. I felt badly about it, but what was I to do? He was coming right at me.

The race took us into the Bronx, but we didn't stay long. Less than a mile later we were back into Manhattan. At 22½ miles I entered Central Park. I was almost home, but I didn't realize how long the Park was. I had three-and-a-half miles to go. The crowds were intense, as I edged by them on First Avenue and near the headquarters of the New York Road Runners Club. My legs ached considerably when I turned right onto Central Park South. After a right at Columbus Circle, the end was near. Wearing bib number 7663, I crossed the line in 4:07:17. It was a great feeling.

I walked a few yards and then sprawled out on West Park Drive by the baggage buses. I didn't care who had to step around or over me. I later caught up with Mike and Denise. Denise was excited telling me how she saw the winner in the park and congratulated him. She said the runner politely informed her he didn't win the race, but that every runner was awarded a medal.

Time was getting away from us. Our train was going to leave within the hour. Somehow, I found the strength in my legs to sprint to another train; the subway back to Penn Station. Unfortunately, we just missed the Amtrak back to Richmond. What a bummer! After a 90-minute wait, we took the next train to Washington. To our surprise, our missed Richmond train was still on the track once we arrived in D.C. The standard delay to change engines lifted our spirits. It was like we never missed a beat.

The next day while reading the paper, I learned a bit more about the New York City Marathon. The winner, German Silva of Mexico, took a wrong turn into Central Park. At 25½ miles he ran off course before correcting his mistake. He caught up with and beat fellow countryman Benjamin Paredes by two seconds.

I felt a special bond with German Silva. I almost missed the train. He almost missed the boat.

In appreciation of New York City Marathon founder, Fred Lebow (1932-1994)

Believing in Miracles
in
BURLINGTON, VERMONT

Vermont City Marathon / VT

Sunday, May 28, 1995
Age 36

The ride was a little bumpy, but no one was complaining. With the sun high in the sky, accompanied by a cool gentle breeze, it was a glorious day. Behind me were the Adirondack Mountains of New York. In front of me were the Green Mountains of Vermont and beneath me were the glistening waters of Lake Champlain. Standing at the rail with my brother by my side, life couldn't get much better than this.

When I signed up to run the Vermont City Marathon, I mentioned to my brother he ought to do it with me. Burlington is across the lake from where Don lives. Just think, springtime in Vermont, running along the shore of Lake Champlain, receiving an official marathon T-shirt. What's not to love? He accepted the challenge and circled Memorial Day weekend, 1995, on his calendar.

It would be his first marathon, but he was no novice in attaining great heights. The Dean of Students at Northwood School in Lake Placid, New York, Don was an expert rock climber and had authored two books. He was the leading authority on rock climbing in the Adirondacks and had logged over 100 first ascents in over two decades. I knew he could climb mountains, but was he going to find himself hanging on the end of his rope in my sport? I was five years younger, Vermont would be my 20th marathon, and I read all the running books. I told Don I was aiming for a 3:20 marathon. "Don't worry," I said, "I'll wait for you at the finish."

On Saturday, we drove away from left Lake Placid for Port Kent to catch the ferry to Burlington. Don, wife Janet, and their pride and joy, three-year-old daughter Elise, traveled in one car. I rode with Tom Broderick, a Northwood teacher who, like Don, was running his first marathon.

At 3 p.m. runner/author Jeff Galloway was scheduled to speak at the race expo offering his views and expertise on running a marathon. That didn't interest Don. That evening, the prerace pasta dinner was scheduled at the Sheraton. That didn't interest Don either. His plan was to run as hard as he could and to see how long it lasted.

75

He was an afternoon runner who never liked getting up early to run. He started each day with a cup of coffee and the next day would be no different. But this wiry guy was tough and he was prepared. He trained hard and ran several miles on hills the likes of Richmond, Virginia, don't have. He was a guy who had spent nights sleeping off the side of cliffs. He was a climber, a hiker, a skater. His lifestyle fit right into where he lived. His house was just a few miles from the rink where the American hockey team won its 1980 gold medal. Do you believe in miracles? Yes, but I still thought I was going to beat my brother in this marathon.

We drove together to the start, but in short order went our different directions. I did my usual marathon warm-ups. I stretched my legs and stood alone to get my mind ready for the miles that awaited me. I had done a lot of road work, put in long miles, and spent weekends on the track. I had endurance and speed. How much? I wasn't sure. But I was confident this run would qualify me to run the 100th running of the Boston Marathon the following April. That was my goal. That was my ultimate goal.

The course offered a beautiful tour of Vermont's largest city. We ran past the shops and restaurants in the town square, past the Ethan Allen Shopping Center, and through Burlington's rural areas. It was a great spectator course too. One could stand at the town square and watch runners coming and going all day. If you stood at Church Street, you saw runners at miles 2.5, 3.3, 9.9, 10.5, and 16.5. With Janet pedaling her bike and Elise strapped in behind her, I waved to them at one of those miles, but I don't remember which. I did see Don when I made the turn past the seven-mile mark. I thought he was going much too fast. I was sure he would pay the price later.

My pace was right on target, but the marathon was 10 miles too long. At 16 miles I looked north on North Avenue as I began a steep climb. I slowed tremendously. My legs ached and I was hot. A lot of runners passed, but none of them shared my last name. I kept looking back waiting for Don to show, but he never came. Tom Broderick passed me. "Have you seen Don?" I shouted. "No," the voice answered. I could hear the drumbeat from the band playing at the top of the hill across from the Sheraton Hotel. I was also listening to my heartbeat as I moved up the hill. With ten miles to go, I was suffering badly. Runner after runner went by, but none of them knew my name.

Near the 22-mile mark, the course turned south as we picked up the bike path along the lake. The wooded area shielded the sun. On any other day I would have thoroughly enjoyed this trail, but this day was different. I kept thinking when is this thing going to end? When is Battery Park going to come into view? Twenty-three, 24, 25 miles and the aches continued while my steps got slower and slower. Still, my brother had yet to catch up with me. He must be hurting too. At least I didn't start the day drinking coffee.

Amazingly, Broderick runs his first marathon and whips me. At least my older brother hadn't passed. Hey, I'm the marathoner here. Less than a mile from the finish, I leave the forest and enter the open field of the park. While running on the right side of the fence, I'm in shock at the face I see on the other side. What's my brother doing with a medal around his neck? How did he pass me? When did he pass me? I finished in 3:37:12. Broderick finished 10 minutes ahead of me. Don finished 10 minutes ahead of him. His time of 3:16:59 qualified him to run Boston the following year. My time qualified me to watch.

Don was sure I was ahead of him. That made two of us. He must have passed me between the 14 and 15-mile mark. I remember a cluster of runners going around me during a narrow part of the course. He had to have been running in that group. I was proud of his strong performance. The mountain running paid off. My brother wasn't smiling much. He was in a lot of pain. He headed to the medical tent and soon his health worsened. He was vomiting and medics were with him for a good 30 minutes. He felt so sick. He didn't look so great either. I, on the other hand, felt pretty good. I was eating cookies, drinking soda, and talking to Elise, who was nothing but smiles. Don said he ran as hard as he could, for as long as he could. He proved to be a true champion.

We decided not to put the cars on the ferry for the return trip. We took another route. I headed back with Tom. Janet and Elise were ·

in the front seat of the car ahead of us. Don was sprawled in the back seat. Back at Lake Placid, Don took his aching body straight to bed. He still felt weak and exhausted. That day Don gave up marathoning. But, seven years later he would return to Burlington for a race of another kind. It would be a race to save his daughter's life.

On February 10th, 2002, 10-year-old Elise was in a terrible skiing accident on Whiteface Mountain in Lake Placid. She was fighting for her life. An ambulance, with a police escort, sped the 90 miles to Burlington, Vermont, where she was to be treated at Fletcher Allen Hospital. Elise spent the next month in a coma as her father and mother stayed by her bedside. Don would later tell me he'd go for a walk, stepping on the same streets he had run on years earlier, while reminiscing about the marathon. That was a good day back then. One couldn't even imagine what his thoughts were now.

Doctors operated on Elise's brain several times. There were moments when her life was in danger and she might not have survived. But she fought back. When it was apparent she would live, doctors were concerned how badly her brain was damaged. After the coma, she didn't speak for three months and many of her basic skills had vanished.

I always thought my brother was tough. He proved it in Burlington when he muscled out a 3:16 marathon. His daughter is even tougher. She battled all the way back. She spent the remaining year with her regular classmates and made the honor roll. She has completed 25K cross-country skiing events and has run half marathons, including a personal best of 2 hours, 9 minutes. As her father says, her trademark is persistence, steady speed, no surges, no stopping.

In the summer of 2018, the college graduate, wife and mother is expecting her second child.

Do you believe in miracles? Yes.

Elise, embraced by her father, on Lake Champlain

Cold, Cold, Cold
in
COLUMBUS, OHIO

Columbus Marathon / OH

Sunday, November 12, 1995
Age 37

P eaceful is how I would describe it. Highway 23 was a stretch of pavement that went through some of the best farmland in the United States. I saw plenty of big open spaces, several red barns, and a number of diners offering a big country breakfast and a great lunch buffet. It was beautiful country in an area that appeared to be a very nice and quiet way of life, and then without warning, everything changed. I never saw it coming.

Those structures standing in the distance were no silos. The formation blocking Highway 23 was downtown Columbus, Ohio. There was no prelude, no introduction, and no warm-up to the entrance to the capital city. It was as if the city sprung right up out of the field. One minute I'm looking at farms, the next minute I'm looking at fumes. There were cars on the roads, people on the sidewalks, and buildings all around. Was this how the city's namesake felt when his ocean ran out in 1492?

The city was gearing up for a big weekend in Columbus. The marathon would attract over 5,000 participants, representing 37 states and 5 countries, but the football participants were going to attract more. The undefeated Buckeyes of Ohio State, playing host to the Fighting Illini, would play in front of over 85,000 screaming supporters. Maybe that's why it was so cold in Columbus. The fans kept coming.

I spent most of Saturday in my hotel room watching the hours of pregame hype to the big game. The local stations covered every angle of the game, including interviewing many of the tailgaters outside the stadium. The enthusiasm never waned. It was amazing, considering the day was cold and rainy. It appeared to be a miserable day to spend outside watching a college football game, but not for Buckeye fans. They were true fanatics. They hollered and howled for several hours before kickoff as the rain never let up. I was happy to be right where I was. I propped the pillows up in my bed and watched all the festivities. The next day would be my turn to face the elements. Forecasters predicted much of the same.

The 1995 Ohio State Buckeyes were winning big each week. The nationally televised game featured one of the greatest halfbacks the school had ever produced. In fact, on this day, Eddie George gained 314 yards, a school record.

It was getting dark when I left my comfortable room to drive downtown to the Nationwide Building, the site for the packet pick-up and pasta dinner. The temperature appeared to be dropping each minute. As I walked through the enclosed skybridge to the marathon expo, the wind and the cold were intense. It was brutally cold. I quickly realized my T-shirt wasn't going to be enough for the following day's long run. At the expo I bought a thermal shirt, hoping it would keep me warm. If that didn't work, I was ready to take out a Nationwide policy, only for their blanket protection.

The pasta dinner was held at Nationwide's spacious cafeteria. I sat with a husband and wife who had completed their goal of having run a marathon in all 50 states. They were easy to spot. The blue and white shirt, with the large USA map, told of their accomplishment. Ever since I began running marathons and learned about the "50 States Marathon Group" and the "50 and DC Marathon Club," I was in awe of these runners.

They were like major leaguers to me. I looked up to them and wanted to join their elite club. Although I was eligible to become a member of both of these clubs after running the minimum of 10 states, I opted to hold off. Like a major leaguer's quest to join the exclusive 3,000 hit club, I wasn't going to join until I reached 50 states. After 50 states, the blue and white shirt you receive has the all-important eight-letter word written on it other shirts lacked. I wanted *Finisher* on my shirt.

As I was sitting at the table with these finishers, a couple of people noticed the shirt and asked about it. "You mean to tell me you've run a marathon in every state?" You could see by the look on their faces how amazed they were that someone had accomplished such a feat. "Yup," they answered. "And he's run in 12 states." The inclusion meant a lot to me for my modest proficiency. For the first time, I felt like I was part of the club. To some, 12 states was a lot, but to me, knowing I had to do another 38 was a lot more.

Just as predicted, Sunday, November 12th, was cold and windy. I stood in the intersection waiting for the start when I noticed a runner wearing a Richmond Road Runners shirt. How about that? Here we were, two Richmonders standing side by side amongst 5,000 people in the middle of a Columbus, Ohio, street. I introduced myself to him and we wished each other luck.

A lot has been written about the runner's high; a euphoric feeling that comes over you after running a few miles. All the runners in the Columbus Marathon were on High for several minutes. They couldn't help it. High Street runs through downtown and was the street for mile markers 1, 2, 3, 25, and 26. It was the street where runners left from and where they would return to. High Street was well named. Not only was it a major street for marathoners, but it was also a major street for bars. From High Street, runners would turn left onto Dodridge, beginning a trek that would take us near the Ohio State campus.

The highest point on the course was coming up. At the six- mile mark we reached 900 feet. I doubt anyone could tell since there was less than a 200-foot variance in elevation on the entire route. However, I'm sure many runners felt lifted when they turned onto Woody Hayes Avenue, named after the legendary football coach. The street passed directly in front of the stadium. The scene looked different than it did on television the day before. There were no crowds, no tailgaters, and no noise. The only thing that hung around was the weather. It was cold and very windy. It would have been difficult to catch a football on this Sunday morning. With the runners spread out near the stadium, the wind was whipping. I still hadn't warmed up, even though the 10-mile mark was behind me.

The course took us back from where we started. At Broad Street, between the start and finish, we ran four miles to the east. Broad Street was a wide boulevard with plenty of room to run. We ran around Franklin Park and continued past the big homes and big trees by Parkview, Maryland, and Drexel Avenue. I was being teased on Town Street. Up ahead I could see runners finishing their work by the state capitol. I was hurting and straining, but I was far from the finish. Just a block from the finishing banner, the course turned left for the remaining three miles. I'm so close, must I turn left? It was disheartening to turn away from the crowds and the noise, but what else could I do. Quit?

On Deshler, I made my final turn on High Street with a little over a mile to go. A short time later, after running for 3:55:13, my job was done. Exhausted and weak, I sat on the sidewalk outside the capitol for about 30 minutes as the wind whipped everything in sight.

In the 16 years of the Columbus Marathon, this was the coldest day in race history. At 22°, I felt sure the record would hold for a long time. Race Director Joan Riegal and her staff did an outstanding job. Her volunteers carried water in buckets from two blocks away in order to fill cups, since five gallon jugs of water became jugs of ice.

I sat in the cold for a long time before I got my legs in motion and walked across the street to where the massages were held indoors. I walked inside, saw the line, and quickly decided I had stayed in Columbus far too long. I exited the building and slowly walked to my car.

I never changed my shirt, never changed my shorts, socks, nor untied my shoelaces. I got back on High Street, better known as Highway 23, and continued past the farms. A mere 479 miles later, I pulled into my driveway in Richmond, Virginia. I know I didn't finish last, but I was quite sure I was the last to take a shower. It almost lasted as long as my run.

A shirt and a medal warms things up

Oh, So Close
in
MIDDLETOWN, DELAWARE

Schweizer's Delaware Marathon / DE

Sunday, December 12, 1995
Age 37

All the training, all the miles, and all the hard work I had put in preparing for the Delaware Marathon, almost came crashing down an hour before the start. The patches of ice from my car to the high school, where the race would start, made for slippery footing. I wanted to "break a leg" in the marathon, but not break an ankle in getting there. As I slid over the ice, I looked to my left down the long road and wondered how much more of this ice awaited me. Maybe I should have worn golf shoes.

The 100th running of the Boston Marathon was four months away. It was the event every runner was talking about. The oldest footrace in America was going to be a grand affair in Boston. I wanted to be a part of it. I had less than a month to qualify for Boston and time was running out. I needed to run a certified marathon in 3:15:00 or less. I would need to beat my best time by almost 10 minutes. That 3:25:25 was almost three years before when I had to deal with the Florida heat. On this day in Delaware, it wasn't the sun I was worried about, but the snow. It was frigid. The temperature at the start of the race was 15°.

At the high school, I picked up my bib number and other goodies in the packet. Unfortunately, I had to walk back to my car to drop those goodies off. I made sure I walked very carefully.

I arrived in Delaware the night before and found a roadside motel less than ten minutes from Middletown High School. I was lucky. It was getting late into the night and there weren't many hotels in the area. When I turned the lights off and settled into bed, I thought about the race that would bring me to Boston. Qualifying for Boston had been on my mind for months. In fact, the words, *Qualifier for the 100th Boston Marathon,* were written on the back of the Delaware Marathon T-shirt.

Yes, I dreamt about Boston for many months. However, to prevent that dream from lasting too long, I made sure I had set all the alarms I could find. I set the radio alarm, my watch alarm, and asked the people at the front desk to do their part.

Saturday morning, December 10th, 1995, was sunny and clear, but the temperature was stuck in the teens and it wasn't about to move into adulthood. Snow covered the ground and all the runners were bundled up. I wore gloves, a long sleeve thermal shirt, and donned running pants, hoping it wouldn't take minutes away from my time. With all I wore, I noticed I was underdressed from what others had on. Most everyone else had more clothing on their upper body and everyone was wearing a wool hat. A wool hat was even on the Delaware Marathon logo, adorned by the sketched figure racing across the map of Delaware. The peer pressure to wear one didn't bother me. I was never much of a hat person, and not even the 15° temperature was going to change my mind.

The start took place in front of the school, a block from where I negotiated the ice. It was the only ice I encountered. The white and icy stuff were well-behaved by staying clear off the road. The wind, on the other hand, didn't obey. It pushed me from all directions.

The route quickly left the neighborhoods of Middletown and headed out of town. I felt strong and kept a 7:10 pace. I chose the proper clothing to wear, and the cold didn't affect me as it had in Columbus a month earlier.

My knee started to hurt about seven miles into the run. It was the first time I had experienced a pain like this. I tucked in behind a group of runners leaving them to battle the wind, as I battled my knee. I limped along for less than a mile and then the pain went away. It never came back. Looking across the open fields, I could see the turnaround for the last 13.1 miles. I was running strong and passed quite a few runners. I must have been running faster than I thought. I noticed a highway marker that read, "*Maryland.*" I knew Delaware was a small state, but I didn't know I was going to be running over state lines. Maryland or Delaware, it didn't matter. I was racing for Massachusetts. At the halfway point I was still on target for Boston. I was running and feeling better than all my previous marathons.

If any runner were to run a marathon in Delaware in 1995, they would be in Middletown on this day. This was the state's only 26.2 miler, even though some of it traveled into its neighbor's yard.

I was enjoying the simplicity of this course. I never noticed any spectators. I didn't converse with any runner. I grabbed water and sports drinks from each aid station. I kept my head up and powered on. There were no cars or bikes on the street and there wasn't a cloud in the sky. I made sure there wasn't going to be any in my head either. I was determined to finish in less than 3:15.

As the miles came and went, I checked my watch. My goal was still within reach, but I was losing some steam on my return trip. An ideal race is to run a steady pace or a negative split. I had never run a negative split, where the last half is faster than the first. The only negative split I had ever done was when I bent down wearing my new tight pants in the 6th grade. As the race wore on in Delaware, I was heading toward a positive split.

Although I was slowing, I was feeling much better than I had in the later stages in Jacksonville. Unfortunately, Boston was getting farther away from me. I continued to run as fast as my legs could go, but hoped there would be a two-mile patch of ice I could slide downhill to the finish. Finally, at 25½ miles into the race, the magic numbers on my watch appeared. I had been on the course for 3:15:00. My bid for Boston was busted. Still, I hustled on. Six minutes later I saw the official clock confirming my disappointment.

If I were a woman, or a man who was 50-years-old, my time would have qualified me to the starting line in Hopkinton. But for a 37-year-old male, a 3:21:20 wasn't good enough. Days after the race, I learned I was oh-so-close. Boston Marathon officials took the extreme cold into account and allowed an extra minute for qualifying times. My 3:21:20 was now just 5 minutes and 20 seconds too slow. I was disappointed, but I didn't dwell on it. I did my best.

It was the fastest I had ever covered the distance. As I sat on the bench in the boy's locker room, a guy came up to me saying I flew right by him at the last mile. That was nice to hear and confirmed I didn't give up. I told him I was six minutes too slow for Boston's 100th running. He said don't despair, and that I could still qualify by running in Edgewood, about an hour north of Baltimore, in three weeks.

December 30th would positively be my last opportunity to qualify for the 100th running of Boston. Appropriately, the race was called the Last Train to Boston Marathon. The race route would be four loops around the Aberdeen Proving Grounds. I wouldn't be the first in my family to go there. My grandfather, Friend Mellor, trained at Aberdeen during WWI. The big question was, would my body recover in time to run another fast time in such a short time period? I had no choice. I registered to run.

My sister, Joan, and her two sons, John and Andy, came up from their home in Northern Virginia. But it still didn't help. I suffered badly and finished in over four hours. As if on cue, at 3 hours and 15 minutes into the race, a train passed near the course. If that was the last train to Boston, then I just missed it. The biggest joy was when five-year-old Andy ran the last 50 yards with me to the finish. Later, my sister said she almost cried as she watched from her car as I walked with my head down to the gymnasium to shower. My sister has a loving heart, but I wasn't sad.

My big chance came in Delaware where I just missed the mark. After that race a blanket was put around my body and a medal around my neck. I walked through the snow and got back indoors. I got something to eat, got a massage, and then sat on the gymnasium floor of Middletown High School. I was tired and beat.

With the red, white, and blue ribbon still around my neck, I reached for the medal that hung from it. After I read the engraving on the back, I realized that's the reason why I run these things. It was the reason why I ran in the rain, woke up early to go to the track, and the reason why I had finished every marathon I started. So what if I didn't qualify for Boston. I tried my best. What more could I have done? I had just finished running a marathon. That's what I needed to remember. The medal reminded me of that with the words, Pain is temporary. Pride is forever.

After a personal record of 3:21:20

Symphony of Splendor
in
CARMEL, CALIFORNIA

Big Sur International Marathon / CA

Sunday, April 28, 1996
Age 37

It's cold and dark as the school bus moves down the highway. It's 4:30 in the morning and I can't see where we're going. I do know we're motoring down the California coast, and I do know there are a lot of turns and steep terrain along the way. What I don't know is if the driver got a good night's sleep. I'm praying he did.

How did I get myself into this position? I'm nearly 3,000 miles out from my home, nearly $500 is out from my wallet, and in nearly 20 minutes I'll be out of the bus, asked to run back to town. Still, I knew I'd be the envy of marathon runners everywhere. I was on my way to running one of, if not, *the* most beautiful courses in the world. The Big Sur International Marathon got high marks all the way around. Its beauty and the way the marathon was advertised separated it from the pack. It wasn't called the 11th running Big Sur ... or the 11th Annual Big Sur ..., but instead, the 11th Presentation of Big Sur. This presentation was going to be special.

Photographs I had seen of the marathon route were simply awesome. It was a must-see, must-run, marathon. I knew the several hours on the plane and the several hundred dollars to get here would be worth it. But you couldn't have convinced me now. It's still dark and the bus continues to roll along. The Pacific Ocean was right off my shoulder, but I couldn't see it. The thing I saw on the long bus ride was only wooden outlines in the shape of cellos. They kept popping up every so often. Finally, I figured it out. The cellos were the mile markers.

In the registration packet, runners were asked to come up with classical music themes for difficult parts of the course, such as *My Aching Bach* or *Decomposing at Mile 26*. Yes, the Big Sur Marathon was a classic in every stretch of the way.

The bus came to a stop a few hundred feet south of Pfeiffer State Park at the park's maintenance area. It was a magnet for yellow buses as more pulled in and more runners filed out. The race wouldn't begin for another 90 minutes and it was downright chilly. I stepped out of the bus and immediately started shivering. I had brought no warm-up clothes, no sweatpants, no long sleeve shirt, and no gloves. I hadn't even checked the day's forecast. Less than 10 minutes from walking off the bus, I walked back on, joining others who wanted to stay warm as long as possible.

The staging area was filling up with several hundred runners. The race instructions were clear. "You cannot drive to the start. You must take the bus." The area consisted of people and Porta-Johns. The beauty of Big Sur had yet to step forward.

Minutes before the start, I walked past the white starting line and turned back toward the runners. I snapped a picture. There would be more shots to come. For years, I had trained hard to qualify for Boston. Four months earlier I ran the best marathon of my life. Now, my marathon focus had shifted, at least for this race. Strapped around my waist was a carrying case. Its sole purpose was storing my camera. Big Sur was to be enjoyed and savored and I was determined to remember it for years to come. I wasn't concerned about time, wasn't concerned about performance. I was concerned with only getting good pictures from my 26-mile trek up the California coast. At 7 a.m., the race began and the photojournalist was off.

The ocean stayed behind the curtain of forest in the early miles. We passed country stores and went by Big Sur Village and Molera State Park. It was greenery and country on both sides of the road. With the morning warming up and the blue sky above, the day was getting better with each step.

The trees gave way to the Pacific, nine miles into the race. It was stunning. There couldn't have been a better way to experience this stretch of the Pacific Coast Highway than what we were doing now. You'd miss so much by zipping down Highway 1 in a car. Running was the only way. Smelling the fresh air, feeling the ocean breeze, listening to the crashing of the waves, and seeing all this splendor was a privilege. It's a wonder where a pair of running shoes can take you.

On our right were soft, green rolling hills. On our left were high jagged cliffs that met the waters of the Pacific. The waves crashing against the rocks changed the water color from blue to white. The setting was spewing greens and blues and whites. If this wasn't paradise, it was at least in the same zip code. To add to this beauty, musicians kept the beat going. At several spots along the course, classical musicians, decked out in tuxedos, entertained the passing onlookers. Violins, trombones, and cellos never missed a note.

The runners needed every ounce of energy they could get. Big Sur was not an easy course. There were many long, tough hills we had to conquer. It was not a course where you would do a personal best, it was a course that, personally, was the best.

After a 400-foot climb from mile 10 to 12, I stopped running. It wasn't because I was fatigued. I was at Hurricane Point when I ran up and my jaw ran down. The view topped anything I had ever seen. I looked down to the cliffs and the coast and saw the Bixby Bridge. The bridge is one of the highest single span concrete arch bridges in the world. It's also one of the most photographed. I know it was on this day. I've seen pictures of the bridge in television commercials, but it's just not the same as seeing it in person. A mile later I was running across it. At the other end of the bridge, I stopped to take a picture of Jonathon Lee. Dressed in a tuxedo, Lee was playing classical music on his piano. This marathon surely was different. I wasn't hitting walls, I was hitting wonders, one right after another.

I was having a ball as I continued north up the coast. Aid stations supplied more than your typical water and sports drink. There were tables of fruit, including strawberries, oranges, and bananas. I couldn't help myself. I ate at every station. I had run 20 miles and I think I was gaining weight. The food kept coming.

Closer to town, more spectators lined the streets. One little girl held a long tray of the biggest, juiciest strawberries I had ever seen. I helped myself to plenty. It was obvious the strawberries originated nearby. Monterrey, California, was known as the salad bowl of the nation. Lettuce, cucumbers, avocados, radishes, and strawberries flourished there. I was getting my fill of California's finest foods. Up ahead was another beautiful sight. In the distance at mile 25 I spotted the Porta John.

The Pacific was out of view as I lumbered the last mile of the race to Carmel. I had finished my roll of film and the race was coming to a close. It was approaching noon when the finisher's medal was draped over my neck. I had been on the course for 4 hours and 59 minutes. With my legs aching, I got on my back, right on the street near the finish. After several minutes, I walked to my car at Carmel High School to begin my 20-minute journey back to the hotel in Salinas.

I showered, ate more food, and drove back to Carmel. I spent the next few hours hiking at Point Lobos, which I had passed on the 24th mile of the marathon. Lobos was lovely. I walked the trails, oblivious to the fact my body had just endured five hours of running. I climbed the rocks and nestled into a spot directly over the crashing waters of the Pacific. I sat for hours, mesmerized by the water's movement. It was an absolutely beautiful setting and I was in my own little world.

I remained in California a few more days experiencing its coastline. I smiled as seals floated on their backs breaking clams with rocks. I was surprised how that lone cypress could survive out by the cliff. I shook when I swam at the beach in Pacific Grove. The Monterrey Peninsula was everything as advertised. Quite simply, it was a top-rate presentation.

California

Pacific Paradise

No going to Santa Cruz today

My cup runneth over

Making note of all this beauty

Through the Woods
in
ANCHORAGE, ALASKA

Mayor's Midnight Sun Marathon / AK

Saturday, June 22, 1996
Age 37

It began while I was enjoying a Dunkin' Donuts muffin and reading the USA Today when I heard those opportunistic words coming over the loud speaker.

Flight 625 is overbooked. Those willing to volunteer their seat for a free travel voucher, report to the ticket counter immediately.

The race was on. It was worth another night stay in Atlanta.

When I received my certificate for a free roundtrip ticket, I knew exactly where I was going. I had heard a lot about Alaska. From its glaciers to its grizzlies, from its midnight sun to its majestic mountains, from its unforgettable whales to its unforgivable weather, I was going to see it all. Yes, my mind was made up. My first choice was The Last Frontier.

If you look at a standard wall map of the United States, you'd think Alaska is directly below Arizona and is a part of Mexico. But with that white border around Alaska, your senses tell you differently. It's definitely a state, but it ain't exactly where *Rand McNally* put it. A better way of locating Alaska is looking at a globe. If you place your right hand directly on top, your thumb will be covering parts of our 49th state. It's the land mass, under Secretary of State William Seward, the United States bought from Russia for 2½ cents per acre. Critics of the purchase called it Seward's Icebox or Seward's Folly. Although Mr. Seward never ventured to the area, he was rewarded years later. Alaskans named a town after him.

June 21st, 1996, was a long travel day. It began at 3 p.m. at Dulles Airport on the outskirts of Washington, D.C. It ended at 1 a.m. the next morning in Anchorage, Alaska. Seven hours later, I'd be standing at the starting line at Bartlett High School to begin my 26.2 mile run in the Mayor's Midnight Sun Marathon. You might say I could have planned it a little bit better. Although the plane touched down in the middle of the night, lights were not needed at Anchorage International Airport. The sun was still in the sky, but it was slowly sinking. I turned the headlights on in my rental car, but I could have found the hotel without them. It was during the

Summer Solstice in Alaska and the sun was working overtime. Knowing it would nap for about an hour, I made sure my curtains were closed at the Merrill Field Inn, because the beams would reappear at 3 a.m. to begin another long day.

The marathon name was a misnomer. The race started at 8 a.m., but it still felt like midnight to me. My body's time clock was derailed from speeding through many time zones. I didn't know what time it was. When the sun came back to visit a couple of hours later, I was waiting for it. I was in no shape to run a marathon, but running wasn't my first order of business. I had to locate Bartlett High School. Fortunately, I arrived to school on time.

The excitement outside Bartlett resembled graduation day. All the faces wore smiles and the chatter heard was the anticipation as to what lay ahead. Many of the runners wore purple singlets representing Team in Training. These runners had raised enough money to fund their way to Alaska. Many of them were first-time marathoners who had worked hard to complete a six-month training program and to obtain donations along the way. My friend, Esther, was running her first marathon and I knew she was wearing purple. I looked for her in the parking lot, but never found her.

The route was going to be like none other than I had run before. We would run 4 miles on a bike path, 10 miles on a dirt road, and a few miles on a road named *Stuckagain*. Hmmm, and I decided to run this thing? The course would take us through tunnels, parks, and along scenic trails.

I took off from Bartlett not knowing what I would see nor what I would come in contact with. I was running in Alaska. I hoped the grizzlies were sleeping. Approaching the first mile, the thought of bears on the trail vanished. I had something else to worry about. A few feet from the first mile marker, I noticed a huge yellow sign with a picture of a moose. Underneath it read *Next 2 Miles*. Next 2 miles? What about the other 24 I'm going to be dealing with?

When we entered the Chugach Mountains, I couldn't help but wonder if the name *Chugach* came from what grizzlies do to you after they sink their teeth into your thigh. Every twist of the trail I kept looking around, waiting to be mauled by a moose or grappled by a grizzly. When I stepped over rocks, I anticipated rattling a snake. I didn't know if snakes were in Alaska, but I was ready for anything that could bite.

It was exciting to be running in Alaska. I couldn't believe I was here. Alaska was a place I had dreamt about. Although I was almost on top of the world, I felt like I was already there. The city of Anchorage was a few miles away, but the trail I was on seemed like I was deep in back country.

The marathon consisted of 70% paved and 30% dirt. The elevation at the start was 220 feet. The finish, at West High School, was at 90 feet. The highest point on the course was 500 feet. The temperature would rise to 65°. So much for Seward's Icebox.

Ten miles into the race, I passed some very slow runners and wondered how they were so far ahead of me. Later, I learned they had gotten an earlier start. I wondered if they saw that moose pictured on the yellow sign.

The terrain was dusty and rocky with no animals in sight. Organizers brought a skeleton on the course to indicate what happens if you don't take in fluids. My feeling was this is what happens if you stray off course in bear country. It was a bit unsettling to see that skeleton. I kept looking for wildlife but came up empty. Finally, at the 23-mile mark, I spotted my first wild beast. I was running through a quiet neighborhood when he appeared. It was standing behind a young boy, only a few feet away. The animal? A cocker spaniel, which just so happened to be on a leash.

Twenty-five minutes later I finished the race. All the fears I had of being attacked never happened. I even kept moving on Stuckagain Road. I completed the distance with nothing jumping on my back, except the weight of that fear which I carried for 26 miles, 385 yards. All the encounters I did face were good ones. In that boy's neighborhood, volunteers handed me fruit pops; a welcome relief after all the hours in the sun.

I began the morning at Bartlett High School and finished on the track at crosstown rival West High. At the finish, I was awarded a medal and my official marathon shirt, but it wasn't going to be worn on this day. The heavy maroon sweatshirt had a few months to go before I'd wear it.

Traversing 26 miles in most states you can gain an understanding of the area. Rhode Island is known as the Ocean State. The marathon ran by its shores. Illinois? You think of Chicago. The course took us to the heart of the city. Nevada? You think of the desert and Las Vegas. The marathon covered both. But what about Alaska? You couldn't possibly understand Alaska by running 26 miles there. The state covers two million square miles. On one end it borders Canada and on the other it's three miles from Russia. Although I didn't see a grizzly on marathon day, the next day I did see a glacier.

The drive from Anchorage to Seward was breathtaking. Driving out of town, I watched Dall sheep maneuvering on the cliffs above. At Seward, the big pigeons in the air were bald eagles. On the boat ride to Kenai Fjords National Park, I watched seals, marveled at whales, and watched more eagles spreading their wings. As the boat stopped in front of a glacier, surrounded by chunks of ice, I witnessed 100-foot-high sheets of ice crashing hard into the Gulf of Alaska. It was the end of June, but it felt like winter. It was very cold and I yearned for that marathon sweatshirt. It all made for the perfect setting. This is how Alaska should feel.

I never saw that moose pictured on the sign, but I saw him from above days later. Sitting in the front seat of a small chartered plane, I watched moose feeding in the stream below and stared at Mount McKinley straight on. With a full tank of petro and an experienced pilot, I peered out the window enjoying the scenery as we circled the mighty mountain dressed in white.

The day before I left this magnificent state, I finally came face-to-face with the animal I had feared most of all. I turned the corner and suddenly, there he was. The grizzly bear's five-inch claws extended toward me as he stood on his hind legs. But this time, I didn't panic and I certainly wasn't going to run. I held my ground, looked at him right in the eye and said, "You don't scare me anymore." Slowly, I turned to walk away, I felt something come down on my shoulder. Still, I never looked back and wasn't fearful, even when the security guard said, "You'll have to leave. The museum is closing."

My fears had faded in The Last Frontier.

(Holgate Glacier
Kenai Peninsula)

Turnagain Arm of Cook Inlet

Whiteout
in
ALAMOGORDO, NEW MEXICO

White Sands / Alamogordo Marathon / NM

Saturday, December 7, 1996
Age 38

From Highway 70 it doesn't look like much. I realize New Mexico is far from any coastline, so when they advertise white sands, what are they comparing it to? Florida has beautiful white sands, as does South Carolina and several other states. How did New Mexico fall into this group? The park was less than a few hundred feet away on my right when I spotted traces of white sand along the crest of the hills. Is this what they call the white sands of New Mexico?

After a right turn into the park, the environment started to change. There was more and more white sand. The sand was on my left, on my right, and even the road became white. It was amazing. The farther I drove the whiter it got. The landscape was covered in sand and completely white.

White Sands National Monument covers almost 300 square miles. The white sand is actually gypsum, formed over thousands of years, when lake beds in the area crystallized to form this tiny grain. Florida and South Carolina beaches couldn't compete with what I was seeing. It didn't matter where you looked, all you saw was sand. Continuing into the park, I had to pull to the right making way for plows to clear the road. I'm in Southern New Mexico, but why do I feel like I'm in Northern New York? It sure looks like snow to me. The dunes looked very smooth and untouched. It was as if they were worked on with the same tool used in smoothing cement sidewalks. Every now and then you could see footprints that disturbed its beauty. I thought, how dare they? But it didn't matter. The sands constantly shifted. Soon, those footprints were covered and another smooth patch appeared.

Picnic tables situated along the side of the road looked nothing like you'd find at other rest areas. Huge wooden shields were strategically placed by each table preventing your sandwich from getting sandy. Like a match approaching a dry forest, the slightest wind would get this sand very angry. After parking the car, I signed the log book at the foot of the trail. It was mandatory you sign in. It wasn't uncommon for Rangers to rescue lost souls. In this kind of environment, the shifting sand can do a number on your ability to reason. Did we come this way? Did we start in that direction? Where's the trail?

There were no landmarks to use to find your way back. This wasn't like losing your car at the mall. At least at the mall you can go back inside and eat a taco at the food court, while the rest of the parking lot clears out. Here, it's like someone gets into your car and moves it to an undisclosed location. Once you got on that trail, you had to be extremely careful to know your way back.

The sand was like a giant playground and too inviting to ignore. Like playing in the ball romp at McDonalds, I ran and dove headfirst into the dunes. I buried myself under the white stuff and did flips and turns and spins. Every few minutes, I kept my eye on the rim of the mountains in the distance to guide me back to the car. I could see how people easily got lost. They really do need to erect a flag pole in the lot. *Oh say can you see ... my way back to my car?* After playing I was out of breath. That's funny, I didn't run that long. Hey, wait a minute, that's not funny, I'm running 26.2 miles here tomorrow.

At the pasta dinner at Alamogordo High School, I sat with Al Becken. The San Antonio runner was one of the first to have run a marathon in every state. His next goal was to run the circuit twice. During dinner, awards were presented for those who ran the fastest, ran the most, or traveled the farthest. The flight from Richmond, Virginia, earned me a painter's cap. Al opted to sit on his hands when the question was asked, "Who has run a sub three hour marathon?" Al whispered to me, "Let him get the prize. I did that over 30 years ago."

December 7th, a day that will live in infamy. FDR was right. At least it was for me on this date in 1996. I drove 20 miles back down Highway 70 for the marathon start. And of all places, it was at White Sands National Monument. The monument wasn't like you'd see in our nation's capital. This monument was all that sand. It was cold at the start with temperatures below 40°. Our route would traverse the roads inside the park for nine miles before we'd head back on Highway 70.

Knowing the effects of altitude from yesterday's jaunt, I decided to go slowly in the early miles. The altitude was only 4,000 feet, but it was about 3,500 feet higher than what I was accustomed to. Plus, the conditions were stark and I wanted to make it out of the park alive. It was a setting unlike any other I had run. It was as if we were running on the moon. The course was peaceful, serene, and undisturbed from 20th century living. It was as simple and pure as the sport I was competing in. However, I feared the wind might kick up and spoil things. It would have helped if I had worn sunglasses. The conditions were similar to a day of skiing with the sun blaring down on the slopes.

I escaped the park, but I couldn't escape the heat. It gets downright hot in New Mexico, even in December. I can only imagine what it's like in June. As I ran by the gift shop, where a day earlier I browsed in shoes filled with sand, I sensed this day wasn't going to produce a fast time for me.

Now this is more like it. I'm running on a busy street and civilization is up ahead. Welcome to the 20th century. From whitetop to blacktop, I continue my run. I can see the town of Alamogordo up ahead, but it's not getting any closer. The people speeding by in cars would arrive within minutes. Start dinner without me. I'm running late. On my left is Holloman Air Force Base. Isn't that the place where they tested the first atomic bomb? Maybe I better keep on running. I do my best to appear composed as cars travel south on this highway that points in the direction of El Paso, Texas. I'd be embarrassed if any motorist had to pull over to administer CPR. I don't need it yet, but my run is far from over. The temperature is climbing steadily. Before my run was over it would climb to 80°.

"Hello Al, how are you?" We chat for a moment before he speeds ahead. For a guy who's 63-years-old, he's in great shape. He was just a few marathons short of having run 200. Now, he's getting farther away from me and is on his way to the zoo for the finish.

There isn't much to look at as I continue my journey. Granted, the mountains in the distance are eye-catching, but I've had the same view for hours. I'm in the middle of one long straight line that doesn't appear to end. I can see billboards on the right-hand side of the road. I'm having difficulty reading what they're selling, but I must be patient. I'll know soon enough what they're advertising. It also gives me an idea as to how far I have left to go. Let's see, if the Best Western Hotel is 11 miles away, then I have to go another ...

I'm getting closer to town. I can see the hotels, restaurants, and service stations. It won't be long now. I turn left, away from the highway, and step carefully over the railroad tracks. The zoo is just around the bend and not a moment too soon. It's feeding time and I grab all the goodies I can before I plant myself under a tree. I've done it.

Not only are marathoners entitled to the buffet of snacks and goodies on the table, but we're also provided a free pass into one of the Southwest's oldest zoo. But for some reason, seeing the monkeys and rabbits didn't interest me. I was dog tired and after getting a lion's share of snacks and wolfing them down, I ducked out of there without ever seeing an animal. No bull.

There was more of New Mexico I wanted to see. The next day I drove through Cloudcroft, home of Smokey the Bear, and then on to Carlsbad Caverns to explore the world below. But first, I had to get the sand out of my shorts.

22 years after he ran by me on Highway 70 near the 14-mile mark, I finally catch up with Al at McAllister Park in his hometown of San Antonio.

He continues to inspire.

For a Good Cause
in
LONG BRANCH, NEW JERSEY

Jersey Shore McMarathon / NJ

Sunday, April 27, 1997
Age 38

T here was no place to go but up. I had people in front of me and many more behind. I started to perspire, yet never thought about quitting. I had come too far to get here and I wasn't about to turn around now. I had already paid my entrance fee and I was determined to press on. Finally, came the moment of truth. After climbing the 354th step, I did what everyone else had done who came before me. I lowered my back and peered out the narrow window affixed to the grand lady's head. New York City looked beautiful.

Have you ever said to yourself, "I plan to do that someday.'"? Maybe it's to take piano lessons or learn a new language. Maybe you always had planned to visit that distant relative or take a cruise to a faraway port. And maybe, just maybe, you planned to climb the steps of the Statue of Liberty.

Most of my visits to New York City had come by way of the New Jersey Turnpike, on my way to visit family in New England. I had seen exits for the Statue, but always kept going straight. As I drove over the George Washington Bridge, I tried to take quick peeks to my right, hoping to catch a glimpse of the city's most famous lady. Usually, those peeks came up short. I had more pressing issues going on, such as staying in my lane and avoiding cars that weren't staying in theirs.

The Statue of Liberty seemed like it would take too much of an effort to visit. The thought of driving around the metropolitan area was unnerving. I wasn't even sure which state it was in. New York and New Jersey each claimed it. New York's mayor, Rudy Giuliani, said if his mother thought the Statue of Liberty was a part of New Jersey, she never would have left Italy. Good thing she was wrong. The Mayor could have been singing to tourists on his gondola if his mom had gotten her facts straight.

The Statue of Liberty, which stands in New York Harbor, was a gift to the people of America from France. Yes, her eyes are fixed on the State of New York, but she stands in the State of New Jersey. Give us your poor, give us your tired, and give us the credit, Jersey residents say.

Once I climbed those 354 spiral steps, I had to get back down. The lady may be grand, but there's no elevator under her robe. My legs were a little sore, but I still felt it wouldn't affect me for the next day, when I would be called upon to take a few more steps for the Jersey Shore McMarathon, 45 minutes away, in Long Branch.

I was somewhat hesitant to sign up for a race titled, *McMarathon*. If I run this race, I'd have to explain it to everyone. I can see it now when I'm asked, "Okay, you've run 24 marathons and one mcmarathon, is that right?" Why couldn't they have left well enough alone and stuck with Marathon? A marathon is what people train for and yearn to accomplish. Why cheapen it? It sounds more like a fast food run than the grueling long run it is. What's next, the Super Size Triathlon?

Years earlier, I had registered to run the Atlantic City Marathon, but never made it to the starting line because of another commitment. I had planned to return to Atlantic City and run on the Boardwalk. I envisioned that to be fun, but the timing wasn't right. The Long Branch event was at the end of April and the weekend was open for me. So, I sucked it up and prepared to run the McMarathon. It seemed better than sucking it down.

To many people, a marathon is an inconvenience. It means roads are going to be blocked and motorists will have to wait for joggers and runners alike. It means an influx of out-of- towners clogging your streets and paper cups littering the curb. But there's so much more to a marathon than mile markers and medals. The marathon is about giving back. The Jersey Shore McMarathon was all about giving back. Proceeds from this race would benefit the local Ronald McDonald House; a program which provides a "home away from home" for nearly four million families since its beginnings in 1974. Providing benefits for children in over 50 countries, the Ronald McDonald House continues to offer families an oasis while their child is in the hospital.

In this race it was the Ronald McDonald House. In other marathons, it would be something else, with proceeds to help the young, proceeds to help the sick, and proceeds to just help. Many runners raise money to help those who can't run. When it comes to going the distance, there's more to marathons than the finish line. The race is always going and the thousands upon thousands of runners who fill out an application and write a check, have helped more people than they would ever realize. The Jersey Shore McMarathon wasn't such a bad name after all. I was glad I came to town.

At the staging area by the shore, I reintroduced myself to Sharon Mordorski or Sam, as she is known. I met her in Greenville and had my picture taken with her. Sam was the first woman to have run a marathon in every state. What an honor that must be. The list of women finishers will continue to grow, but Sam can say she got there first. Her marathon days had not slowed. She talked about doing one the following weekend and doing another after that.

The parking lot to the beach house was crowded with runners. I got on my back and stretched my legs. It seemed odd doing this across the white lines of the huge lot. If this had been on a weekend in the summer, I would have been run over. The Jersey shore attracts vacationers from New York and Pennsylvania. On this day it attracted vacationers from 20 other states, but no one came to swim.

After I stretched my legs, I got up and explored the path by the high grass. I never thought much about it until a few days later. My leg must have brushed up against poison ivy and I was itching for another week. But for now, I was itching to start running. The course traveled north toward the tip of New Jersey. It was a perfect day on the north shore. The ocean was on our right and the coast was clear.

Organizers gave us a history and geography lesson about the area where we were running. A question on a placard would appear and miles later another placard would have the answer. It was a great way to not only educate the runners, but to help keep their mind off of the miles they were running. One question was "Which country lies due east of New Jersey?" I got it right when I guessed "Portugal." More marathons should follow New Jersey's lead. We're out there for hours running the streets of the community. Why not take advantage of it and teach? There's nothing wrong with building sound mind and body.

At Sandy Hook, near the lighthouse at Fort Hancock, I could see across the bay to New York City. I saw the Twin Towers and the Verrazano Bridge. It seemed bizarre I was running a marathon in New Jersey and could see part of a marathon course I had run on in another state. I don't think that happens often. We circled the lighthouse on Hartshone Drive on our southern swing. On my left was the Atlantic Ocean, on my right was Shrewsbury River. In front of me are two girls who are destined to stay together. On the back of one shirt it read, *I'm with her.* On the back of the other it read, *She's with me.* It would be tragic if one dropped out.

Any disappointment of not running on the Boardwalk in Atlantic City was gone. McMarathon took us on another Boardwalk, this one only a few miles from the finish. My legs began to tire as the race continued down the coast of Jersey. We trot by a few towns in this race, but none is more impressive than the town of Deal. The area is beautiful, with wide streets, immaculate lawns, and exquisite pricey homes. I seem out of place bringing my sweaty, tired body down its streets, but I have no choice. Passing through Deal is the hand I'm dealt. It's part of the yellow brick road to the finish.

From South Lake, to North Lake, to Ocean Boulevard, to a left on Bath, past the Ronald McDonald House I ran. A left on Sairs and onto the high school track to the finish. I had been running for 4 hours and 37 minutes. My legs ached and I was exhausted and starved. I was worn out.

As I limped away from the track, I could almost hear the voice call out to me. *Give me your poor, your tired, your huddled masses who have been on their feet too long.*

Finishing Up

Home away from home

Off Exit 74
in
EAST LYME, CONNECTICUT

East Lyme Marathon / CT

Sunday, September 28, 1997
Age 38

As the nation's most traveled highway, Interstate 95 carries millions of cars and trucks each day. The section from New York to Boston can be especially busy, including late into the night with a stream of red lights and white lights. I know. I've traveled that stretch too many times to count.

When you leave the George Washington Bridge and drive into the Bronx, you would think it would be clear sailing through the Constitution State, but Connecticut can get clogged. Stamford, Bridgeport, New Haven, and New London are Connecticut towns I've driven through at speeds of 70 and speeds of 7. It always seems to be a long stretch through the state with the long name. When I drive east, I'm thinking about getting into that next state to visit family in Rhode Island. When I drive west, I'm thinking about getting past the congestion that can get me by the GW Bridge. Connecticut is caught in the middle. All these years, all these miles, Connecticut meant chasing down Interstate 95. Other than sitting in a car, I hadn't explored much of the state, even though I spent my childhood less than 25 miles from its border.

My fondest memory of Connecticut wasn't a happy one. Our Rhode Island Junior College (now known as Community College of Rhode Island) baseball team was in a playoff game with Housatonic Community College of Bridgeport. It was late in the game, with one out, when I took my lead off second base. The next batter hit a grounder between third and short. I was taught you hold your position if the ball is hit in front of you. I remembered that, but I was sure the slow-footed shortstop wouldn't be able to reach the ball. And if he had, he couldn't have thrown me out. I was wrong on both counts.

As I walked back to the bench, my coach went crazy. He dropped his clipboard and hollered at me for what seemed like an eternity. I felt as tall as the man whose museum I had visited the previous day. P. T. Barnum said, "There's a sucker born every minute." Not only did I feel like P.T. in statue, but sucking was what I was doing to my thumb at the end of the bench.

The years have long passed, but the memory of the tag and the temper surface each time I drive through Bridgeport. I step on the gas a little harder from Exits 24 to 30. Farther up the interstate are Exits 44 to 48. You can get to Yale University by taking any of them. As the goaltender on the Cranston East Hockey team, we traveled to New Haven to play the junior varsity squad of the Bulldogs. The ice rink was not your typical hockey arena. It was shaped like a whale. As I recall, I didn't have a whale of a game that day. I blamed it on my face mask. I don't think the holes were lined up to my eyes. Needless to say, baseball and hockey had not treated me well in Connecticut, but I was far from giving up. There were a few more exits to go on the interstate. I was hoping Exit 74 and a different sport would be kinder this time around. I registered to run the East Lyme Marathon.

Old Lyme, Connecticut, is a beautiful New England area. They have good schools, good neighborhoods, and good people, but it's known for something else. In 1975, an arthritis epidemic had occurred near Old Lyme. Physicians first thought it to be a geographic and seasonal cluster of "juvenile rheumatoid arthritis." They termed it *Lyme Disease* and learned it's a complex multi-system disease that results from an infection with ticks. Between 1982 and 1996, nearly 100,000 cases were reported across the United States. It was also a period for record sales of tweezers.

The East Lyme Marathon was highly regarded as one of the most picturesque courses in the country. As quoted in the race information packet from Amby Burfoot, a 1968 Boston Marathon winner and editor of *Runner's World*, it was the most beautiful marathon course he had ever seen. Yes, I'm sure the course was nice, but my response to that would be the same if Amby asked me to run 27 miles. "I'm sorry Amby, but I would not go that far." Maybe it was because I had become so familiar with New England, I wouldn't have ranked it as the most beautiful. The course was only 50 miles from my hometown. The landscape was nothing I hadn't already seen; fall colors, stone walls, state parks, and miles of shoreline running. Hmmm, maybe Amby was on to something.

Cruising past Exit 74 two days before the race, I continued for another hour to my guest room in Rhode Island. I had a wonderful visit with my parents and reluctantly waved off the desserts my mother was trying to feed me the night before the race. I really did want that apple pie and bowl of ice cream, but I couldn't chance it. I didn't want to lose my edge.

As I sat in my parent's living room watching the Red Sox on television, I wasn't motivated to run a marathon the next day. I had already driven 500 miles the day before and I wasn't ready to leave. The marathon was like a job or a test I had to study for. If I weren't on this quest to run a marathon in every state, I would have stayed to see the Sox on Sunday afternoon.

There was no hype to East Lyme. The event didn't offer a pasta dinner, where I would have had an opportunity to sit and mingle with other runners. Packet pick-up was scheduled an hour before the race. My parents weren't motivated to come see me. In fact, if the race were televised, I'm sure the runners they would have preferred to watch would have been the ones going from first to third at Fenway Park. And to make matters worse, as soon as I finished the race, I'd get back in my car to drive home.

I hugged my parents good-bye and backed out of their driveway to begin my trek to marathon country. When I saw signs for the University of Rhode Island, I realized I had made a major mistake. Remember that split in the road 10 miles back? I should have stayed to the right. Now I'm on Route 4 instead of Interstate 95. If the race is considered right in my backyard, then this move shows I haven't been cutting the grass. However, the extra miles did not delay me. I had left in ample time. I wasn't even disturbed during the moments I hadn't a clue as to where I was. I knew I was heading west and Connecticut was going to greet me any minute.

I got to East Lyme High School in plenty of time. I sat in front of the rows of lockers and stretched. Afterwards, I got on my back and raised my feet to the ceiling, hoping there were no hall monitors working on Sunday.

At 8:30 a.m., we headed west on Boston Post Road and quickly turned right onto Pattagansett, and by the lake with the same name. From there we worked our way down Scott Road, under the interstate, and continued to Rocky Neck State Park near the ocean. We ran on narrow country roads and passed those stone walls Southern New England is famous for. During one stretch, we passed apple trees. I didn't have to see them to know they were there. The smell splashed me right in the face. This was the taste of New England. All those times I zipped by Exit 74 without knowing what was nearby. Now, I was experiencing it the best way, by getting out of my car and lacing up a pair of running shoes.

On Old Black Point Road, which jetted out to the ocean, I noticed two race volunteers standing in the middle of the road. The women, a few feet apart from each other, were dressed in costume standing by the aid station. I ran a few hundred feet toward them. Like deer caught in headlights, these "dears" held their ground as I "threaded the needle" between them. I said "hello" and never slowed. The scene represented the uniqueness of the marathon. You could see tables of refreshments, strangers applauding your efforts, and people dressed in costume to keep you amused.

From the serenity of the shore, we passed into the turbulence of the town. With less than five miles to go, East Lyme traffic got busy. I paid extra attention to the cars and trucks cruising a few feet on my left. As I pressed on through Main Street, I ran by townsfolk getting out of their cars to shop or run errands. A few miles later, I was under the interstate on my way up the hill to the high school. At 1:33 in the afternoon my race was over.

I had been running for over five hours. I didn't hover long over the refreshment table because another long run was looming. The finish line in this marathon was off Exit 79 in Richmond, Virginia.

It had already been a long day for me by 2 o'clock in the afternoon. After awakening in Rhode Island, driving for an hour, and running 26 miles, I wasn't exactly looking forward to this 450-mile drive home. On this day the thought of living in Bridgeport didn't seem such a bad idea after all.

Home of the Vikings ... and the start of the
East Lyme Marathon

Getting ready for a barrel of fun

The Toppled Trees
in
OMAHA, NEBRASKA

Omaha Riverfront Marathon / NE

Sunday, November 2, 1997
Age 39

When J. Sterling Morton and his wife moved from Detroit to the plains of Nebraska in 1854, what he missed most were the trees. Morton, a lover of nature, quickly planted trees, shrubs, and flowers. The trees acted as windbreakers by keeping the soil in place and were needed for building materials and fuel. Also, underneath those trees was a comfortable spot to hide from the hot sun. As the founder of Nebraska's first newspaper, Morton had an excellent channel to spread his love of trees and the benefits that came from them. Through Morton's efforts, Arbor Day was born.

Located west of the Missouri River, Nebraska's largest city was a treasure trove of trees. J. Sterling Morton would have been pleased to have seen what Omaha had become. However, on October 25th, 1997, all that changed when close to 10 inches of snow fell on the metropolitan area. It also crippled the trees when the snow landed on the already leafy branches. The branches were no match to the weight of all that white. Omaha Mayor Hal Daub said, "We've never had every inch of our city damaged like it was by this storm." The storm damaged or destroyed 85% of the trees in Omaha. On a less important note, the storm almost destroyed the Omaha Riverfront Marathon, which was one week away.

I was looking forward to going to the marathon. I had spent a summer in Omaha during college. I worked for Southwestern Company, selling books door-to-door. Working 80 hours a week, there wasn't a house I walked past that I didn't walk up the steps to knock on its door. There were many days I would have rather gone to the park to knock my head against one of Omaha's trees. Now, 17 years later, I was anxious to return. I was excited, especially knowing I would run by all those homes without knocking on a single door and carrying a heavy book case in my right hand. My mother still claims it's the reason for my slumping shoulder.

I had read in my local newspaper about the severe storm that battered Omaha, but hadn't heard any word about the marathon's cancellation. With the packet pick-up and pasta dinner hours away, I spent part of the day at the Henry Doorly Zoo. One of the nation's top zoos, the acclaim did not disappoint. While walking through the

123

jungle exhibit, a monkey almost jumped on my head. Thank goodness the snakes were behind glass.

Next door to the zoo was Rosenblatt Stadium, home of the AAA Omaha Royals and site of the college World Series. I've toured the homes in the area, but never the field. I had fun looking around the grounds.

During the walk from my car to the site of the marathon expo, I passed a marathon registrant who said, "Did you hear? The marathon has been downgraded to a half marathon." My heart dropped. I walked inside to find answers, but the person in charge wasn't there. I learned the storm had wreaked havoc on the marathon course. Downed trees had blocked many of the streets on the planned marathon course. Even the fastest runners would be hitting a wall in Omaha. The race director would arrive later and the dozen or so "*50 Staters*" were anxious to talk to him, none more than Tony Lopetrone. Tony and his wife, Nancy Broadbridge, depended on Omaha. The couple was on track to running a marathon in every state in 1997. If Omaha was downgraded, there wasn't another marathon in Nebraska for the rest of the year. Tony was worried, but Nancy was confident everything would work out.

The expo was busy with many people buying shorts, hats, and singlets and looking forward to 13.1 miles of running the next day. The thing I only wanted was to get my hands on the director. I had come too far to run half. A few miles away at the pasta dinner, the race director was at the front door taking tickets. He also took the polite pressure from the few runners who came from faraway places to bring the marathon back. He obliged, but said the route would have to be changed. Since a half marathon was already scheduled at 8 a.m., he said those wanting to run the full marathon could do the half marathon twice. Our race would begin at 6 a.m. It made sense to us, and Tony was able to enjoy his dinner. The director maintained his power. His house wasn't as lucky. It was beginning its second week without electricity. The city of Omaha was still suffering.

It was cold and dark outside the convention center at 5:30 in the morning. The race director gave last minute instructions to the handful of marathoners who were getting a two-hour jump on the half marathoners. The route would take us north for six miles and then back to the start. Because of the changed course, this race could not be certified. It was agreed upon that on the return trip, we would make a full circle around the block-long convention center, guaranteeing we went at least 26.2 miles.

The race began like a group of friends going out for a Sunday morning jog. We knew each other's names and we enjoyed the quietness of the early morning. The snow had melted, but we could see the damage left behind. Yard after yard was covered with fallen trees. Chain saws were at a premium. Every resident wanted to get their hands on one.

I didn't talk much with Tony. He was far down the road. He had been running a marathon every week since January, sometimes doing two a weekend, but his speed was hardly ever compromised. He was averaging 3:30 marathons.

The wind was very stiff. I fought hard to move forward as I was constantly being pushed backward. I was hoping the wind direction wouldn't change when my direction did. At the turnaround, I caught up with four people. Our pace was right on schedule to join the hundreds of runners who were doing the half marathon. As we approached downtown to turn left on Dodge Street, we could see the runners waiting for their 8 o'clock start. This was going to work out perfectly. We started as a scarce pack in the dark, now we were going to run with hundreds in the light. Most of these runners didn't know what we had been up to for the last two hours.

A few steps away from cutting in front of the half marathon start, the 8 o'clock race began. We were a few seconds too slow. We had to weave through them to make our way around the building for our last leg of the trip. As I fought through the crowd, I turned to wait for the four people I had been running with. There was Lois Berkowitz, but where were the others? I kept looking back waiting for them to appear, but it was no use. They joined the half marathoners and ran with them. Lois and I ran together around the convention center, while the other three runners were already running north. What a shame. They were so close to running a 26.2 mile race, but they didn't do it. They might have run 26 miles, but they didn't go the full distance. They finished the race by cutting corners. Nobody wins when you cut corners.

As the miles went on, I slowly caught up with those who were running 13.1. Most of them were local runners who were running with family or friends; men, women, and children who were getting out of their house after a week of being shut in. With just a few miles to go, while all alone, I could hear the noise of chain saws up ahead. National Guardsmen were clearing both sides of the street. I ran right between them, but they never looked up from their work. Soon, I powered up the hill, turned left, and continued on around the corner to the open door inside the convention center. I had finished the marathon just in time. It was getting colder by the minute. Snow was hitting the windshield as I drove to the University of Nebraska-Omaha campus to shower.

Organizers of the Omaha Marathon never imagined their race would be turned upside down. The streets were like a war zone, with debris in front of almost every home. Trees were split in half, branches were splinted, and destruction littered the sidewalks. When I saw the frozen turkey out by the curb, I knew this was no ordinary day in Omaha. Over 125,000 residents had been without power, most for over two weeks, and almost everyone in this city of 345,000 had been affected by the storm.

After the Omaha Marathon, I never received my finisher's certificate for all that time I had spent on my feet. I wasn't surprised. Omaha was still trying to get back onto theirs.

Debris and Victory in Omaha, Nebraska

Getting the Dirt
in
DETROIT, MICHIGAN

Detroit Free Press International Marathon / MI

Sunday, October 17, 1999
Age 40

Through 80 years, two name changes, four world championships, and one long season after another, the corner of Michigan and Trumbull had brought millions of people through its gates. They came to cheer Kirk Gibson, Al Kaline, Hank Greenberg, and my grandmother's childhood friend, Mickey Cochrane. Built only a few months after the Titanic sank, Tiger Stadium hadn't changed much at all. On any given weekend, there would always be a grounder to short, a fly out to center, and a home run in the right field stands. In the 1971 All Star game, young Reggie Jackson connected on a pitch that sent the sphere flying into the lights high above right field.

Almost 30 years later, here I sit, in the box seats behind the third base dugout, visualizing the flight of the ball and seeing it hit the tower. It's a thrill sitting in this Detroit landmark, knowing I'm one of the last who will ever do so. The final out was called on Tiger Stadium three weeks earlier. The following year, the team would move a few bus stops away to a new ballpark. The fate of the ballpark on Michigan and now Cochrane was uncertain. One thing was certain. Tiger Stadium would play a major role in the 22nd running of the Detroit Free Press Marathon. Runners would start in front of the ballpark and would be rewarded by finishing inside. Another thing was certain too. I wasn't going to waste much time on the course. I was running for home.

Although it had been two years since my last marathon, my running hadn't suffered. I believed I was going to put in a good time. My driving was putting in a longer time. The first day, I drove from my home in Richmond, Virginia, to Sandusky, Ohio. The next day, I finished the last leg into Detroit. I knew only a few things about Detroit. They had a good hockey team, an old baseball stadium, and on Halloween night the fire department worked overtime. I knew there were some bad areas I needed to avoid, but I wasn't sure where they were. What I did know was that I was in for an adventure.

Between the start and finish in downtown Detroit, runners would enter Canada for six miles and then return through a one-mile tunnel. Had anyone alerted the Michigan Department of Transportation about this? It would be terrible if the light at the end of the tunnel were an oncoming truck. That's something the lead runners would have to worry about. I was thinking about more important matters, such as will I able to breathe while running in a tunnel and will I be able to see? If there ever was a time for tunnel vision, let this be it!

On Sunday, October 17th, 1999, I drove in the early morning mist to a parking lot across from Tiger Stadium. The ballpark was ready. All the lights were on, including the ones Reggie had hit a long time ago. I walked inside and sat in one of the 45,000 seats and reflected back to the time I last came to Tiger Stadium. It was 1976 when I watched Mark "The Bird" Fidrych strike out Reggie Jackson of the Baltimore Orioles.

Fidrych, and many of the old-time Tigers, came back to the stadium a few weeks earlier to bid their farewells. The former pitcher walked to the mound and scooped up some dirt as a memento. I planned to do the same.

On the walls inside the stadium, fans had written good-bye messages showing their appreciation and sadness to the facility that brought them many joys throughout the years. It was truly the end of an era. In the hallway behind home plate, I hopped onto an old concession stand and stretched my legs. Thirty minutes later, I was out the door to the starting line. It had just begun to rain.

The quickest way to get to Canada was to drive south. It was also the quickest way to run. Soon, we were running over the Ambassador Bridge to Windsor, Ontario. Although we weren't stopped at the border, we were required to register weeks before the event to make sure our paperwork was in order. Off the bridge, we turned left onto Huron and then a right on Riverside Drive along the Detroit River. On my left was the beautiful skyline of Detroit, with the 73-story cylinder, Renaissance Center, standing tall. I saw the Joe Louis Arena, where the Red Wings played the previous night, and saw a city that looked mighty impressive. The structure that stood out in Windsor was the casino that brought all that traffic from over the Ambassador Bridge.

From Riverside Drive, the route took us inland and down Wyandotte

Avenue. The street was almost deserted. Windsor residents must have had more important things to do than stand on the sidewalk cheering on 4,000 runners who invaded their country. After our six-mile jaunt in Canada, it was back home to the good old "U.S. of A." It was the first time vehicular traffic was prohibited from entering the Windsor Tunnel. On this day the traffic came by foot. All I heard was the pitter-patter of feet. It was almost deafening, but all part of an experience few runners have the opportunity to experience. The tunnel was clean, well lit, and ventilated. Regardless of these comforts, I was happy to come out of it. When I reappeared above ground, downtown Detroit, Michigan, had the freshest air on earth. The tunnel was like running indoors on a treadmill. There's never enough air to satisfy me.

The Renaissance Center was directly in front of us, as we were greeted by cheering spectators. Only in America. The course then proceeded northeast along Jefferson Street to Belle Isle Park. The park consisted of several softball and baseball fields. It was at one of these fields my father played in a softball tournament in 1939 and '40. Now, close to 60 years later, his youngest son was racing to another home plate, 15 miles away.

My pace was falling back on the return trip to downtown, but I was still ahead of Rudy. Whoever Rudy was, he was popular. Spectators all along Jefferson Avenue cheered for him. I'd hear, "It's Rudy. Way to go Rudy." Up ahead I'd see people standing quietly by the curb, until they looked at the runner behind me. Suddenly, their enthusiasm would rise and the cheers would follow. *"It's Rudy."* For six miles I kept hearing "Ruuudy, Ruuudy, Ruuudy." Closer to downtown I was passed by several runners. Rudy passed me too. I still didn't see the front of his shirt, but the cheering continued.

We passed the new ballpark on our way to the old one. Comerica Park was in the early stages of being constructed. It looked nothing like a baseball park. Only the sign in front told me it was turning into one.

On Rosa Parks Avenue, I was getting excited knowing Tiger Stadium was coming up soon and I was going to be running inside it. When I turned right onto Michigan Avenue, I still couldn't see the front gate. Come closer, come closer, I muttered to myself. Minutes later I saw runners up ahead, but they weren't going inside. They were turning left around the stadium and disappearing. I followed their steps until the course took us to the opposite side of the ballpark. Feeling like a VIP, a race official pointed me to the open gate. I pierced my way under the center field stands to another open gate that led to the playing field of Tiger Stadium.

It was an incredible rush as I followed the warning track to right field, and raced down the foul grounds by first base to the finish. It was the greatest finishing area I had ever experienced. It took me only 3:40:42 to get to first base. Behind the ropes on the third base foul line, I sprawled out on the greenest lawn in the state of Michigan. I looked up to the scoreboard, the stands, and to the pitcher's mound, and thought about Mark Fidrych. I slowly stood, reached into the tiny pocket inside my running shorts, and pulled out a plastic baggie.

Like most runners, I'm proud of the finisher's medal I got that day in Detroit. But I wouldn't trade anything for all that dirt.

Valuable prizes obtained in Detroit

Good Times
in
GOODLAND, KANSAS

High Plains Marathon / KS

Saturday, June 2, 2001
Age 42

No one could tell me I wasn't in Kansas anymore. The miles and miles of open highway was nothing but Kansas. It's a long way from the Kansas City, Missouri, airport to Goodland, Kansas, 407 to be exact. On June 1st, 2001, I drove the distance to run the High Plains Marathon. The next day, I would drive back for another event. I told myself I could do both, but knew working the room for the audience of the Kansas Court Reporters Association would be limited. Speaking on Memory Skills would be easy, but doing it while standing could be more of a challenge.

I had taken a long layoff from my last marathon and anticipated sore legs the following day. Thank goodness the rental car was equipped with cruise control. My feet would have had to work too much to be putting the pedal to the metal for eight-plus hours of driving.

The drive to Goodland from the Kansas City airport was very relaxing. The rolling hills and open plains was a welcome sight from the buildings, buses, and billboards I was used to seeing on stretches of I-95 on the East Coast. It gave me a feeling of being "Out West" and I could envision Indians on horseback coming up over the crest. Except for city traffic around Topeka, Interstate 70 was smooth sailing.

I drove past Abilene, home of Dwight D. Eisenhower. I drove through Russell, home of former Senator Bob Dole and the huge Russell Stover Candy Company. Seventeen miles from the Colorado border, I exited the interstate in Sherman County; one of four of the state's 105 counties in Mountain Time Zone. Shaving an hour off my time wasn't going to be as easy for the next day's race.

What better place to run than a place called, *Goodland*. Kansas is nothing BUT good land. It's that good land, with its rich soil, that helps put bread on tables across America. How do I know? I read the sign between Lawrence and Junction City that said so.

Less than 40 people had signed up to run the marathon. This would be the smallest field I had ever entered. Not wanting to finish last and not wanting to get lost would be two of my concerns. With larger fields, such as New York or Marine Corps, you would know some runners would be on the course for six hours. That was a given. With 39 runners, there was no telling if they were all elite runners who would leave me in the dust or 39 runners I would leave in the dust. My guess it wouldn't had been the latter. I wanted to finish with some of the pack and finish before harvest time.

At the pasta dinner at Goodland High School, I got my first look at the competition. With both hands holding a plate of spaghetti, bread, salad, and a drink, I sat down with Jim Davis and Roxana Lewis. I couldn't have picked a better table.

Jim Davis, from Burns, Kansas, had run in 23 ultramarathons. In the next few weeks, the 59-year-old would run another near Buffalo, New York. His goal, along with Roxana's, would be just to finish. This was my kind of group. Roxana Lewis, a 55-year-old from Los Angeles, was no stranger to marathoning and adventure. She had run in 25 marathons and had climbed over 15 major mountains, including McKinley, Matterhorn, and Rainer. The only thing high about tomorrow's High Plains Marathon would be in the name. I was confident she would finish.

The smallest field was combined with the earliest starting time. I set my alarm for 4 a.m. at the Best Western Hotel. I had a hunch traffic on Saturday morning would be light for the 5 o'clock start. The television news that evening was focused on the weather. Tornados had been spotted near Wichita, 325 miles away. I was amazed by the sophistication of the local television stations pinpointing streets that were in the storm's path. The stations were set up like a war room with live feeds and tracking devices keeping viewers informed. Obviously, Kansans take tornado watches very seriously. Forty days earlier, the town of Hoisington, 30 miles south of Russell, was almost wiped out by the powerful winds. Summertime in Kansas can be deadly. However, on this night in Goodland, the skies were calm and beautiful sunshine was forecast for the next day.

The race began right on time in the predawn darkness. After a prayer and ground rule check from race director, Michael Skipper, we runners took off. It was chilly, but the sun would soon change that. In the meantime, it was one foot in front of the other around the neatly kept lawns and homes of Goodland and out by the fields for 26 miles.

Highway 24, parallel with I-70, runs east to west. It was on this roadway the runners met up with the sun, which was coming up in the opposite direction. There was no escaping the bright yellow ball, but to just squint and bear it. The wheat fields weren't high enough to conceal it. It was a beautiful course running from Goodland to Edson, and back to Goodland, on a two-lane highway, between wide open fields. It was quiet, serene, and simple, just the way running should be. The runners' equipment is shorts, singlet, socks, and shoes, nothing complicated, nothing overwhelming. This course had it right.

Marathoning can be a lonely sport. It's just you and the elements and the miles upon miles that await you. Whether it's a small race, like this one in Goodland or a large race with 30,000 runners, it's lonely for each participant. There are no teammates to pass the ball to and no teammates to take your place. My training runs are done without partners. The pace and route are solely up to me. It's my decision to go faster or slower or to turn around and go home. I seldom talk when I run, but in Goodland it was different.

I caught up with Jim near the six-mile marker and we talked for a few miles along the way. It was a nice change. He told me his wife would have been on this trip if she had been feeling better and told me about his work. We chatted about our love of running and the peaceful surroundings we were enjoying. I asked him how he manages to run 50-mile races. He answered, "Slowly, and with many walking breaks." A few miles later, Jim took one of those walking breaks while I kept going, but I knew I'd see him again approaching from behind later in the race.

In the distance stood a huge, white grain elevator which never seemed to get closer. We kept running toward it, but it seemed like it was moving backward. The grain elevator represented the Land of Oz. It was near the turnaround site. I was anxious to get there. I kept a steady pace, not concerned about time, but concerned about keeping my legs moving. The aches would happen soon enough. In the meantime, I told myself to enjoy the run and the scenery. After meeting up with the grain elevator, the turnaround still didn't show itself. Up ahead I could see runners still moving in the same direction I was. I kept thinking, when are they going to turn? A few miles later the turnaround appeared. I just had to follow my footsteps and I would finish.

With the sun no longer a factor, I increased my pace on the march home. I was smelling the finish, although the crop duster plane, near mile 22, gave me something else to smell. Past the High Plains Museum, telling about Goodland's place in history with the invention of the helicopter, I continued on. A right on 17th street and a left on 8th brought me to the finish in front of the Recreation Center. I felt I could have gone another five miles. I felt great and was astonished with my 4:09 time, considering my yearlong marathon layoff. After consuming cookies and Coke at the rec center and picking up my finisher's medal and certificate, it was back to the hotel for a shower.

Driving east on I-70, on my way back to Overland Park, I looked to my left and smiled upon the state highway I knew all too well. It was a wonderful day with wonderful people. A runner mentioned the marathon T-shirt was different than other race shirts. This one had no advertisements on it. It was simple, yet colorful, just like my experience in Goodland, Kansas.

High Plains with low pains in Goodland

Runners and Wranglers
in
SALT LAKE CITY, UTAH

Deseret News Marathon / UT

Tuesday, July 24, 2001
Age 42

It arrived in the mail several days before the marathon. I didn't have to go. I could have stayed home, worn it, and no one would have ever known. I didn't need to travel over 4,000 miles in a day and half to run 26.2 miles. However, the Deseret News Marathon T-shirt had to be earned to be worn. I went to Salt Lake City, Utah, to earn the privilege of wearing it.

About 1,000 runners were prepared to run the 32nd Annual Deseret News Marathon. The city of Salt Lake City was preparing too. The 2002 Winter Olympic Games were just seven months away. July 24th, 2001, was a strange day to hold a marathon. Tuesdays aren't typically marathon days, but on this day, it held special place in Utah history. It's so important that every July 24th is marathon day. It's also Pioneer Day, where on July 24th, 1847, Brigham Young and his followers came upon this valley and declared, *"This is the place."* Mormons have settled there ever since. The marathon traces the route Brigham Young took on Emigration Canyon Road.

A clean, bustling city ringed by mountains in the Wasatch Range, Salt Lake City is a beautiful setting for a marathon. It's also a beautiful setting for a parade. Over 200,000 people would line the downtown streets to watch one of the West's largest parades celebrating its pioneer heritage. The final two miles of the race would be on the parade route, but only for those arriving by 8:30 a.m. After that time, an alternate route would be set up so as not to interfere with the parade.

The marathon, like High Plains, started at 5 a.m. However, unlike the Kansas race I didn't have a car. Runners were required to take the shuttle from the Delta Center to the start. I almost felt as if I had to explain myself when I asked for a 3 a.m. wake-up call. Decked out in my running gear, I braved the chilly temperatures to walk to my bus stop about a mile away. Walking down Salt Lake City streets at 3:30 in the morning was a little unnerving. I had never walked down any street that early and I was glad to reach my destination. There was life at the Delta Center. People in shorts and T-shirts were there too. I had a feeling of belonging. I felt safe.

The bus filled quickly and we headed off. There was no point in looking out the window. It was as if we were sitting inside a black kettle. The view was only the reflection of other runners. The bus kept moving and downshifting. Every few miles, the driver shifted into another gear and you could tell we were climbing in elevation. Finally, the bus stopped and we filed out by the clubhouse at Mountain Dell Golf Course. With several buses transporting runners to the start, ours wasn't the first to arrive. When I exited, I saw many runners looking like homeless people, huddled in blankets and sleeping along the banks of the golf course. It was cold and dark, yet beautiful with the silhouette of the mountains and the bright stars shining down on us. Another 45 minutes would have to pass before the race would begin.

The finish line in downtown Salt Lake City was a long way from where I stood. Soon, the buses would leave and I'd have to make my way to the city by foot. I cannot see a thing. Those were the words going through my mind when the race began. It was pitch dark. The police lights up ahead were a welcome sight, but they were the only sight. The course became more and more spectacular as the minutes passed. As the sun began to rise, the Utah scenery was everything the guide books had promised with majestic mountains and beautiful lakes, and yes, a lot of uphill running.

At one stretch we powered up for six miles. Just prior to the last hill was an aid station. A volunteer, holding a drink, said "Who wants Splash?" I assumed it was a new sports drink. I answered, "Me." Immediately, he splashed it into my face. I no longer ask for "Splash."

The lone wheelchair participant struggled during the first half of the race. I passed him on the uphills, he passed me on the downhills. Beginning at mile 13 he passed me for good. The course was downhill the rest of the way. On the downhill, I watched a fawn run across the road, then fall in front of two runners ahead of me. The deer quickly got up and dashed into the brush. Was the animal startled by the runners or the bagpipers playing close by? The following day Emigration Canyon Road would be quieter.

Reaching the 24-mile mark at 8:30 a.m. was all that was on my mind. I wanted to run up the parade route in front of the throng of people. The minutes were moving faster than I was. At 20 miles, as I passed the University of Utah with its big white letter U exposed on the side of the mountain, I started to hurt. Finishing began to be the only thing on my mind. It was almost like another day. The race started in the cold and quiet darkness. Now, the day was warm and people were playing golf, while traffic was snarled by the university. I kept moving, but slower. The course had bottomed out. The downhills were over, and so was my chance to run on the parade route, as race officials had now redirected runners parallel to the festive gathering on the next street.

While crossing each block, I caught glimpses of the parade and was anxious to see more of it. A little work had to be done first. The alternate route lacked one important thing - mile markers. I wasn't sure how much farther I needed to go. I'd ask others, "Have we hit 25 miles?" They didn't know either. The parade was over two miles long. I knew if a majorette could go that far while twirling a baton, then I could go the distance too. Of course, I would have preferred to do it while riding on a float.

After several minutes of straight line running, the race route turned left toward the park. The finish would soon appear, but race officials had something else in mind. The course turned left away from the park and I had to press on. When you've been on the course for over four hours, climbed over 1,000 feet in elevation, having begun running in total darkness, you're ready to stop. This left turn went against everything I wanted to do, but I had no choice. I knew the banner would soon come into sight.

It was worth it. The Deseret News Marathon had a buffet waiting for us. Tables and tables of bananas, apples, bagels, yogurt, cookies, and drinks were there for the taking. I grabbed a handful of each and made my way under a tree to begin my personal picnic. Bending down to sit was difficult. I knew getting up would be too. I'd have to deal with that later. For now, my focus was strictly on removing the cap off my yogurt.

Thirty minutes passed before I was back on my feet. My marathon wasn't over. I could have taken a shuttle back to the Delta Center, but I wanted to see the parade. So, I followed the parade route back to its origin, which was also the part of the route back to the hotel. I waved to Salt Lake City mayor, Rocky Anderson, and waved to Governor Mike Leavitt. I watched horses, cheered for marching bands, and gawked at floats and floats and floats. Spectators, five deep, lined both sides of the street as I rambled by them, sweaty and slowly, from my 26-mile ordeal. I immediately took the finishers medal off my neck when I began walking past the crowd. I didn't want to explain myself if I heard, "Congratulations for winning the race." My legs ached, but not enough to make me stop. The parade was a welcome distraction.

I took advantage of every minute during my 24-hour Salt Lake City visit. After the hotel shuttle picked me up, I spent the next several hours on foot. Monday afternoon, the day before the marathon, I walked throughout the downtown area visiting bookstores, shops, and the famed Mormon Temple. That evening, I attended a rodeo at the Delta Center and the next day I ran 26.2 miles and watched a parade while walking about four miles back to the hotel. I arrived home in Richmond on Wednesday at 3:30 in the morning.

Sore Foot Pity in Salt Lake City? Not at all. It was a fabulous adventure, the weather was gorgeous, and the people I met were a delight. It didn't take me long to realize this trip was going to be special. The hotel shuttle driver got it started when he said, "We're just waiting for some cowboys."

Special delivery from Salt Lake City

The Horse Race
in
ELMA, WASHINGTON

Puget Sound Marathon / WA

Sunday, August 19, 2001
Age 42

Y ou notice it as soon as you get off the plane. The air in the Pacific Northwest is different. There's crispness to it. No wonder all those coffee houses succeed in Washington State.

Seattle, Washington, is growing. Newcomers arrive each year because of the color green. The job market and the area's beauty make it so. It's a world of flannel suits and flannel shirts, corporate ladders and kayak leaders, rugged buildings and rugged mountains. Seattle has the best of both worlds. In the summer of 2001, Seattle also has the best of both leagues. The Mariners have the best record in baseball and are on their way to a divisional championship. As for me, I was on my way to the Puget Sound Marathon.

Washington State schedules several marathons each year. There's the Christmas Marathon, the Halloween Marathon, the Valentine's Day Marathon, and the Easter Marathon, to name a few. There are marathons in almost every month. This month was no different. In this state, recreation means outdoors, and marathons fit the bill. The city of Seattle holds a marathon each year, but it wasn't on this August weekend. On this day the town of Elma would play host.

Population 3,000, Elma is located 30 miles west of Olympia off Highway 12. I found it by lining up H-4 on page 108 in the Rand McNally Road Atlas. Even that took some doing. Other than the steady stream of patrons at the Rusty Tractor Restaurant, Elma, Washington, is quiet. August 19th, 2001, was quiet too. The marathon field was very small. I had an excellent chance to finish in the top ten, but then so did everyone else.

I learned about this marathon from the Internet. I printed the registration form and mailed $60 to Kristine Salazar. I had never heard of the race, but I knew Kristine existed. The cancelled check confirmed it weeks later. I was on my way.

Generally, marathons aren't postponed or cancelled. They are held no matter the weather condition. I've run them in snow, rain, strong winds, and bright sunshine. If a race is listed, you can be certain it will be run. There is, however, a slight fear that comes over you, especially when you travel over 3,000 miles to participate. You say to yourself, *perhaps this is the one cancelled ... perhaps I got the date wrong ... perhaps my plane will be late ... perhaps*. There was no pasta dinner for the Puget Sound event. The instructions were simple: *The race begins at 9:30 a.m. The directions from Olympia are as follows ...*

Stopping by the Exxon gas station in Elma, before the race, provided relief for me in two ways. I was asked by a guy wearing shorts and a singlet where the restroom was. It was now confirmed. The race was on.

In the Puget Sound area, the word *slough* gets mentioned often. There are sloughs everywhere. Turn left over the slough and then you'll pass a slough, and there you'll see the hotel right by the slough. I looked the word up: *A muddy hollow in the ground, a swamp, a bog.* I saw a lot of that. One didn't have to be a sleuth to find a slough. If you found Wenzel Slough Road, you would find the starting line for the Puget Sound Marathon. About 75 runners came to Elma on this day. As the morning wore on, fewer and fewer runners were left on the course, with many running the 5K or half marathon. The rest were going 26.2 miles.

I got to know the course very well. Turn right at the stop sign, run six-and-a-half miles up South Bank Road, turnaround, run back to the start line, and go back out again. I knew I wouldn't get lost. I was hoping I just wouldn't lose count. South Bank Road was dotted with a few homes, a few barns, and one large greenhouse by the bend near the turnaround. Volunteers at aid stations served refreshments to runners coming and going. The road was open to traffic, but I saw few cars. The road looked like any other road in the back country of Michigan, Minnesota, Maine, or Massachusetts, but the air gave it away. It had to be Washington State.

Early into the race, I spotted two horses grazing by the fence along the side of the road. Moments later, the most unusual event occurred. As I ran along even to them, one horse broke off from the other to run with me. Separated only by a fence, we were running side-by-side for what seemed to be at least 100 yards. No other runners were around us. It was a special moment between horse and runner. Life can be a lot like that. We compare ourselves with others and go the pace they go without utilizing our full potential. This big, strong animal on four legs was running just as fast as I was. Was he aware he could go faster? I couldn't. I looked forward to seeing the horse three more times that day for another run. He obviously didn't feel the same about seeing me. He paid me no attention.

Most of the spectators were lying in a field by the intersection of Wenzel Slough and South Bank. Their facial expressions said it all, "What in the world is going on here?" It's not surprising. Most likely, these cows were never informed a race was coming to town.

I struck up a conversation with Jane Nigra from Georgia early in the race. After getting well ahead of her, we high-fived each other on the turnarounds. With four miles to go, she passed and waved good-bye. She was the first to congratulate me at the finish.

I mentally divided the race into four parts; *up, back, up, back.* I told myself I had to run only six-plus miles four times. *Up, back, up* went well. The last *back* took some doing. My legs began to cramp. I stopped and stretched at the aid station near the 24-mile mark. My calves were very tight. I thought the other calves, lying in the field beyond the fence, might see me at night if things didn't change. I was in a lot of discomfort. I drank a lot of fluids, gave my legs a good stretch, and continued my run. It made a world of difference. I began to move faster, and before I knew it, my race was over.

I had the endurance and strength, but proper stretching is where I lacked. Stretching is very important, easy to do, and should be done daily. However, by not adhering to it, I paid the price for it on this day.

The finishing area was not elaborate. It was near the three picnic tables with the cookies and drinks under the shelter. The white turning signals chalked on the road were getting lighter by all the foot traffic throughout the morning. One runner almost missed it. He was hollered at with the words, "No, this way." No more than 35 runners completed the marathon. I was sure I traveled the farthest, to run in this low-key race in a place called Elma. A finisher overheard me when I mentioned I was from Richmond, Virginia. "You're from Richmond? I work there," said Julie Overy.

I didn't finish in the top ten, but I did get a trophy. As I was leaving, I shook the race director's hand, thanking him for his hard work. He said, "Let me get you something." He walked over to the awards table that had more miniature gold runners than runners who ran. He gave me a trophy. Did I deserve it? I completed all the necessary paperwork to compete. I traveled through three time zones to get there. I was the only athlete that had run neck and neck with a horse. I kept the hardware.

Getting ready to tie one on

Elma's streets are getting crowded

Honoring America
in
KEENE, NEW HAMPSHIRE

Clarence DeMar Marathon / NH

Sunday, September 30, 2001
Age 42

Flags were everywhere. They were plastered on cars and trucks, hung from store front windows, and tied to fences atop interstate bridges. America was in a patriotic mood. There was good reason. Sixteen days earlier was September 11th, 2001. A day America would long remember.

The Clarence DeMar Marathon in Keene, New Hampshire, was the reason I was travelling up Interstate 95. The weather was pleasant, similar to that fateful day over two weeks before. It was past midnight when I passed by New York City. I craned my neck in the direction of lower Manhattan. The bright lights illuminated the dark sky. Workers were continuing to haul away debris from the rubble of 220 stories of the Twin Towers, known now as Ground Zero.

That tragic day in American history would change the way we live. There would be more security checks at airports, more security checks at public events, and more security checks on our children after we tucked them in at night. Americans began to rethink their priorities. Love of family and love of country were on the top of the list. Friday was that kind of day for me. It was homecoming, visiting my parents in Cranston, Rhode Island. It had been a couple of months since I'd been back. This visit would be for a day-and-a-half before I'd make the 110-mile trip to Keene.

Late September was tourist season in Northern New England. Foliage fans frolic to the region each year. I had a sense this year would be different because of recent events. People weren't travelling. I was going to Keene without making hotel reservations. My mother kept telling me I'd have trouble finding a room and urged me to get on the road as Saturday afternoon moved on. Still, I kept delaying the departure. My brother and his wife stopped by to say "*hello*." My sister-in-law, Kathy, brought me a small American flag, with safety pins, to wear on my shirt during the race. I eagerly accepted. Finally, at 5 p.m., I hugged them all and headed north. On my way out, I bought a Kodak disposable camera to capture marathon moments. A trend was about to begin.

The drive out of Rhode Island, into Massachusetts and onto Keene, New Hampshire, came quickly. It was beginning to turn dark and I was praying my "no decision" was not a "bad decision" for finding vacancy signs. Marathoners are famous for hitting walls. On this night, this marathoner hit one with a hole in it.

After Keene mayor, Michael Blastos, welcomed runners during the pasta dinner at Keene State College, I chatted with Deo Jaravata. The 36-year-old Los Angeles school teacher had his sights on running a marathon in every state too. The next day, he checked off New Hampshire about 30 minutes before me.

Back at my "quaint" hotel, I started getting into marathon mode. I pinned race number 250 on the front of my singlet below my American flag. Before settling into bed, I set my watch alarm for 6 a.m. for the 8 o'clock start.

Sunday, September 30th, 2001, was cold. Wearing flimsy shorts and a flimsy shirt, I scraped frost off the windshield of my rented, white pickup truck with a plastic library card. While pushing the white powder off in the morning darkness, I questioned my commitment to this 50-state marathon quest. A day earlier, I was sitting in the comfort of my parent's home enjoying good fellowship and good food. However, I decided to leave all that to do this. It's September, I'm in shorts, I'm shivering, I'm insane. Thankfully, the heater came on quickly and I drove the two miles to the college. From there I boarded a school bus for the ride to Gilsum, a town about 26.2 miles away. Surrounding a Gilsum church, runners waited and chilled. The temperature was on the rise and the sun was on its way.

Inside my runner's pouch was my camera. I carried no crackers, no water, and no food supplement. I would be a runner/photo journalist. I decided I would snap pictures during the rest of my quest. I had so many wonderful memories from each event, which I wanted to remember long after the suffering had passed. My early marathon goals were only to finish them. Later, my goal was to run them fast. Finally, my goal was to capture them and to enjoy each passing mile and each passing smile.

I missed a Pulitzer Prize photo op by not taking the shot of the smoker at the starting line. It was a sight I had never seen before and one I haven't seen since. Standing in full running apparel, he was puffing away moments before the race. I don't know how he finished, but what I do know, is he was one runner who was smokin' from the start. Coincidently, the finish was just off Marlboro Street.

The course was pure New England. We traversed on beautiful country roads, including a swing through Sawyer's Crossing Covered Bridge at 19.2 miles into the run. We ran on Route 12, Route 10, and Route 32, passing under bright colored leaves, under a bright blue sky through the towns of Gilsum, Surry, Swanzey, and Keene. We passed Monadnock Regional High School, Frazier's Factory Furniture, and race sponsor, Peerless Insurance Company.

The brochure indicated the course would be fairly flat. I heard one runner make note of that, as we began tilting our heads upward, during one steep stretch. Some runners like to drive the course before a race so they know what to expect. Others like to be surprised. I fall into the latter. I want to see the course once and be done with it. I've checked out courses in the past and it didn't help. It was always easier in a car. There are, however, times when I wished I had studied the last three miles. It's during these miles when I ask myself, "When is this thing going to end?"

Sometimes you start to believe you're really something to be able to run these distances, and then you meet a guy named Tom Matti. He's known as "Hi Guy." Having read an article on him, I introduced myself to him during the race. Tom's a strange man and he'd be the first to tell you. He runs in sandals and he runs often. The day before, he ran the New Hampshire Marathon in

155

Bristol. Tom didn't talk long. He sped ahead. No sooner did Tom pass, when another outstanding runner approached. This runner had an artificial leg. His stride was fluid, and minute by minute, the distance between us got farther and farther. "What a Guy" and "Hi Guy" were two of the many runners at the Clarence DeMar Marathon. Clarence DeMar was quite a guy himself. A seven-time Boston Marathon champion, DeMar was a Keene resident. It was because of him that a few hundred visitors came to town during this September weekend.

It was approaching noon and the day was warm. I had forgotten about the cold morning when I defrosted my windshield with my Chesterfield County Virginia Library card. I had forgotten the shivers and insanity of coming to the Granite State. The race was fun. I met Deo from L.A., who was attired in red, white, and blue. I met Jessica Lacroix from Salem, Massachusetts. She successfully completed her first marathon, accomplishing it with hard work and no witchcraft. I met people young and old who pushed hard to the end and succeeded in making it happen.

The thrill of seeing the finishing banner by the commons of Keene State College was great. I had finished and I was fatigued. Twenty minutes later, the thrill of seeing Mary, the massage therapist, was greater. Taking her picture finished the roll.

I drove away from Keene State College, with the finisher's medal around my neck, feeling proud of what I had accomplished. I thought about that run for most of my trip home, until I got around New York City when reality settled in. I looked over to lower Manhattan and realized the people who really deserved a medal were those under the bright lights. The next day was the first day of the month, a new beginning. But September, 2001, would be a date and time that would linger on in the heads and hearts of everyone.

With Deo Jaravata of Los Angeles, CA

Arch Support
in
ST. LOUIS, MISSOURI

Spirit of St. Louis Marathon / MO

Sunday, October 21, 2001
Age 42

It stands on the grounds at Jefferson National Expansion Memorial, named after the President who authorized Meriwether Lewis and William Clark to explore the American West. The gray, shiny steel structure reflects much more than the bright sunshine that hits it. It reflects the efforts of trailblazers and pioneers who wanted a new way of life.

The welcome sign is 630 feet high. It's the St. Louis Gateway Arch, better known as, the Gateway to the West. Its symbol is everywhere. It's part of the logo for the Chamber of Commerce, printed on souvenir shirts in every gift store in town, and shown repeatedly with each turn of the postcard stand at Lambert International Airport.

Completed in 1965, the stainless-steel structure stands just an "Albert Pujols fly ball" from the Mississippi River. Millions flock to it each year. Not only is it amazing but knowing you can go inside is even more amazing. Two large entrances, on each side, take visitors to an "underground city" directly below the arch. Underneath, you'll find the Museum Store, offering collectibles of your St. Louis visit, as well as the Museum of Westward Expansion, a nifty look into the life of the Old West. After you've explored the ground floor, it's time to explore the top.

Eight tiny capsules, unlike the ones Tylenol sells, take visitors inside the arch to the top. The elevator is a crammed tram that seats no more than five. After the four-minute ride, you get to know your comrades quite well. The view from the east windows are of the mighty Mississippi River and Illinois. The view from the west windows are on the city streets of St. Louis. I spent most of my time looking west, concentrating on 26.2 miles of streets I would be running on the next day. Hopefully, my arches would hold up as well as this one.

I traveled to St. Louis directly from a speaking engagement in Arkansas. While sitting in the Little Rock airport, I noticed a man wearing a marathon shirt. As soon as I saw it, I knew why he was going to Missouri. I met Glen Hendrix, his wife Charlene, Ali Bachari, Julie Kurthausen, and Voula Weaver, all runners. We talked for over a half hour, right up to the minute we were called to board the plane.

Runners are easy to spot. There's a reason why T-shirts are given to all participants. We wear them. Advertisers love us for that. The St. Louis shirt had plenty of them listed. Written on the back was *Jerome Group, Civic Entrepreneurs Organization, Emerson, FastSigns, NextStart.com, Pepsi-Cola, Saint Louis Bread Company, Saint Louis Track Club, Schnucks, Saint Louis Sports Commission, The Booksource,* and *The Standing Partnership.* Compared to other shirts, that wasn't a lot. However, I did notice what they do a lot is spell out Saint Louis. I wondered if they did that in St. Paul? At the St. Louis Science Center, site of the pasta dinner, I saw many advertisements listed on backs. One gentleman didn't have any on his. He was wearing a coat and tie. He was 59-year-old Jose Nebrida of Chicago. The next day would be his 112th marathon. He would be carrying a small American flag.

A shirt you'll always see at the pasta dinners are the blue and white "50 State Marathon and D.C. Group" shirts or the gray "50 State Marathon Club" shirts. Although they're two separate groups, many runners are affiliated with both. There are no ads on these shirts. The wearers are usually over 50 years old. I love talking with these people. I ask them where they're from, the number of marathons they've completed, and where their next race is. I've never met a member who was pretentious or didn't want anything to do with you. Many of them are very humble about their remarkable achievement. I've always been in awe of them.

Another person at the pasta dinner I was in awe of wasn't wearing one of those marathon club shirts. He was Joe Henderson, columnist for *Runner's World*. The featured speaker was very humble. After his talk, we chatted for close to an hour. It was a privilege for me to sit with him. Mr. Henderson is not the average Joe, but he comes across as one.

I couldn't have told you exactly where the marathon started. All I knew was that it was downtown. A thousand runners were converging there so I figured I'd find them. With a late start out of my suburban hotel, the 15-mile drive in the dark gave me more than a few minutes of anxiety. However, seeing three guys in shorts and singlets was all I needed for reassurance that the starting line was near. I parked my car and walked the three blocks toward City Hall. I followed the music of Lee Greenwood's, *God Bless America*. It was blaring and I got as close to the speakers as I could. With the tragedy of September 11th a month earlier, a rush of emotion came over me and I teared up. It was a cool, dark morning in downtown St. Louis, and I was right where I wanted to be.

In Monday's edition of the *St. Louis Post-Dispatch*, there was a front page full color picture of Jose Nebrida during the National Anthem. He was looking upward, his right hand was over his heart, and his left hand was holding the American flag. I almost teared up again.

The 26.2 miles ahead of me was about to be the best city tour any guide could provide. Think of St. Louis and what do you see? Busch Memorial Stadium? Ran past right field. Budweiser Brewing Company? Ran right through the gates, but unfortunately, no fluid station. St. Louis Zoo? Ran past the entrance in Forest Park. Washington University? It was on my left. Enterprise Center (formerly Kiel Center) home of hockey's

Blues? It was on the right. Gateway Arch? I have pictures to prove it. Yes, St. Louis was on full display.

With temperatures barely topping 70°, I wasn't affected by the heat. I was too busy enjoying the sights and snapping pictures. I took a lot of them. I took pictures of people running, and I took pictures of people looking at people running. Those are the pictures I enjoy the most. They cheer and laugh and raise their hands in jubilation. Often, after I move on, I can hear the crowd talk about how funny it was that a runner took a picture of US. I look for big and enthusiastic crowds. Sometimes, I'll take a picture of just a couple of people sitting in lawn chairs in front of their home. Other times, I take pictures of volunteers handing me water.

There were two spectators I passed three times. I assumed they were cheering for a friend or loved one. Once that person ran by, they'd get in their car and move farther up the course. Their runner must have been going the same pace as me, because every few miles I'd spot them. She was wearing a red hat, red sweater, and holding a stick attached to a red heart with the word *Courage* on it. The man was in red too. He was also holding a rectangular sign that read, *Persist*. They weren't cheering or yelling, but just holding the signs. Their presence helped motivate me and reminded me that we all need people like that in our lives.

Heading back downtown after four hours of running, I saw hundreds of spectators on both sides of the street. After a hard left turn and then a right, the finish was about 50 yards straight ahead. I thought about taking a picture of the people as I was coming in, but decided against it. At this moment, I felt like an Olympic champion coming into the stadium for the final lap. I covered the camera in my right hand and finished in 4:10:59. I was elated.

Afterward, I met up with my Arkansas friends. I gathered them together for a group shot. They were beaming. They had just run 26 miles, 385 yards, but you'd never know it. With medals draped around their necks, they stood straight, smiled into the camera, and looked liked champions. On this day in Saint Louis, MO, they were.

Band of players

Wait For Me
in
CHICKAMAUGA, GEORGIA

Chickamauga Battlefield Marathon / GA

Saturday, November 10, 2001
Age 43

Near the border of two states, I was in another - panic. What started out as a simple drive, with plenty of time to spare, turned into an a-MAZE-ing adventure. I was lost. The race was about to start. The Chickamauga Battlefield Marathon is run in Georgia, 12 miles from the site of the packet pick-up and hotel in Chattanooga, Tennessee. On the morning of November 10, 2001, those short miles turned into almost a quarter of a tank of driving. Although I carried no weapon, I was up in arms during my march to the battlefield.

The directions to the start were included in the race information bag. In fact, I had those directions a month earlier when reading about the event online. Arriving Friday evening in Chattanooga didn't afford me the time to make a dry run to the start. Upon checkout at the hotel, I doubled checked the directions to the start. The clerk asked me a question that would haunt me for the next 30 minutes, "Do you want the shortcut?"

After my hands scraped frost off the windshield and my teeth chatted in Chattanooga, the journey began. The shortcut was turning left at a gas station, and then turning right at a daycare center, and then straight into the park and you can't miss it. I found the park, it was a big one. What I couldn't find was the single chalked line in front of Cherokee Elementary School. Many people I talked with didn't even know where that single school was. I was driving very fast through the park, passing cars in areas I had no right to pass. Like the soldiers before me, I was regrouping, retreating, and recounting my directional orders. The minutes were slowly ticking away, as I watched the second hand's assault. There was nothing I could do. The race had now begun.

I was so distraught. What should I do? Should I bag this event and try again next year? Should I run and work my way up the leader board by reeling in the runners ahead of me? Of course, that's provided I find my way to the school. I was totally lost, believing I was way out of the way, when I followed a car into a driveway. With all the self control I could muster, I slowly and calmly walked toward the woman getting out of her car and asked where the school was. Her directions included a right at the fork and then a left. I ran back to the car and sped off. When I made the last turn, I was stunned. Up ahead the runners were waiting for the start. I couldn't believe it. The race hadn't started. My concern was whether the pack was coming toward me or away from me. I pulled the car off the side of the road and sprinted into the sea of bodies, whose backs were away from me. I had my answer. I was so happy, yet out of breath, minutes before the start.

The first person I saw was Tom Pebworth of Richmond. I met Tom years earlier at a Toastmasters meeting and learned he was a state away from completing his personal goal - running a marathon in 50 states, including D.C. Days before his Delaware marathon that would clinch it, I mailed him a pencil sketch of my Delaware Marathon medal and added, "the first state shall be the last." Tom is still running. At Chickamauga his T-shirt read, "*Age and Treachery Beats Youth and Skill.*" Also in the crowd was Jose Nebrida holding the same American flag he carried in St. Louis. I took their picture.

Down Johnson Road, left on Five Points, left on Wilder, over the Battlefield Bypass, and into the Battlefield we ran - no wonder I couldn't find the start. It was an absolutely beautiful setting. From one edge of the pavement to the other, runners had the entire use of the roads. We ran past open fields and along shaded roadways. There was a good mix of uphill and downhill running and lots and lots of cannons. The Battle of Chickamauga was fought on September 19-20 in 1863 of the Civil War. Union and Confederate casualties numbered over 34,000. On this clear fall morning, 138 years later, the only Rebel Yell was the word, "GO" signaling the start of the race.

There was plenty of room to spread your arms, yet enough people on the course so you didn't feel isolated. I chatted with a woman from Chicago and asked if she saw the Bears' amazing comeback victory in the closing seconds a week earlier. She told me the big gang at her house was watching. She chuckled when describing how her husband left the room minutes before the team came back and won. Her husband now came back for her sweatshirt that she discarded to him on Highway 27, six miles into the race. The next day, the Chicago Bears won in a similar fashion. I had hoped he stayed to the finish, as he did when his wife competed in Chickamauga.

Early into the race, I was talking with a couple when he accidently got in his wife's way and she fell. After they made contact, I could see the mishap unfold. I wanted to take a picture of it, but thought it would be in bad taste. She tried to catch herself, but her momentum took her down. She was unhurt and was able to spring up. He felt badly about tripping her. I saw them after the race and said to their kids, "Did your dad tell you what he did to your mom?"

Also in the race was 17-year-old Brenton Floyd. I had heard about him. He's the youngest runner ever to have completed a marathon in each state and has run in well over 100 marathons. His grandmother, who got an early start, was up ahead and had walked over 100 marathons. The following week, they were off to another race in another state. I wondered how he managed his schoolwork and the money to run so often in so many places. I knew chances were good I would see him again in some other state. I could ask then. I couldn't imagine how someone that young had run in that many. Most marathon runners are in their 30's and 40's. It's not a young person's sport.

I felt strong upon seeing the 23-mile mark, but I knew I still had a few more hours of running. The nine-mile loop course was to be run twice. One stretch of the course was run three times. The small 23, 14, and 5 yellow mile markers were placed a few feet from each other. Hopefully, I'd feel just as good the next two times I'd see them. Generally, I'm not fond of loop courses. It's like running on a treadmill and seeing the same scenery. If I'm going to run 26 miles, I'd rather see new scenery around each turn. This loop course was different. It gave me another chance to read the placards describing events that took place on these hallowed grounds.

It was a country setting with horseback riders to the left fitting in nicely with the cannons. The race was closed to traffic, but that didn't stop the horse trailer from passing. It was going a little bit faster than I was. I was, literally, right on the horse's tail and hoped he wouldn't drop landmines to slow me.

Like so many marathons I had run, the day started off cold and warmed up. I took a picture of a race official sitting by the 11-mile marker. She looked like Grandma Moses. She was hunched over and bundled up wearing a heavy coat, white gloves, and hat. Ninety minutes later she looked like she was 20 years younger. It's amazing what the sun can do.

With four miles to go, I picked up my pace. After being on the hoofs of the horse, now I was on the heels of a human. I was running a few steps behind her strong pace. I didn't pass her, but was able to pass other runners. After the race, she told me hearing my footsteps helped her kick it in. I finished in 4 hours, 11 minutes. I was sore, but satisfied.

The beautiful, white, mock marathon T-shirt depicted the Wilder Tower with an emblem of the race. I was glad to wear it, until someone mentioned to me I had it on backwards. How appropriate. My Chickamauga experience ended the way it began.

Road Work
in
TOWNSEND, TENNESSEE

Smoky Mountain Marathon / TN

Saturday, March 23, 2002
Age 43

It was a typical afternoon in eastern Tennessee. The bumper-to-bumper traffic, off Exit 407, led into the nation's busiest National Park. People come to the Great Smoky Mountains for its natural beauty of deep forests, beautiful flowers, and rushing waterfalls. People also come here to see another park. A few stop lights ahead is Dollywood, surrounded by an abundance of hotels, fast food restaurants, and gift stores. If you forgot to buy your postcards at one shop, you had another chance up ahead. The next shop also carries moccasins, stuffed bears, and your official, *I Love Great Smoky Mountains* T-shirt. I could almost hear the voices in nearby cars. *"Hey Dad, are we there yet?"* *"Yes, son, we have arrived."*

Seeing the Smoky Mountains brought back memories of my college years. Twenty years earlier, I had graduated from Western Carolina University, near the North Carolina side of the park. During that time, I never would have imagined I'd be back in the area running a marathon. Every once in a while, I'd run ten miles near the campus. I was pooped after the loop and thought how a marathon included 16 more miles. Forget it. I really didn't enjoy running. It was boring, but I knew it was good for the body. It was unlike playing other sports with the variety of catching a pass, fielding a grounder, or sliding into third. In the sport of running, you run, and then you run some more. It was, however, an activity you could do anytime and the track was always waiting. The improvements came quicker and the endurance got better. Hitting a curve ball wasn't so easy.

The traffic in eastern Tennessee began to move. It wouldn't be long before I'd take the right fork to Highway 321 on my way to Townsend, the site of the Smoky Mountain Marathon. The steady stream of autos, eateries, and souvenir items, gave way to thick forest, sheer rock, and hairpin turns which even a chiropractor couldn't straighten. Following along the edges of the National Park, I drove on making sure both hands were on the wheel and both eyes were on the road. When the eyes did blink, they couldn't have done so simultaneously. If they had, I would have driven right through Townsend.

After I checked into the hotel, I pulled the car around to the side of the building and saw one other car parked. I was 450 miles from home, but I knew I had a friend nearby. The Tennessee license plate indicated he was a marathon runner. It told me I'd see him at the pasta dinner later that evening.

The prerace meal was one of the best I had encountered. There were several types of pasta, bread, salad, and cake. The food was good and plenty. The $8 - $12 prerace dinners are also open to family and friends of the participants. A family came from Michigan to cheer on their daughter, a wife came from South Carolina to cheer on her husband, and there were other supporters who, the next day, would high-five and hi-ho their hero by the finish line.

You never want to assume who the runners are and aren't at pasta dinners. It's better for them to correct you after you say, "Good luck tomorrow," instead of after you say, "Who did you come to cheer for?" Runners with speed can usually be detected. Runners with endurance can look deceiving. I struck up conversations with many of the people there, including Jeff Porter, from Clarksville Tennessee, who owned that Tennessee license plate I had seen at the hotel. I chatted with a couple from Connecticut, a man from Maryland, and a guy who ran in Goodland. We all had a lot in common. The next day we would run 26.2 miles. The only thing wasn't perfect about the night was the misspelling on the banner hanging from the wall. It read, *Smokey Mountain Marathon*, but maybe the *e* was added for *effort*.

About 100 runners gathered behind the bank to take their mark for the start of the race. As I looked around, I noticed I was the only one wearing shorts and a singlet. The cold temperature brought out a lot of sweatpants, long sleeve shirts, and gloves. I was shivering, but I knew once the race got started I'd warm up. Still, I was cold. My red legs gave it away. The photograph of the start, mailed weeks later, showed I wasn't the only one half-dressed. I saw two other runners who looked just like me. The only difference was they were standing on the starting line with the look of winning the race. I was deeper in the pack with the look of surviving it.

Early into the run, I snapped a picture of a highway sign by the side of the road. *Road Work Ahead* represented the next four hours for me. We crossed the bridge to the other side of the Little River on our way to our big challenge. The course would take us out for six-and-a-half miles before we'd make the turn to come back. Two miles into the race, I turned and snapped a picture of runners coming up a small hill. The marathoner who led the way pointed to his race number and said, "You can tell people you took the picture of the winner." However, we would soon discover the truth. His speed was only in getting his race entry in before anyone else.

The scenery was rustic. There were signs reading *Cattle Crossing* and *Equestrian Xing*. There were beautiful log homes and run-down shacks with piles of junk cars and other collectibles covering front yards. It was the best and worst of Appalachia. There were moments in the race when the faces I saw were only curious cows looking at me. There were stretches reminding me of my 10-mile runs 20 years earlier. The winding roads, the mountains in the distance, the wooden posts, and wire fences brought back fond memories. I stopped and took pictures of a lot of these sights, while ignoring the pinned black number 94 on my chest. After all, I was running a race.

Is it any wonder I never felt sore? I took the race very slowly. The times I stopped were only to look through the viewfinder. I powered up the hills and ran a steady pace. Returning to town felt like one of my easy training runs. I finished under the banner and spun around for my second trip out. The first half was easy. Let's see what the second half would feel like. I took less pictures and paid little attention to mile markers, which were going to pass anyway. I concentrated on the familiar landscape, passed the same cows, and took water from the Tennessee volunteers who served me earlier. Like the fisherman I had noticed on the banks of the Little River, I was reeling it in on the final leg of my trip. I moved quickly past the RV trailer park on my left and over the bridge on my right. I passed runners with a little less than a mile to go.

Up ahead I noticed a runner with confederate head gear and wearing a Kiawah Island Marathon T-shirt. It was Bobby McAlister of Hopkins, SC, whom I talked at length with the night before. After catching up with him, we ran together toward the finish. Fifty yards from the end of the race, he took off sprinting, while I just tucked in from behind without challenging. Bobby bolted like it was going to be a photo finish, while I took a photo at the finish.

I picked up a few treats at the refreshment table and collapsed on the grass, cheering on the other runners. About 30 minutes later, I got my crooked legs going and walked along Highway 321 to a

convenience store to buy an ice cream bar. In the store, I was asked how I did in the race. I answered, "Great." If I had shown the picture I had taken of the sign at the construction area near the finish, he would have known why. It read, *End Road Work.*

Cowboy Up

"Get off my land!"

Friends and Feuds
in
GOODY, KENTUCKY

Hatfield & McCoy Marathon / KY

Saturday, June 8, 2002
Age 43

I f reading the rules and regulations didn't scare you, then maybe the sound of the shotgun would. If that didn't make you jump, then maybe the picture of those two outlaws on the T-shirt would. This was no ordinary event. This was the Hatfield and McCoy Marathon and it was to be run in the heart of feud country. *So be careful out there. There's trouble in them thar hills.*

```
3. ALL RUNNERS MUST PASS ALL THE CHECK POINTS OR YOU MIGHT BE LOST IN
   DISQUALIFIED OR EVEN WORSE SHOT OR WORST OF ALL YOU COULD BE LOST IN
   THEM THAR HILL AND NEVER BE HEARD FROM AGAIN.
4. WATER STOPS WILL BEGIN AROUND MILE #2 AND THEN APPROXIMATELY EVERY
   MILE AFTER THAT.
5. PLEASE BE AWARE THAT PEOPLE FROM THE HHILLS AIN'T USED TO SEE'N
   RUNNERS ON THE ROAD SO WATCH OUT FOR TRAFFIC AND POTHOLES.
6. FINISH THE RACE BEFORE DARK!!! CAUSE THAT' WHEN MOST OF THE SHOOTIN'S
```

When I mailed my $25 check to race director, David Hatfield, I realized there was nothing fictitious about this marathon. This was the real McCoy.

The entire route was stamped with Hatfield's and McCoy's. It was a 26-mile outdoor museum with historical markers describing the fights, the shootings, and the stabbings of the two families. There was the election night fight of 1882 when three McCoy brothers killed a Hatfield. Farther along, another marker described the three McCoy brothers who were tied to a Pawpaw tree and killed in retaliation by the Hatfield clan. The families could never find a peaceful way to resolve their differences, but all that changed. As recently as the year 2000, a reunion brought the families together for the first time. Each June, for three days, it's a festival of friendship. Now, when they hit, fight, and throw, it's with tennis balls, fish, and horseshoes. When they square off, it's about dancing, and when they clench their fists, it's during the tug-of-war competition. Both families seem to like it that way.

Pasta wasn't the only thing on the plate during the prerace dinner. Actors, portraying Hatfield and McCoy, exchanged barbs and insults at each other. Their words, like the food in front of us, were well-heated. Following the performance, another Hatfield spoke to the group. Carl Hatfield had led the West Virginia Track Club to the 1978 AAU National Championship.

I was fortunate I was at the dinner. If it weren't for the graciousness of John and Jeannie Rivard, I would have still been looking for hotel space. The marathon was during the reunion festival and rooms were occupied with Hatfield's and McCoy's and a few hundred other last names.

I usually make hotel reservations. This time I hadn't. I believed I would have found something in or around Goody, Kentucky. Instead, I found John and Jeannie. John Rivard overheard me when I asked the volunteers at the registration table if there was a hotel nearby. He said, "You're not going to find anything. You can stay with us." He then looked at his wife, who was handing out T-shirts and said, "That would be okay, right?" She answered, "Sure."

It was a tremendous blessing for me. John had stopped in from work to give something to Jeannie when I asked my question. Immediately, he had me follow him to the house. From the parking lot to this West Virginia hotel, I trailed his Verizon telephone truck across the Tug River into Kentucky. We traveled about five miles, took some turns, and headed up a narrow street with small homes on each side. I followed him up the steep hill, until we parked our vehicles outside a big, beautiful log cabin in Turkey Creek, Kentucky. I had just hit the lottery. He showed me the room I'd be staying in, explained to me how to work the television remote, pointed me to the refrigerator, and gave me the key to the house. Talk about trust. He went off to work, and I went back to the hotel for the pre-race dinner.

Later that evening, their son, Josh, made a surprise visit from his Lexington, Kentucky, home. I was the athlete, but Josh was the good sport. He slept on the living room floor. That evening, half

178

the house was filled with marathoners. Jeannie was running her first.

The 26.2 mile race couldn't make up its mind which state to stay in. We began in Kentucky, then went into West Virginia, then back to Kentucky and finished in West Virginia. There were a few "50 Staters" running the race who counted it as a West Virginia run because that state had only one other marathon within its borders. I counted the race as a Kentucky run because of its long distance from Richmond. According to the rules in both the 50 States Marathon Club and 50 & DC Marathon Group, if a race enters another state, you could only count it as one, providing it either started or finished there. However, if you ran the marathon again you could count the other state.

Phil Little was running the race a second time. The 59-year-old Floridian, whom I met on the course during the Smoky Mountain run, was going to add another race the following month to his 100-plus marathons. It would be a marathon that would give him a feeling of being on top of the world, but that's where the race was. Phil told me the cost to race above the Arctic Circle was costing him over $3,000. But Phil, you do get the free T-shirt.

There were stretches on the Kentucky side where houses stood inches from the road. A homeowner, standing on his porch, could lose a hand while waving to a friend if a truck barreled down the road. Running along Highway 49, I spotted the mailbox of V. R. Hatfield and Lucas McCoy. During the race I'd see more Hatfield and McCoy mailboxes. It was exciting for me to be running through this historic region. For years, I had heard about this famous feud, but didn't know where it all started. On this day I knew.

The region was also coal country. The long trains rattling nearby confirmed it. Twenty miles into the race, the trains took over. The lights were flashing and the gate was coming down when I was about 100 yards away. I was so happy. It came at a time when my legs were extremely stiff. I caught up with Darren Boas and Dudley Fontaine, who both had nowhere to go. The aid station was by the crossing gate and I drank several cupfuls. I stretched and loosened up the muscles in my legs. Four more runners had now shown up, including Phil Little. The train kept rolling and I wasn't the least bit annoyed with its passing. A full five minutes later the gate went up and the six of us went through.

The unexpected rest added a spring to my legs and I felt strong, until I passed Uriah McCoy's house. A tour was going on with the guide holding a shotgun in the front yard. I said, "Point your rifle this way so I can take a picture." He moved close to me and directed the end of the barrel to the sky, and then BOOOOM! The noise was deafening and my heart jumped. I asked for it. I concentrated on running after that.

Soon, I was back into West Virginia, finishing in front of the Coal House in downtown Matewan, as an antique car show was taking place. The scene reminded me of a *Back to the Future* movie. Runners, who spent most of the morning alone, were thrust immediately into crowds. No one paid much attention to us. I sat on the sidewalk in front of a store, with a cup of water in my hand and a medal around my neck. A short time later, I maneuvered my way through the crowd and the cars to retrieve my own car, which was parked in another state.

I drove back to my log cabin and showered. Jeannie and Josh returned a half hour later. I thanked them for their generosity and returned the key. My last photograph  of the trip was of them with their arms around each other standing on the deck. As I drove away, I thought about my good fortune. I wound up with the best hotel in town, including a built-in swimming pool, full refrigerator, and a big television in my room. What would have happened if John Rivard hadn't stopped by to see his wife?

I left Kentucky and drove over the bridge into West Virginia. I passed railroad car after railroad car of black West Virginia coal and drove farther and farther away from my new memories. On Highway 52, I pulled into the lot of a small diner to eat lunch. There were two Verizon telephone trucks parked outside. I approached two men sitting in a booth and asked if they knew John Rivard. Immediately, one of the men said, "Are you the guy who stayed with John?" The next sentence was, "Sit down and join us."

For many people, the Kentucky/West Virginia border is famous for its fightin' and feudin.' It used to be for me, too. The summer of 2002 changed that.

"Now, now, no more fight'n boys!"

Gasping For Air
in
MANITOU SPRINGS, COLORADO

Pikes Peak Marathon / CO

Sunday, August 18, 2002
Age 43

Thirteen miles would take me over six hours to complete. I would be on the course for 9 hours, 49 minutes and 49 seconds. I would spend 30 minutes on a cot hooked up to an IV. The race was billed as "America's Ultimate Challenge." There was truth to its advertising. One didn't have to look at the course to know what was in store, the length of the waiver agreement would do it instead. Even in its fine print the words kept coming. I noticed words such as *hypothermia, shortness of breath, loose gravel*, and *heatstroke*. This was the Pikes Peak Marathon. Enter at your own risk.

Pikes Peak, located just over from Colorado Springs and just under from Colorado's sun, stands at 14,110 feet above sea level. It's the mountain that inspired Katherine Bates to write, *America the Beautiful*, with its purple majesty and amber waves of grain. However, the only purple majesty and amber waves of grain I saw was after I threw up the grapes and crackers near the summit. Still, the view was breathtaking, but boy, how I wanted that breath back.

The Pikes Peak Marathon is one of the more popular events in the country. The 800 slots are quickly filled months before the mid-August race. After I sent my registration in, I took a deep breath and asked myself, what am I getting myself into? Without visiting the mountain and experiencing the altitude, there was no way to get a grip as to what was to come, but there were a few basics. Train like you have never trained before. I heard that advice plenty. It was strongly advised you carry a water bottle and drink, drink, drink. At high altitudes, it's easy to get dehydrated, especially if you're over exerting yourself or lest we say, running a marathon at high altitude.

I did a lot of running in preparation, but I was concerned about the altitude. I didn't know what it was like to *not* breathe. However, friends thought the day I sent my registration in was a moment my brain lacked oxygen, but there was no turning back. I was headed to Colorado. I arrived the day before the race and checked into the Apache Court Motel in Manitou Springs. I had the hotel owner walking around the lot in search of the big mountain. She said, "I think it's that one over there." From the street, Pikes Peak is hard to distinguish like Mount Fuji or snow-covered Mount Rainier. The area is ringed with mountains so to an out-of-towner you wouldn't know where to find the famed peak. One thing was certain, no matter where it was, 14,000 feet was up there.

I drove to Soda Springs Park to pick up my runner's packet, and talked to runners who had just been shuttled back down after finishing the Pikes Peak Ascent. Some of these hearty souls would run the marathon the next day. After reading and hearing so much about Pikes Peak, I was looking at the runners in awe, knowing these people had just returned from the Promised Land. I asked many of them how they felt and about the weather conditions at the summit.

I spent a lot time with 72-year-old Lyle Langlois. He was amazing. Lyle not only had run a marathon in every state, but he had bicycled all over the globe, and is considered a leading expert on subways, having visited almost every subway system in the world. We talked about life underground and what he just experienced atop it on the summit of Pikes Peak.

The day was warm, and Pikes Peak, with its ever-changing weather, was warm too. Forecasters predicted the same for the next day. At the outdoor pasta feast, Pikes Peak legend, Matt Carpenter, spoke about what to expect on the mountain. Carpenter, a Manitou Springs resident, is the epitome of fitness. A world-class trail runner, Matt has won the Pikes Peak Marathon several times and knows every boulder, rock, and stretch of the mountain. Neal Beidleman, another world class climber, also spoke. Neil had climbed Mount Everest and was on the fateful expedition in May of 1997 that claimed seven lives. His story is mentioned in Jon Krakauer's best seller, *Into Thin Air*. Beidleman tells how the conditions were so bad on Everest that he felt like he was in the middle of a milk bottle. On this day he appeared to be a lot more comfortable. He was in shorts.

The race began on pavement in downtown Manitou Springs. The pavement didn't last long. The course headed through the open fence and started up the mountain. The narrow trail turned into a bottleneck for the hundreds of runners. The running was replaced with walking. It was a steady climb and I thought at this pace, I shouldn't have any trouble at all. I was walking before hitting the two-mile mark. The trail was beautifully groomed. It was nature at

its best with dirt, rocks, trees, and fresh air, while heart and muscle constantly moved upward. I soon realized the best training I could have done was to stay on a treadmill at its steepest incline for hours. I was feeling a strain in my inner thighs.

Less than five miles into the race, I saw a mountain peak far in the distance. I asked a runner what it was. He said, "It's Pikes Peak." I thought he was kidding. The climb hadn't even begun. In the race to the top, there were a few down hills, but there was always an uphill around the next bend. Volunteers, attired in their official Pikes Peak Marathon purple T-shirts, doled out refreshments and fruit along the

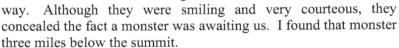

way. Although they were smiling and very courteous, they concealed the fact a monster was awaiting us. I found that monster three miles below the summit.

My walking pace slowed as I moved above tree line. "Above tree line" means living things don't last long up there. Birds, however, do. I was quite annoyed with this one bird that kept flying in stealing grapes from the tray the volunteer had placed down. "How dare you?" I said to that bird. "Isn't there a worm you can pluck instead?"

The scenery was gorgeous as I entered the boulder field. The ants above me were runners/walkers working their way to the top. I was moving very slowly when I came to the sign that read, "*1 Mile to Summit.*"

With about a half mile to go, too many people to count were passing me. I started getting nauseous. I stopped and hung my head over a rock and started throwing up. I never should have complained about that bird, because the grapes were coming up and the crackers were on their way too.

Word got down the mountain a runner was sick. A medic was heard asking, "Who's sick up there?" I slowly lifted my head and raised my hand. He offered me oxygen, but I refused, knowing I would be disqualified from the race. He slowly walked with me and gently persuaded me to press on. If I weren't on the summit, the halfway point, by 1:30 p.m. I would not be allowed to continue. Race officials state any participant who can't make the summit by six-and-a-half hours is not going to finish the race. It's a safety measure that is strictly enforced.

I was taking baby steps. My pace was not going to get me to the top in time. As one medic left and another took his place. She walked with me and stressed time was running out if I didn't move faster. I had a choice to make, but I was determined to continue. I was so sick. I was getting the chills. I was nauseous, lightheaded, and tired. I was on the mountain for over six hours and I hadn't even reached the halfway point. It also didn't help that during the past week I had been sporting a mild cold.

I continued and walked a little quicker. Finally, I looked up and saw the yellow banner I so desperately was searching for; *Pikes Peak Marathon Summit.* Somehow, I managed to have the sense to pull out my camera and snap a picture. A volunteer approached me with a marker and stroked a green line over my number, indicating I had made it to the top. I arrived in 6 hours and 13 minutes. I kissed a lady on the cheek and then enjoyed the view from 14,000 feet for several minutes. I was standing on top of the world, but time was running out. I had to get back down and finish by the 5 p.m. cutoff time. It took me 6 hours and 13 minutes to go halfway. I needed to do the other half in three and a half hours. Fortunately, it was downhill.

I said good-bye to the many volunteers and started running down the mountain, while yelling "thanks" to the medic who seemed surprised I was very much alive. It was an emotional moment and I was almost in tears. I was racing to my dream of completing the Pikes Peak Marathon. Every step I made I was losing altitude and that in itself made me feel better. I was determined to get back down by 5 p.m. I was not going to be denied. I zigged and zagged running all alone down this famous mountain. I followed the trail and stepped over and between boulders and continued below tree line. I still felt nauseous and knew anything I put inside me would soon come up. I drank very little and continued to run, while taking minimal walking breaks. Constantly checking my watch, I plowed on. The trail, which earlier was littered with runners, was clear sailing. Nobody was in sight, as I raced in search of the other banner draped in downtown Manitou Springs.

Moving down the mountain, I encountered a few runners who were slowly, but steadily, making their way home. I passed them, but felt they weren't going to make it in time. Toward the end of the trail, a couple of cyclists went by me. Up ahead I'd hear them stop and then they'd start up again. It finally dawned on me they were picking up the mile markers to clean up the course. I was right behind them as they were robbing me of important information. I didn't know how much farther this ordeal was and the time was getting too close to 5 p.m. for my comfort.

At about 4:45, when the sun was going down, my spirits were going up. I hit pavement and I knew the end was near. When I passed the Pikes Peak Cog Rail, I knew the expression on my tired and sick face was not a flattering look to those who were crossing the street from the depot. I turned the corner and ran under the banner that read, "Finish" with 10 minutes and 11 seconds to spare. I did it! I did it!

I was escorted to the back of the tent and laid on a cot, as a medic stuck a needle in my arm, set up an IV, and put two bags of fluid into me. The tent was on the side of the road next to an open lane of traffic. As I was sprawled out throwing up into a bag, a car pulled up to the light. A young boy sitting in the back seat glanced over to me with an expression that said, "what is this?" Before he could find out, the light turned green and his dad drove off. If the kid never runs a marathon, I'll feel somewhat responsible.

I was the last runner to be treated. The medical people planned on folding their tent at 5:30 p.m. and they adhered to their schedule. They could administer no more than two IV bags. Anything more, I would have had to check into a hospital. They advised me what to eat and that I should take it slowly. I wasn't about to differ. Shortly after I finished, a runner approached me saying, "I saw you near the summit and I can't believe you made it." He was so surprised I was under the finish banner because I was in a terrible state. It made me feel proud of what I had accomplished.

I walked to my car. It was easy to find. It was the only car parked on the side of the street. As I did when I drove to the start, I turned the headlights on. It was a long day. I got back to the Apache and flopped onto the bed and flipped on the television. Rich Beem was talking about his PGA Championship win over the late charging Tiger Woods. After a short rest, I went to an Italian restaurant and indulged.

The next day I headed back to the airport. As the plane lifted from

Colorado Springs, I looked out the window and saw the mountain I had trouble distinguishing a few days earlier. Soon, the plane was at 14,000 feet and climbing. This time, I was breathing a lot easier.

America the Beautiful

Springs and Spuds
in
POCATELLO, IDAHO

Pocatelli Marathon / ID

Saturday, August 31, 2002
Age 43

It was beautiful in its purest form; the blue sky, the green fields, the mountains in the distance. It was open spaces and open roads in a place that opened its arms to over 100 marathon runners from across the country. This was Pocatello. Welcome to Idaho. The slogan for the Pocatello Marathon was exactly what I needed after completing Pikes Peak less than two weeks earlier. I could live with *Running the Gap*.

The two-and-a-half hour drive from the Salt Lake City airport was straight up Interstate 15, passing through Ogden, Brigham City, and the Caribou National Forest in Idaho. Billboards reminded you of natural hot springs in the area. I vowed I would find them before my marathon mission was over.

At the Ramada Inn in nearby Chubbuck, I picked up my runner's packet with its usual goodies of pens, notepads, aspirin, and T-shirt, but there was more. The next table was overflowing with potatoes. I grabbed my five-pound sack and thought about how I was going to get it into my small suitcase for the trip home. Mashing them wasn't an option. Another item I found in the packet wasn't edible, but did whet my appetite; the brochure for Lava Hot Springs. I got in my car and found it.

Located about 30 miles from Pocatello, Lava Hot Springs is a runner's delight. Natural underground springs, ranging in temperatures from 102 to 112°, bubbled to the surface. I could have stayed in those "healing waters" all day, instead of the two hours I did. Young and old sat quietly along the benches of the gravel bottom pool or stood in the three-foot water. It was a place I needed to be after a marathon, but time wasn't going to be on my side. Any "cold feet" I may have had of stepping into the hot springs disappeared as soon as I touched the water. It was hot, but absolutely soothing. I had entered the state only a couple of hours earlier and already had my potatoes and hot bath. No wonder they call Idaho "The Gem State."

Around the corner from the hot springs was an Olympic size municipal pool with three platforms, the highest being 33 feet above the water. I stopped there first. After I paid my admission, I was asked by the teenage girl from behind the counter if I was going to go off the platform. I told her I probably would. She then handed me a pen and told me to *"sign here"* and gave me a wrist band to wear, indicating I was good to go. When I got a closer look at the platform, I prayed there wasn't going to be another band put around my toe. I climbed the ladder and walked to the edge of the platform. I peered below while holding onto the railing. I had never stood that high from a diving board, yet I was only on the second platform. The lifeguard gave me the clearance to go and I jumped.

As I was falling feet first into the water, I thought, this was not a good idea. My foot stung for several hours. As I swam painfully away, I noticed a skinny young girl jumping off the platform above mine. She surfaced smiling and headed back for more. Thankfully, the hot springs were around the corner.

The pain in my foot was gone when I awoke Saturday in anticipation of the 3rd running of the Pocatello Marathon. I drove in the predawn darkness to the train depot to board the bus that would take runners 26 miles out of town. I sat in the front seat across from Carmen Baggett from Marietta, Georgia. She and her husband came to Idaho to visit family. She would finish the race in 4 hours and 15 minutes. Not bad for someone running with cracked ribs. Sitting behind Carmen was Mike Sullivan, the winner of the inaugural Pocatello Marathon in 2000. On this day Mike would finish in 3rd place with a time of 2 hours and 54 minutes.

Paul Piplani of Phoenix and Art Stanger of Boca Raton were seated behind me. Paul had run in over 300 marathons. The next day he would add another in Albuquerque. Art was preparing for his 100th marathon. On this day the 43-year-old would become a centurion. Two weeks earlier, he almost claimed Pikes Peak as his 100th, but Pikes Peak claimed him. He dropped out near the summit. The following year, the Floridian dentist went back to sink his teeth into the mountain one more time. He succeeded. It would be one of 20 marathons he would run that year. Also running in Pocatello was Boonsom Hartman of Chicago. It would be a memorable day for her, but aren't most birthdays?

The bus kept motoring down the highway. I questioned the driver, "You mean we haven't gone 26 miles yet?" He only smiled. What did he care? He was going to be driving the empty bus back to town later that morning. The rest of us had to run back. The bus finally came to a stop just south of the town of McCammon on Marsh Creek Road. It was a long way from any kind of civilization and there was nothing around, except for a handful of volunteers, a police car, and an older gentleman holding a pistol. My hunches told me he was the starter.

We ran parallel to Interstate 15 and the Portneuf River, which those Lava Hot Springs flow into. The scenery was spectacular as we headed toward Idaho's second largest city, on this beautiful sunny August day. Most of the spectators were the four  legged ones, who looked at us sheepishly and sounded "horse." It was the most traffic they had ever seen on Marsh Creek Road.

The first human spectators I noticed were a couple seated in lawn chairs, at the end of their driveway, near the 13-mile mark. As I approached, I asked if I could take a picture of them from behind with runners in the background. However, when I turned around, there weren't any runners in view. Instead, I took a picture of them. She wore blue denim cutoff shorts and a blue American hero shirt. Her husband had on blue jeans, plaid shirt, and a white NRA cap. They wished me well as I continued on.

Although I didn't see a soul behind me, I knew there were rubber soles back there. There were times when a cluster of runners would pass me, but I would overtake them on hills. Then slowly but surely, they would narrow the distance and pass me again. This went on three or four times with this particular group. I told them they were in a "No Passing Zone," but they didn't obey. I passed one runner who I had seen at another race. As I passed her I said, "You did Great Smoky, didn't you?" We kept talking with our voices getting louder and louder, as I moved farther and farther away.

I was hurting approaching the 21-mile mark. My calves were very stiff, and I was happy to make a pit stop at the aid station. I gulped down several cups of water and stretched for a long time. Before I ran on, I rounded up the six volunteers for a group picture. They each held a cup of water in each hand and reached out toward me when I snapped the picture. I labeled it, *A Tip of the Cup to my Friends at Mile 21*. I had a strong feeling I'd stop and meet new friends a mile later.

I had a little more than five miles to go and they were going to be tough. I kept the camera in my pouch the rest of the way. I had more pressing matters to deal with. The stretching helped and surprisingly, I took water on the run at mile 22 through  25, as the scenery changed from open land to neighborhoods. I saw more of 4 wheels than I did of 4 legs as I came into the downtown area of Pocatello. Appropriately, I finished on all 4's myself with a time of 4 hours, 44 minutes, 40.4 seconds. However, the "4" that stood out in my mind was the time I needed to be at the Salt Lake City airport for my trip back. That race was just beginning. Hopefully, the potatoes wouldn't slow me down.

Horsetails & Ponytails

The Moon and the Fires
in
APACHE JUNCTION, ARIZONA

Lost Dutchman Marathon / AZ

Sunday, January 19, 2003
Age 44

Playing from the car's CD player was Jamie O'Neal's, *"There Is No Arizona."* The popular country music song is about a broken promise from a man who assured his girlfriend, that after he situated himself in Arizona, he'd send for her. The months passed when she realized she'd been lied to and that there was no Arizona. It's a sad message, but a beautiful song. I played it constantly. I played it while looking at the beautiful saguaro cactus. I played it while gazing up into the majestic mountains. I played it while squinting under the huge Southwest sun. I was now convinced. There IS an Arizona. Thank God for that.

I had a day-and-a-half to spend in this wondrous state, and I was going to take full advantage of it. My first stop was to see *BOB*, better known as, Bank One Ballpark (now known as Chase Field), home of baseball's 2001 World Series Champion Diamondbacks. Discouraged because of the locked gates preventing me from peering in, I decided to eat lunch at the restaurant adjacent to the ballpark. After getting off the elevator, the hostess led me to a table out on the terrace. It was spectacular. I was sitting in the left field stands in one of America's most beautiful stadiums. I pictured Randy Johnson on the mound and the excitement of the D'backs winning it all. I ate my pasta, read the Arizona Republic, and simply gawked. After lunch, I walked to the next block and circled U.S. Airways Arena (formerly America West Arena) home of NBA's Phoenix Suns. Afterward, I left town.

I drove 35 miles east of Phoenix to Apache Junction, site of the second annual Lost Dutchman Marathon. I had no trouble finding it. After checking into my hotel, I drove several more miles to the registration site at Gold Canyon Golf Resort. Looking at the green grass of the golf course up against the desert terrain, suggested the grounds crew should be well compensated. It looked everything like the postcard mailed to me a month earlier.

I reintroduced myself to Tony Lopetrone and Nancy Broadbridge. I met the husband and wife team in Omaha during their successful quest to run a marathon in every state during one calendar year. They've logged thousands of miles over the years, but Nancy's bad knee was going to keep her out of this race. I assumed the injury was a result of high mileage or that she twisted it from pushing too much during a race. I was wrong on both counts. Nancy's knee injury came from crossing paths with her cat in their Michigan home.

During the pasta dinner, runners were enlightened by a slide presentation by local legend, Tom Kollenborn. He spoke about the history of Superstition Mountain and the search for gold in the Lost Dutchman Mine. Unfortunately, things did not pan out for all the runners whose route would take them near that mine.

The next morning, I drove to the Rodeo Grounds to wait for the bus that would transport us to the start. I arrived very early and pulled my car alongside Don Lang's. The Los Angeles resident doesn't spend a lot of time in Los Angeles. Don had run over 300 marathons around the world. Avoiding the predawn chill, we sat in our cars and talked for about 30 minutes.

I got on the first of four buses for the ride to the start. The sun had yet to surface when we left the grounds, as the bus headed down the road and up the mountain. Turning left, turning right and then up, up, up we went. When the bus stopped, I was one of the first out. I walked from around the front of the bus and was awestruck by the beauty that stood before me. The staging area was atop a mountain, where the moon and bright stars shone on us. The cactus, disguised as referees signaling a touchdown, was all around. Centered on all this beauty were about 30 flickering fire logs, spaced a few feet apart, to keep runners warm.

It was the most beautiful setting I had ever seen. I felt privileged to be there. I felt thankful for my good health and what running had brought to me. As time went on, more buses arrived and the "*Oh, Wow's*" were heard by almost everyone who exited. As the crowds got bigger, I was even more thankful I was on the first bus and was able to experience this setting by myself. I immediately huddled up to a log with the flames just inches away. Attired in shorts and a singlet, I was cold. The Arizona sun had yet to arrive.

At 7:30 a.m., while the sun and moon occupied the sky, the race got going. While running down the dirt road, I felt pockets of hot and cold air, depending upon where the sun was hitting. It didn't take me long to realize the day was going to be hot. I smiled at the singing cowboy, waved to the kids on the bus, and snapped pictures of the Arizona desert. We got off the dirt and onto the pavement, turning right on Apache Boulevard. We passed golf courses, ran through neighborhoods, and gave an extra look to the belly dancers who were inspiring us on as they appeared to be shaking things off. The scenery constantly changed, but there were always mountains in view. I enjoyed the sights and took several pictures. The running seemed secondary.

The last few miles, the course entered a dirt road closed to traffic. The sun was high in the sky and there was no place to hide. It was getting hotter each minute. Around the enthusiastic purple-dressed ladies at the aid station, the course turned left. Directly ahead of me was the biggest hill of the day. I kept my legs in motion and ran through the entrance of a cardboard wall.

Officials had placed it on the top of the hill to inform us the worst was over.

With four miles to go, I spotted the sign reading, "*It's almost all downhill from here.*" The word *almost* was unsettling to me. Was the person who planted that sign a runner? After the sign was placed, did he drive his pickup truck to the finish? *Almost* doesn't count, except in horseshoes, I remembered being told.

Well, the sign was truthful. It was almost all downhill. So was my energy. Near the 24-mile mark, the temperature was well into the 80's. Hovering over the fire logs seemed as if it were days before, instead of the few hours it really had been. The finish was around the corner from the rodeo grounds. I moved painfully by the site, yearning to be on the other side of the fence at my car. I would have to wait. I drank water at every station, but still felt dehydrated. I was thirsty, hot, and anxious to finish. The end didn't come soon enough. Why couldn't the race end at 26 miles? The 385 yards seemed a lot longer after I had made the last turn.

A few yards from the finish, a runner started doing push-ups. It might have been his way to show he was still feeling strong after covering 26.2 miles. I couldn't resist. I ran over to him, and good-naturedly, put my foot on his back. It was the highest I had raised my foot all day. Moments later, I crossed the finish line and accepted the most beautiful medal I'd ever received. The purple, black, and yellow half-inch-thick medal depicts a prospector and mule with the words, *"Run for the Gold."* The next day, I replaced the ribbon with my car keys.

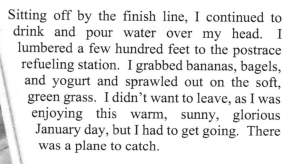

Sitting off by the finish line, I continued to drink and pour water over my head. I lumbered a few hundred feet to the postrace refueling station. I grabbed bananas, bagels, and yogurt and sprawled out on the soft, green grass. I didn't want to leave, as I was enjoying this warm, sunny, glorious January day, but I had to get going. There was a plane to catch.

After boarding the bus to the rodeo grounds to retrieve my car, I headed toward Phoenix. On the way, I stopped at a mall and limped inside to buy a towel to inquire about a school or YMCA where I could take a shower. I was told the recreation center was about six miles away and was open on Sundays.

On the shuttle bus to the airport terminal, I was joined by several passengers with golf bags. With many of the bags looking the same, passengers remaining on board were very observant of those who were getting off at their respective stops. It proved the simplicity about marathoners. My athletic equipment was contained in a small

blue nylon carry-on bag. Golfers don't have it so easy. I laughed when a gentleman in the back exclaimed, "The clubs that are bent are mine."

Hog Heaven
in
FAYETTEVILLE, ARKANSAS

Hogeye Marathon / AR

Sunday, March 30, 2003
Age 44

With a name like "*Hogeye*," I just had to enter that race. Arkansans are devoted to their hogs and hogs were everywhere in Fayetteville. Located in the Ozarks of northwest Arkansas, Fayetteville is home to the University of Arkansas, and on this day, it was home to the Hogeye Marathon. Watch out everybody! The runners are coming and they're hogging the roads.

The 200-mile drive from Little Rock to Fayetteville was as smooth as the three-hour flight from Baltimore. The scenery on I-40 included trees, cows, and a lot of trucks. It seemed as if every third truck had the name, *Tyson* or *Walmart* on it. My path was taking me toward their corporate headquarters. It was evident the two companies employ excellent drivers. Unlike their prices, the Wal-Mart trucks never "rolled back" and the Tyson trucks prevented me from knowing, "*How do chickens cross the road?*"

I arrived in Fayetteville on Saturday, the day before the race. After checking into my hotel, I drove down North College Avenue to the Radisson Hotel to pick up my runner's packet. The Radisson, located in Downtown Square, was the host hotel. I opted for a hotel several miles away that was less expensive. I do know, when I turned the lights off at night, my room looked like the Ritz. I prefer to stay away from race headquarters to see another part of town, and to get another flavor of the city. Plus, I can always find a hotel at a better rate. The drawback is the longer commute to the starting line.

After picking up my yellow bib number and Hogeye Marathon T-shirt, with the picture of an Arkansas hog on it, I walked around the square in search of a good eatery. I found one. It was extremely busy with college kids and parents. I sat at the counter, quietly reading the Arkansas Democrat and eating my salad and meatball sub. I was caught off guard by the brisk weather that greeted me when I arrived in town. The day was cold and windy. The singlet I was planning to wear would only be worn if the temperature climbed 20° by race day. It wasn't encouraging.

I drove off to explore more of Fayetteville. While driving down Highway 71, I saw supporters on one side of the street, protestors on the other. I was glad I was driving north. I slowed the car and lowered the passenger side window, as a gentleman handed me an American flag. A television news photographer caught the moment. America had recently gone to war with Iraq to oust Saddam Hussein. That day on Highway 71, I saw a lot of American flags and a lot of support for our troops. My Fayetteville flag is still in my home.

I continued down the highway and stopped at Barnes & Noble across from Northwest Arkansas Mall. Near the entrance, a huge poster advertised the following day's 2 p.m. book signing by Arkansas's own Susan McDougal. McDougal, who spent time in prison for her Whitewater doings in connection with Bill Clinton, was known for keeping quiet. All of that was going to change. Her book had recently been published.

Darkness had fallen over Fayetteville when I headed back to the Radisson for the evening's pasta dinner. The runners had exclusive rights to the hotel's restaurant upstairs. I sat with Cathy McCarty, Ron Christen, and his wife, Cynthia. The three Floridians were well on their way to running a marathon in each state. We questioned each other as to see if we had ever crossed paths. Once Cathy mentioned she sings while she runs, I asked if she ran High Plains in Goodland, Kansas. When she said, "Yes," I told her, "I remember you!" Eight months later, when the three came to run Richmond, I picked them up at the airport. We've kept in contact ever since.

The runner's expo was long over and my opportunity to get a long sleeve shirt had passed, until I found Mike. The race director also works at Fleet Feet Sports store in town. He made a call to a coworker, and a shirt was going to be dropped off at my hotel. I gave Mike my credit card information and the shirt was on its way. Later that night I asked Mike, "How much did I pay for this?"

The morning of the race, attired in my running garb, I handed my room key back to the hotel clerk. He said, "The race starts at 7:30, you know." This wasn't comforting as it was 7:25. I said, "No, it starts at 8 o'clock." Gosh, I hoped I was right. It gave me an uneasy feeling. I drove the 10 minutes to the town square and saw runners loosening up, not running. My uneasy feeling subsided. I stood atop a brick wall, held onto a tree, and stretched my calf muscles. The day was chilly, but the shirt worked wonders. My legs would quickly warm up once the race got underway.

The race took the runners past the huge Donald W. Reynolds Razorback Stadium. I could only imagine what Saturday afternoons during the fall was like in Fayetteville, with the town hopping over its hogs. The course traveled over country roads, under overpasses, and went parallel to Interstate 540. I caught up with Cathy, and we ran and chatted for about a mile before I sped ahead. It also gave her an opportunity to start singing.

The day was clear and sunny, but still cool. I snapped a picture of two hearty spectators, wrapped in winter coats, sitting in lawn chairs. They were enthusiastic and it was nice to see their support for the runners. I was anxious to see them on the turnaround, but miles later when I turned the corner and looked up at the hill, they were gone. The marathon is a long event and runners are grateful for any support they get. I think running four hours is easier than sitting by the street in the cold for that long.

I ran a slow, steady pace and hardly suffered any discomfort the entire way. I chatted with many runners, enjoyed the Arkansas landscape, and smiled to all those who handed me a cup of water. The route was 13.1 miles out and then back to the town square. We passed hospitals, golf courses, farms, and even a Tyson building. There were turns, hills, and mile-long straightaways.

At the 24-mile mark, I grabbed a drink from director Mike. He tossed a Hawaiian lei around my neck, as he had for the two runners just ahead of me. I felt energized. I moved past the football stadium, up the hill, and turned the corner. I ran past my car, a block from the finish, and was gentlemanly as I moved out of the way for a female runner who sped by me at the finish. I hoped she reached her goal. I know I reached mine. I finished with a smile on my face in a time of 4 hours, 33 minutes.

I ate bagels, Twinkies, yogurt, and drank Coke back at the hotel, and then got a massage from two women. Kelly worked on my legs, while Lisa worked on my back and shoulders. Strangely, after 15 minutes I was feeling better than I had ever felt before. I wondered why.

My day was far from over. I needed to shower and needed to catch a plane. I drove a short distance to the University of Arkansas and located the field house. While a baseball game was playing nearby, I headed to the men's locker room and showered. Afterward, I drove back to the capital city to board my flight.

My odyssey began at 3:30 Saturday morning. Forty-eight hours later, I was home in my bed having covered over 2,000 miles in the air, 600 miles on the road, and 26.2 miles on my feet. There have been days I questioned if that whirlwind weekend was just a dream. I met wonderful people, I experienced no pain from the run, and I was massaged by two lovely women. But if it were a dream, how did I get this Arkansas hog T-shirt?

Lisa and Kelly getting the kinks out

The Marathon
in
MARATHON, IOWA

Marathon to Marathon / IA

Saturday, June 21, 2003
Age 44

The year was 2003, but it felt like 490 BC, and I felt like Pheidippides running through the streets by Marathon. However, I'm sure Pheidippides didn't run through cornfields, take water at aid stations, and have the luxury of proper footwear. But the Greek runner, whose job was bringing news of a Greek victory over a Persian Army, was determined. My job was far less important. I just had to finish. It didn't seem fair. Pheidippides died after his run and never got a medal. As for me, not only did I get a medal, but I got a bus ride back to my car. Yes, the marathon can be cruel.

A marathon to Marathon tells you the race began 26 miles, 385 yards from Marathon, Iowa. The town of Storm Lake had the honors of the white painted starting line. Storm Lake was easy to find. All you had to do was to drive up Highway 71 through Northwest Iowa and look for the lighthouse. It was as pretty as they have in Maine and a lot less weathered. Iowa was everything one could imagine with its open fields, John Deere tractors, and quaint quiet towns. I was surprised to see the lighthouse.

My connecting flight from St. Louis to Omaha was filled with a lot of baseball fans. On this weekend, Stamford would battle Rice for the national collegiate championship at Rosenblatt Stadium. I was the only one interested in running a marathon.

I sped off from Omaha and crossed the Missouri River into Iowa. I passed towns familiar to me from my door-to-door book selling days almost 25 years earlier. I recognized Council Bluffs, Missouri Valley, Logan, and Woodbine. I had lunch in Harlan, and thought back to when I sat in the town square in 1980, waiting for my friend, David Sawyer, to finish taking his driver's license test. On that day, David walked down the courthouse steps with his new license. On this day, I walked up the same steps to find a restroom.

Harlan, Iowa, was more beautiful than I had remembered, but back then I was a young college kid working 80 hours a week knocking on doors. This day was different. I was going to leave right after lunch. I ate lunch across from the mammoth courthouse at Joe's on the Square, a pleasant little restaurant with exposed brick. I even met the owner. Joe lent me his newspaper. I read about the news in Harlan and the surrounding towns. I read about the Henderson's having friends from Arizona visiting and about the Wagner's whose son had just enlisted.

After the prerace pasta dinner at Storm Lake High School, I drove 15 miles back to my hotel in Sac City. Unlike the ease in finding the lighthouse, the Sac City Motel was hidden behind a gas station off Highway 20. However, once you're in Sac City you can find any business. The hotel room was very homey and looked like a room a grandmother would have waiting for you upon your visit. There was the rocking chair, the colorful curtains, lamp, and old style faucet handles that made it very charming. There was also the television. I watched the White Sox beat up on the Cubs 12 - 3 and listened to Sox fans boo Sammy Sosa, who weeks earlier, was caught with a corked bat.

The local news had the temperature at 60° on race morning, but it seemed a lot cooler. Having spent a summer in Iowa, I knew summer days can get very hot. The weather on this day was perfect. We circled Storm Lake High School and stormed out of town. The course could have easily been planned with a

ruler. There was a straight line here and a straight line there. We passed wide open fields and ran down one country road and turned on another. It was pure Iowa at its best.

With very few cars on the road, the day was peaceful with the sound of feet pounding the pavement, and an occasional farmer plowing the field. Above, there were a lot of beautiful redwing blackbirds flying from one telephone line to another. Aid stations, spaced every 2½ miles, competed for Best Theme. Runners voted after the race. I took water from an ape representing the monkey and gorilla station. I grabbed water from the beach bums who were playing Jimmy Buffett music. I accepted water from kids with green painted faces, and accepted a cup from an Amish family. Although, I don't think the latter knew about the competition.

There were stretches when the wind was stiff and I was glad to turn away from it. After I drank a cupful of water, handed to me from a volunteer who walked down from an aid station, I went to toss the cup into a container. The wind got hold of it and raced it about 50 feet straight up the road, until it stopped at the table it came from.

There weren't a lot of landmarks to focus on, as each stretch of road looked like the next. After passing the painted 24- mile marker in the road, I'd guess the next marker would be up by that red barn. I wasn't off by much.

Approaching the 5-hour mark, I came into the town of Marathon. On the edge of a cornfield was a huge wooden sign with the word, "MARATHON" written on it. It was above an Iowa map with a silhouette of a runner across the state. The board below it read, "MARATHON TO MARATHON," June 21, 2003. It was exciting to see other Marathon signs and landmarks too.

211

I took many pictures, including one in front of a bar of the man with the long, white beard, dressed in a white T-shirt, blue jeans, suspenders, and holding a bottle of beer. A few yards up, I stopped to take a picture of the seven people sitting on the bench in front of Robinson Auto Sales & Service. They all seemed amused by me.

 I snapped a picture of the 26-mile marker stuck in the flower basket. The word "MARATHON" was written on the grain elevator in the distance. I turned left and headed straight for the finish, but stopped to take a picture of the people who were seated on the bleachers, as my time slipped past the 5-hour mark. I didn't mind at all.

After the race announcer called my name and hometown, Rodney Johnson introduced himself to me. When he heard, *"Richmond,"* his ears perked. I learned Rodney lives six miles from me. He was a lot of fun to be with. With a time of 4:08:25, the 63-year-old picked up an age division award.

After a nice lunch at the rec center, I sat with Rodney on the school bus for the ride back to the start. As we passed Crossroads Motel, Rodney pointed out his room and told me the hotel clerk gave him his room key and a fly swatter upon checking in.

Sitting across from me was Lisa Spence, a Houston resident who works at NASA. She helped train many of the Shuttle astronauts. She lowered her head and nodded after I asked if she knew the seven who died four months earlier aboard Columbia. In 2007, the NASA engineer completed her goal as having run a marathon in every state. Her next sight may be on the moon. She had already conquered Antarctica.

Back in Storm Lake, I got in my car and drove to Buena Vista University to shower. Afterwards, I was off to Omaha. I immediately headed to Rosenblatt Stadium, hoping to get a ticket for that evening's game. On my walk to the stadium, I bought a general admission ticket from a guy outside the park and then waited in line. The stadium was sold out, but officials were letting people enter in shifts. I finally got into the ballpark in the 3rd inning. It was a beautiful night in Omaha. The game was exciting with Rice University beating Stamford to even the series. The next night Rice claimed the title.

Like most of my other trips, I accomplished a lot during my short stay. I attended an exciting ballgame, ran a 26.2 mile race, and met some wonderful people in the Midwest. Pheidippides never had it so good.

Six miles to go ...

One mile to go ...

Hey, we've been waiting for you

Staying Awake
in
WAKEFIELD, MASSACHUSETTS

Run Around the Lake Marathon / MA

Friday, August 1, 2003
Age 44

Awake-up call wasn't needed for this one. I could have partied all night, taken a sleeping pill, and been knocked out with a blow to the head, without missing the start. As it was, after I had a late breakfast, a good-sized lunch, and spent most of my day in another state, I was ready to run. Many marathons begin at 7:00. Wakefield was no different, except for one minor detail. This race started at *7 p.m.*

The 7th Annual 24 Hour Run Around the Lake Relay, Marathon and Ultra, gave runners a lot of choices. I was one of the wimps who signed up for the smaller race. As much as I enjoyed Lake Quannapowitt, I felt as if eight times around was enough. Having spent my childhood in nearby Rhode Island, I should have heard of Wakefield. I was familiar with Rhode Island's Wakefield, a beautiful New England town by Narragansett Bay. But Wakefield, Massachusetts? Where's that?

I learned Wakefield, Massachusetts, is about 15 miles north of downtown Boston. It's a beautiful town with a beautiful lake. Runners would have that lake on their right-hand side deep into the night. Some would circle the lake eight times, while others would go around and around and around and probably lose count. I made sure I went around the minimum, and that Beatrice and the other race officials, put a check by my name each time I came into sight.

With the wipers working on the car, I got off at Exit 39 and quickly turned left into the Best Western Hotel. At the end of the parking lot it looked like a lemonade stand was set up. Thankfully, it wasn't. It was the race registration table. They knew what they were doing. Each runner was given two bib numbers eight inches high. If they didn't track you coming, they were certainly going to track you going, before you made another lake loop.

After getting my shirt and number, I escaped the drizzle and waited in the hotel lobby until we were called back out. I met Freeman Gerow of King, North Carolina, and Dana Reising of Danville, Kentucky, who just recently finished running a marathon on her 7th continent. There was Carolyn Krumrey and Susan Sinclair of

Houston, whom I had met two months earlier in Iowa. Chris Allison, a restaurant owner from Greely, Colorado, was also there. I asked Chris if he were a "50 Stater". He replied, "It's the only reason I'm here." I offered to drive him back to Boston after the race, but he had long since finished when I ended my run. The next time I saw Chris, we were in another hotel lobby in Alabama. I jokingly apologized to him for my slow Wakefield run. He had gotten a cab instead.

The skies opened up 10 minutes before race time. It was pouring rain. Initially, I tried to dodge the drops, but soon came to my senses thinking, what's the use? I thought the race was going to start in the parking lot, until I saw everyone head off to the back of the truck. Feeling like an illegal alien attempting to cross the border, I walked up the makeshift ramp and joined the other runners who were packed inside. The 20-foot length back had very few inches not taken up, as I quickly met several new acquaintances.

The engine started shortly after the foot-high safety rail was put into place. It was appropriate the driver took us to Church Street because I was praying for my safety. The truck rattled down the street, as I used my experience in riding in subway cars to keep my balance. What were the drivers of cars thinking when they pulled up behind us at traffic lights? It must have been quite a sight to see all these people crammed in like sardines into the back of this truck. Fortunately, none of those cars had flashing lights affixed to them.

We were let out in front of Colonel James Hartshone's house at 41 Church Street. Hartshone was a town treasurer and a cavalry commander. He was also a shoe manufacturer. Too bad he died in 1870. He had a lot of potential customers at his doorstep. There was no letup in the rain, as I positioned myself under a tree. A jovial fellow up front shouted the race instructions, "The race begins by this tree. When you get to the corner, turn right." Suddenly, we were off. The right-hand turn was all we needed. The entire race was right-hand turns, as we circled the lake on our concrete sidewalk track. We passed the baseball field, the cemetery, the church, Colonel Hartshone's house, the bank, and the hotel parking lot. We did it again seven more times. I could smell the pizza cooking on

Main Street, could hear the puddles being stepped on, and see the dusk slowly slipping into the night.

The sidewalk path was a popular trail for Wakefield's runners, walkers, and dog owners. We were informed the path could be busy on a warm, summer night and to give a right-of-way to townsfolk, but the townsfolk were too smart. They stayed home and stayed dry. A few runners opted for the asphalt roadway, instead of the concrete walkway that can be punishing on knees and legs. Seeing these fleet footers passing into the arena with cars, fog, and rain was a bit nerve-racking to watch.

The most critical part of the race was when I turned into the Best Western lot. I made sure the officials, now wearing miner's caps, could see my number so they could mark off one loop. My worst nightmare was not being counted. The parking lot wasn't the only place to avoid a Dodge. Following down the small embankment, runners had to dodge tree roots and standing water. I kept my head down and moved very slowly, maneuvering through the minefield, before jumping back on the pavement. What followed was the darkest stretch of the course. I studied the location of the puddles to avoid them for my return visits. It was nice the rain had stopped.

I saw the guy with the white knee-high socks a few times. He was looping me as if he had to be in bed before his parents came home. I think he succeeded. He won the race at 9:49 p.m. I ran the race like a rebel. I was out all night. I never stopped during the 26.2-mile run. Yet, I was surprised as to how long it was taking me to finish. The time on the bank clock kept jumping farther ahead each time I ran under it. I was so tired, I was yawning.

Ninety-nine percent of my races took place shortly after getting out of bed. This race took place shortly before I'd be getting into one. The day before, I spent swimming in my parent's pool and playing with my niece and nephew. I played like there was no tomorrow. I paid the price the next day. I ate two good meals, didn't nap, and then borrowed my parent's car later in the afternoon to begin my journey from Rhode Island into Massachusetts. It seemed strange to be getting ready to run a marathon at the end of the day.

I didn't bring a camera to Wakefield, so I just concentrated on running, but the lake seemed to be getting bigger and bigger after each loop. Without mile markers, the gauge was the loop around the 3.16 mile lake. After my third time around I finally memorized the spelling of *Quannapowitt*. It was a good thing, because the next few trips to the lakefront sign it was too dark to read. On my last loop, while on the opposite side of the lake from the finish, my pace quickened. I raised my head and started passing runners. I caught those who I could see under lamp posts who were far in the distance. Down the curb, up the next, by the gated entrance to the cemetery I ran. I moved quickly past the church and by the uneven concrete sidewalk near the Colonel's house.

The bank clock read 12:16 and soon I would turn right for the final push. Two minutes later I was done. I walked over to the refreshments and grabbed some cookies and a drink. But before I walked to the car to begin my 90-minute ride back, I asked a gal holding a clipboard one very important question: "You have me down for eight . . . right?"

Time spent with parents and pool

Searching For Elvis
in
TUPELO, MISSISSIPPI

Tupelo Marathon / MS

Sunday, August 31, 2003
Age 44

If Elvis Presley were spotted on August 31st, 2003, it would not have been during the first hour of the Tupelo Marathon. The occasional flashlight and police lights were the only things visible for the hundreds of runners making their way to the starting line outside the Tupelo Furniture Market. At 5 o'clock in the morning, most Mississippians were in bed.

Located in Northeast Mississippi along the Natchez Trace Parkway, Tupelo is a bustling little city of 30,000. Its claim to fame is a tiny, white frame house off Highway 78. It was here on January 8th, 1935, Elvis Aaron Presley was born. The house and nearby museum, with its Presley paraphernalia, draws thousands each year. You can look at Elvis's clothing, including suits, coats, and boots. You can read about his White House visit with President Nixon and look at photos of his young bride, Priscilla. All this, while listening to the continuous music, makes you think Elvis never left the building. Of course, before it's time for you to leave the building, you can take a piece of Elvis home. Registers ring with the sale of key chains, coffee mugs, pencils, sweatshirts, dinner plates, and hats of the man whose career as a singer and entertainer redefined American music. Yes, the legend lives on.

If the legend never dies, then the person who designed the Tupelo Marathon T-shirt was thinking of someone who did. Written between the picture of skull and bones were the words, *Trample the Weak* and *Hurdle the Dead*. The psychedelic long sleeve shirt would be acquired by visiting the packet pickup table at the mall. I was in shock when I saw the shirt. It was the most horrible thing I had ever seen. Who in the world designed this? I quickly studied it, shoved it into the plastic bag it came in, and vowed I would wear it only on cold winter nights in bed.

The Tupelo Furniture Market wasn't just one furniture store. It was a warehouse of many buildings, with many entrances, as I found out by making a dry run before race day. However, seeing it at 4:30 in the afternoon didn't prepare me for seeing it the next day at 4:30 in the morning. I had a good hunch the steady stream of turning vehicles was on target. I was right. When I arrived, I saw Brenton Floyd, the youngest to have run a marathon in every state. The Tupelo Marathon would be one of 38 marathons he would run that year, twenty more than his age.

It was a strange scene watching hundreds of runners making their way to the start behind the furniture mart. All these people walking in pitch darkness with a mission. At 4:50 a.m. in Tupelo, Mississippi, I tried to remind myself what that mission was.

I was running with a jovial group. I asked the man to my right what his name was and where he was from. He answered, "Glen, from Arkansas." I thought a second and said, "Glen Hendrix? I met you at the Little Rock airport in 2001 on our way to run St. Louis." I asked if Charlene was running. "Here I am," a voice in front shouted. I asked if Julie was there. Another voice was heard, "I'm over here." In the early morning darkness, when you couldn't see a face or your own feet, I told them they looked beautiful. They laughed...and kept running.

If homeowners on Chesterville Road had looked out the window, they would have probably thought their town was being overrun by bandits. There was a lot of chatter and patter going on all morning. I heard a woman in front say, "Watch out for the dead rat." I was watching, but I didn't see it. At this hour, there was no way runners could see mile markers. The leaders probably had gone to the halfway point before they first spotted the orange painted numbers on the pavement. Motorists would later be able to tell a

222

race had come down this country road by seeing the numbers, but what would they think when they'd see the words, *"pee pee"* in large white letters printed across the street? The lettering appeared it would stand a lot longer than the two Porta Johns placed by the side of the road.

I felt a bit apprehensive attempting to run a marathon in the middle of a Mississippi summer, but the weather was ideal. The early morning start was a huge factor. The sun made its first appearance at the 7-mile mark. Near the 12-mile mark, the sun was directly in front beating down on me, but a quick right turn into a plush neighborhood allowed for a welcome retrieve from the glare. Approaching the 13-mile mark, I remembered at the Elvis museum there was a statute of the young entertainer at age 13. A placard read, *"Elvis at 13."* Thanks to a race volunteer, I have a picture in my marathon album labeled, *"Paul at 13."*

As with many marathons, the field grew smaller midway into the run. Many runners were participating in the 14-mile race and their route would soon end. For the rest of us, we had to retrace our steps back to the furniture market. Of course, this time I was able to see where I was going. As the lead runners made their turn, I saw men and woman with fit and strong bodies. As more runners passed, the body types changed too; strong legs, but maybe not strong arms, or strong shoulders, but not muscular legs. When you weren't impressed with the arms or legs, you'd know the turnaround was coming up soon.

The water stops were few and far between and the sun was doing its best to punish those who remained on course. At one aid station, I dumped three or four cups of water over my head. My only regret was not moving my feet out of the path of the flow. At least an inch of water fell into my left shoe. I squished on.

The course had a good combination of hills and straightaways and my pace was steady. It wasn't as fast as Glen's. He passed me with a few miles to go, and I finished behind him with a time of 4:37:22. If I hadn't stopped to take pictures, my time would have been much faster. I even took a picture of Chuck Engle on his return trip. With a winning time of 2:11:11, Chuck finished strong. A week later, he finished strong again by winning the New Mexico Marathon.

The race finished outside the door to the furniture market, about 385 yards from the start. A table full of pizza and drinks waited for us, but another race loomed. I had to get back to the airport to catch my afternoon flight. That airport was three hours away in another state. The early start still meant I was well ahead of checkout time at the hotel. I quickly showered and was soon on my way to Birmingham.

As I put Tupelo in the rearview window, I had fond memories of my Mississippi stay. There weren't a lot of turns to the race, but the sights varied. There was darkness and light, horse farms, neighborhoods, and about eight wonderful people who came out to cheer. I never did see that dead rat.

When I got home, I took another look at the T-shirt. I put it on. It started to grow on me. I even walked outside in the broad daylight with it, but hoped no one would try to read it. As the weeks passed, I didn't care if they had read it. It has become one of my favorite shirts because it's just plain different. I've seen it worn at other races, and I am proud it's a part of my collection. A shirt I vowed I would never wear, has turned out to be one I wear often. It's funny. The shirt, like Mississippi's 1960's image, has changed. I'm glad I made the trip.

Feeling HIGH in Tu-pe-LO

Celebration of Life
in
WALKER, MINNESOTA

Walker North Country Marathon / MN

Saturday, September 27, 2003
Age 44

When the plane touches down at Minneapolis - St. Paul International Airport, the trip is far from over. I would have to drive another 150 miles to reach my destination. My northward journey began on Interstate 94, continued on Route 15 to St. Cloud, where I crossed the Mississippi River to Route 10. From there it was on to Little Falls, home of real life hero, Charles Lindbergh. Thirty miles later I arrived in Brainerd, home of fictional hero, Paul Bunyan. Legend has it that for the past 50 years a gigantic Paul Bunyan statue sat in the center of town. The legend continued after asking the girl from behind the counter at the Chamber of Commerce where it was. "They moved it last week." she said.

At Brainerd, I picked up Route 371 to Pine River, Backus, and Hackensack, and billboard after billboard selling boats and bait, fishing poles and fun Northern Minnesota offers. I also passed many of the 10,000 lakes Minnesota is known for. It's no legend the state has close to 15,000 lakes. I quit counting after 11. A few miles on Route 200 my journey ended. I arrived in Walker. For a slow marathoner like myself, could there be a better name?

Walker is such a small town that it wasn't difficult to find the hotel on 4th Street. By the time you got to double digits, you were out of town. It also wasn't difficult to find Walker-Hackensack-Akeley High School, site of the Walker North Country Marathon registration and pasta dinner. Four minutes after I left the motel, I had the car parked in front of the school.

After getting my number and long sleeve, nylon pullover shirt, I walked to the trophy case admiring the success of Walker's athletes and teams throughout the years. With a population of about 1,000, the teams have been competitive. In fact, on this cold Friday night, a large soccer gathering watched the Wolves win again.

At the dinner in the school cafeteria, I sat with Canadian Bob Lester and Minnesotans John Gunther and Burt Carlson. Carlson is not only an ultramarathoner, but has also run a marathon in every state. The next day, the 78-year-old would complete the distance in 5 hours and 38 minutes. After dinner, I walked along the long pier at Leech Lake. Even if I hadn't been eating the large ice cream cone from Dairy Queen, I would have been cold. The wind was whipping right off the water and I was shaking. I kept eating and kept walking back and forth. I watched the birds, looked out to the trees, and looked down at the water while thinking, Baby, it's cold out here. Fortunately, the motel was right around the corner.

I didn't need to set the alarm for Saturday morning. My body was still running on Eastern Time. The schedule showed a 9 a.m. start, while my body was trying to tell me it was at 10 a.m. I had to eat something. At 6 a.m. in the predawn darkness, I walked two blocks and found the Outdoorsman Café. I was out of my element. The patrons looked outdoorsy, but as I moved away from the smoke, none of them looked like they knew or gave a hoot about the footrace later that morning. When I ordered the eggs, bacon, and home fries, I looked like I didn't give a hoot either. But, I was hungry, and so be it.

It was cold as I waited with the other 120 souls in preparation for the big race. I was anxious to start running. After a lap around the track, we exited the gate and explored Walker and the surrounding area. Little did I know, the best of Northern Minnesota awaited me. We quickly left town and hit bike and snowmobile trails. We ran on dirt roads by lakes, ran on pavement entering the Paul Bunyan State Trail, and covered many miles on narrow, grassy paths in the thick forest. The trails were beautiful and far from any civilization.

I was so glad I came to Walker. Other marathons in the state are more popular. Thousands run in the Twin Cities in October and Duluth in June. Walker is a low-key race that doesn't get much attention. I've talked to a few people who highly recommended Walker when I mentioned I needed to do a Minnesota marathon. "This race," they said, "is different from all the others." On this day I was finding that out. It was an effort to get here and it was turning out to be an effort to run here. Although running on grass is better on the joints, it takes more of an effort than running on pavement because you can't push off as easily.

Race officials did a great, painstaking task of alerting runners of tree roots that were waiting to trip us up. The orange painted roots were easily seen and avoided. The trail kept twisting and turning. There were stretches we ran up and stretches we ran down.

Autumn leaves had begun falling and the bright colors helped take my mind off running 26 miles. The trail, part of the Chippewa National Forest, covers over a million acres. It includes thousands of lakes, several types of birds, including the largest breeding population of bald eagles in the lower 48 states, and 14 kinds of mammals. It was the mammals I was thinking about. I was definitely in bear country. Wearing running shoes wouldn't help me either. There were many miles when I was all alone, and if a bear approached, there was no other human to outrun. I'm glad it was AFTER the race when I heard that the race director had seen a bear and timber wolf on the course the day before.

We left the trail and I was feeling hungry. Maybe I should have ordered pancakes. I wanted to finish and go back to Dairy

Queen. My pace quickened in the later stages of the race, while all I thought about was "ice cream cone" on every step… and that's a lot of steps.

Four hours and 50 minutes after the start, I re-entered the football field and ran on the track in Lane 3 to the finish. A friendly, bearded gentleman, dressed in winter clothes with a wool cap, draped a finisher's medal around my neck. Yes, this is what I live for. I had done it. A tent, set up in the corner of the field for runners, kept race tallies and food. I was only interested in the latter. There were cookies and Cokes and a freezer full of ice cream sandwiches. I grabbed two and then sat. Afterward, I grabbed two more and then two more. I think I ate about a dozen. I no longer craved Dairy Queen.

After showering at the high school, I headed out of town. On the drive to Walker the day before, I had passed through the city of Sartell. I had remembered my father's WWII Navy buddy lived there. I called my parents while in Walker to get Rollie and Janette Weis's address. On Sunday afternoon, I took the Sartell exit and found their house. When Mr. Weis came to the door, I said, "I'm Don Mellor's son." Those words got me in his house, got me a home-cooked meal, and got me three hours of memories from a man who served with my father in the South Pacific over 50 years earlier. I saw photos of my Dad I'd never seen before. It was the highlight of my trip.

The memories I took home from Minnesota were extraordinary. The beauty of the state and its people is one I'll always treasure and remember. The Walker North Country Marathon had been held for 21 years, and with the motto depicting their priority, it will be run another 21 years as well. My experience truly was, "A Celebration of the Life and Land that is Northern Minnesota."

Waving the Checkered Flag
in
INDIANAPOLIS, INDIANA

Indianapolis Marathon / IN

Saturday, October 18, 2003
Age 44

I was fortunate. Most races in Indianapolis go 473.8 miles farther than the one I signed up to participate in. My race traversed a city, instead of going around in circles. My race awarded each participant a medal, instead of a bottle of milk to the winner. My race lasted just over four hours, instead of ... oh well, three out of four ain't bad.

An Indianapolis Checkered Flag ... but the race continues

The Indianapolis Marathon didn't draw the type of crowds that frequent Indianapolis Speedway each May. In fact, the Indianapolis Marathon wasn't even run in Indianapolis. The race took place in Lawrence, located northeast of the capital city, but like the Indy 500, this race had a lot of turns, a lot of excitement, and a lot of roadwork.

A white curtain separated the runner's expo from the pasta dinner. When I turned in my meal ticket and walked past the curtain, the first person I saw was a familiar face. I sat down with Deo Jaravata from Los Angeles. The last time I saw Deo we were above tree line at Pikes Peak. He was running down. I was walking up. We've talked on the phone a few times over the past few years, and it was a nice surprise to see him in Indiana. It was a chilly night when I left the dinner. I knew the next morning I'd be attired in a long sleeve shirt.

I had a 30-minute drive across town to my hotel room. Wanting to see the speedway during my stay in Indy, I got a hotel nearby, but far from the marathon start. As things turned out, I failed my time trial and never saw the famed Indianapolis Speedway. I almost failed to get to the start in time too. My routine seldom changes. I awake in plenty of time. I set the radio alarm, set my watch alarm, and call the front desk for a wake-up call. I stretch while flipping through the television channels, and make frequent stops to the bathroom. Time was beginning to get away from me after I stopped in the hotel breakfast bar for juice and a bagel.

After I filled the car's tank, I drove to the start. The traffic was light until I started hearing noises I didn't like. Up ahead I could see runners making their way to the start, but there was nothing I could do. The train whistle was blowing and the railroad gate came down right in front of my car. The railroad cars kept coming and coming. I was cutting it very close and was sweating like I was already running the marathon. I was hoping for the opportunity. Finally, the train passed and the gate went up.

The parking for the marathon was a good distance from the race. I had read comments about the Indianapolis Marathon and remembered how one runner wrote, *"The parking is three miles from the start."* He exaggerated, but it was at least 385 yards away. I pulled into the lot driving over the painted arrow that was pointing toward me. I skillfully moved by the runners getting out of their vehicles. The temperature was warm and I knew a long sleeve shirt was not the way to go. I grabbed my singlet, pins, and bib number and jumped out of the car and hustled to the start. I had made it with less than 10 minutes to spare. I pinned my number on and walked under the huge American flag that was hoisted on the fire truck.

I was faced with another dilemma. I wasn't going to have a lot of leeway after the race, because of my flight. I asked a few runners about the fastest way to get to the airport from the finish. I would have to run no slower than a 4 hour and 30 minute race. I couldn't afford to be slow and I couldn't afford to get lost. Still, I was confident I could pull it off, but I couldn't think about it now. The race was about to start and it was time to enjoy it.

It was a beautiful, fall color day, and with the football Colts having a bye week, this was the only game in town. After a mile loop, the race course headed west on 56th Street, circled a neighborhood around the streets of Boy Scout and Wallingwood, before coming back on 56th toward the start. The course then headed east toward the sections of Oaklandon and Indian Lake.

In the early stages, the course gave the runners a few hills. A dead deer by the side of the road was the only thing that wasn't moving. The course was on wide streets by beautiful homes, with a handful of cheering residents, including a boy who was clearly a race fan. I moved behind him on the sidewalk and snapped a picture of him waving an Indianapolis checkered flag, with runners in the background. Unfortunately, it didn't represent the end of the race, nor the halfway point.

As we entered Fort Harrison State Park, a cluster of runners veered to the left for their 13.1 mile finish. The marathoners stayed to their right to continue their long journey. Shortly after entering the park at mile 13, I glanced to my left to check the mile marker faced in the opposite direction. The red number read "25." I wouldn't see that number again for a long time. The park was a huge open field, a nice change of pace from the neighborhoods I had spent in the last couple of hours. Named after Benjamin Harrison, the 23rd President lived and practiced law in Indianapolis.

The race moved past the park and onto Fall Creek Parkway. It was a long, steady, slight incline that continued for miles. I was looking forward to running down it on the return. Deo and I shouted at each other in passing. Once again, he was going in the direction I was working toward.

I never passed up water at aid stations. I always reached for water in the early stages and would switch to Powerade later on. I also grabbed packages of GU that were offered me. GU is a packet of

goo that goes straight to where your body needs it. It comes in a variety of flavors and you just suck it down. Near the 15-mile mark, I grabbed a chocolate flavored packet. After downing it, my fingers were covered with chocolate goop. I did my best to lick them and pour water on my hands to clean them. I promised myself no more of that flavor.

I began to tire while crossing over a parking lot and running a few hundred feet on grass. My steps were slowing down, but it didn't last long. Near the 18-mile mark, close to the turnaround, my pace quickened. Eight miles left and I was running faster than I had all day. I passed several runners and was unchallenged the rest of the way. I kept my head up and told myself, I'm a marathon runner. I've run several of these and I'm conditioned. I clicked off mile 22 through 24 as I reentered the park. I felt strong past mile 25 and powered up the short hill and back toward the finish. I could hear the music in the distance and could see the finish from across the commons.

As I made my way home to the finish line, I saw Deo with a finisher's medal around his neck, standing behind the roped off area taking my picture. I returned the favor.

My finishing time was 4:03:49. I made up a lot of time by my eight-mile surge. I caught up with Deo and handed a stranger my camera so she could take a picture of us. I've stood with Deo in New Hampshire, Colorado, and now Indiana, but our reunion didn't last long. I had to get going. I grabbed a couple of drinks off the refreshment table and briskly walked to my car for my race to the airport.

The airport was at the opposite end of town, plus I needed to find a shower. Another concern I had was the B1 bomber. A B1 bomber was being transported on Interstate 70 from Richmond, Indiana, to Indianapolis. News reports said it would slow traffic. I was going to be right in the mix of it. It was just my luck. I competed with a train to start the race. I was competing with a plane at the end of it. Driving down I-70, you couldn't help but notice the bystanders standing atop the bridges waiting for the huge plane to come through. I decided I would shower at the gymnasium at Indianapolis University, located a short distance from the interstate. I hoped the delay wouldn't put me behind the aircraft.

Less than an hour later I was back on the interstate. The bridges were clear, indicating the big plane had gone through and that *MY* plane would still be there.

After dropping off the rental car, I hopped on the shuttle for the ride to the airport terminal. With less than an hour for my flight, I was joyfully relieved knowing I had made it on time. It was a great feeling, but it didn't last long. The feeling turned to disappointment with the seven letter word stretched across my flight information at the gate. My Indianapolis checkered flag wouldn't be waved yet; "*Delayed*" had won out.

Rocket Power
in
HUNTSVILLE, ALABAMA

Rocket City Marathon / AL

Saturday, December 13, 2003
Age 45

Race Director Malcolm Gillis had gotten his money's worth when he received his third check from Paul Mellor. I had sent him checks the previous two years without ever lacing up in Huntsville. I wasn't going to allow any Christmas party to get in the way in 2003. Fortunately, I was never invited to any.

I strongly considered running in Birmingham in February. It would have been a fun weekend running in conjunction with the Men's Olympic Trials. I thought about running in Mobile in late December. There certainly would be no party to go to then. Plus, I had once spent a summer in Mobile and thought it would be fun to revisit. However, I couldn't shake Huntsville, so I sent my money in again. It had a great reputation. Home to NASA's space camp, the race had a great name in *Rocket City Marathon*. Home to a flat course, it was famous for its fast times. Home to hospitable and dedicated volunteers, it was welcoming to have your name printed in large letters on your bib number. Huntsville had another advantage. It was the closest Alabama marathon city to Richmond, Virginia. It's now or never.

The race to Huntsville had a slow start. I chose to rent a car for the long trip and was stunned when I learned I couldn't leave my own vehicle in the lot. I had no choice. I drove two miles away to my office complex and parked, then I ran back for my rental car. As I huffed and puffed while buckling up in my new SUV, I couldn't help but think, maybe I'm not meant for Huntsville.

West on Interstate 64, south on Interstate 81, and west on Interstate 40 I drove. I entered Tennessee, then Georgia, and then back into Tennessee on my way to Alabama. I saw exits I had taken for marathons I ran at Smoky Mountain and Chickamauga. After nine hours of driving and two years of planning, I saw the sign I had been searching for - Welcome to Huntsville.

At the pasta dinner, I sat with veteran marathon runners and those who were about to run their first. Elizabeth Gottfried was part of the latter. The wife of Alabama Men's Basketball coach Mark

Gottfried, the mother of five would finish the marathon in 4:59:14. Unlike her husband's players, Elizabeth never called time-out.

Overcast skies greeted the 1,200 runners on race day. With snow predicted later in the day in the foothills of Tennessee and Georgia, I was anxious to finish. After welcoming remarks from Mayor Loretta Spencer and the playing of the National Anthem, the race began east of the Hilton Hotel on Church Street. During the early stages, with wall-to-wall people, my focus stayed on the heels of those in front. If you stopped you'd get run over. If you sped up you'd run up the back end of someone else. I maintained a comfortable pace and looked for pockets to settle into.

A marathon is quite an event. You begin the journey with hundreds of people, yet as time goes by, the field thins out and there are moments you are all alone. It happens in every race. I knew it would happen on this day too. Without the race marshals and runners up ahead, you'd need a AAA TripTik to find your way around the course. We constantly turned corners. We sped on Lincoln Street, Governors Drive, Drake Avenue, and Airport Road. We made strides on Mira Vista, Weatherly, and Mountain Gap. We high stepped on Hillwood, Camille, and Dell Avenue. It never got boring.

On one of those streets, a man was at the end of his driveway retrieving his newspaper. With all the runners going by his house, he probably wished he was wearing something besides his bathrobe. However, he looked like he didn't care. The support from the few spectators along the course who braved the cold, raw day was helpful. I especially appreciated the gentleman holding the *You Can Do It* sign. I saw him at least three times during the run.

We turned on Bailey Cove Road at the 10-mile mark. A sign at the corner read, *Welcome to the Escalator.* Unfortunately, the power must have been shut off. I had to use my own power to go on. The next four miles was a straight line, as was the headwind. I slowed and waited for a group to pass before tucking in behind them. At the 11-mile mark, an official, wearing a heavy jacket, hood, and gloves, called out our times. I had 15 miles to go before I could be bundled up as well. During this stretch, I met Karen Culp of Stafford, Virginia. Her husband, Vic, was a couple of miles ahead. They both had covered a lot of marathons together. Karen had her work cut out for her. She had just gotten over bronchitis.

I was taking baby steps between miles 16 and 19. I sucked it up when I had to go over a speed bump. Then almost magically, I changed into a runner again at mile 20. I picked up my pace, similar to the Indianapolis race months earlier. I felt strong and kept my head up. I passed runner after runner. I got compliments on my "new legs" from Cincinnati's George Stump and Karen Culp, who had passed me miles earlier. For the next six miles, I passed runners on my left and runners on my right. I wasn't passed the rest of the way. As I blitzed by one group, I heard the woman say to her partner, "I wish I had a rope." I would like to have thought she was referring to harnessing my power.

My finishing time of 4:18:59 might have been slow for many runners, but I made up a lot of time once I hit 20 miles. I easily could have gone another five miles (I think). I was treated like a champion when I finished. A medal was put around my neck and a volunteer walked with me the short distance back to the hotel, explaining to me how to find food and drinks. It was as if he were at the finish line waiting only for me. This was the reputation I had heard about this race; they took care of you. They had enough volunteers to cater to all runners.

After refueling and trading war stories with my fellow warriors, I drove to the campus of the University of Alabama at Huntsville (UAH) to shower. In the early afternoon as I walked to the gym, I felt the cold temperature. It seemed a lot colder now than it did at 8 a.m. Twenty minutes later, I drove away from the spacious campus and passed the towering rockets by Space Camp. I was embarking on another marathon ahead. Richmond was only 435 miles away.

241

The rain was falling when I pulled up to the drive-thru at a McDonald's to get a large drink. Little did I know, the biggest gulp I'd take would be a few hours later when the snow began to fall outside my windshield. The Virginia line and the snow and ice arrived at the same time. For the next eight hours, my average speed would be 25 mph. I passed trucks that had jackknifed on the icy roads. As I moved up the interstate I saw fewer and fewer vehicles. I kept thinking about the biggest test to come - Afton Mountain. The area is famous for its bumper cars during the winter. It was an amusement ride I wanted no part of. Afton was six hours away.

Listening to the radio, I heard disc jockeys saying good-bye while others were saying good morning, as I snailed my way toward home well past midnight. Later that day, the disc jockeys would be reporting the capture of Saddam Hussein. It was past 2 a.m. when I successfully conquered the mountain. My six-mile surge at Rocket City would have left this vehicle in the dust. The dust was what I wished for. The snow and ice kept coming. After the mountain, I thought about my next hurdle. I had to return the rental car, and then run to retrieve my own car. There has to be a better way.

When I arrived in Richmond at 4 a.m., I pulled into the lot at the all night IHOP restaurant. Once inside, I explained my situation and convinced an off-duty employee to ride with me to get my car. I gave him $10 when the job was done.

After being awake for 23 hours and after being on the road for 14, I learned a valuable lesson: The next time I go to Huntsville I'm taking a rocket.

You're in Huntsville, Alabama

Scouting for water

The long road awaits

The Staple Gun
in
KINGWOOD, TEXAS

Texas Marathon / TX

Thursday, January 1, 2004
Age 45

Beginning at a playground, held on a Thursday, and having a pick of old bowling trophies to take home, made the marathon in Kingwood unique. The result was a huge success. There's a reason why we shouldn't mess with Texas.

For the 129 participants, the nation's first marathon of the year was a great way to make good on a New Year's resolution of getting fit. For me, I had a resolution of getting well. While many Houstonians were out partying and toasting in the New Year, I was in my hotel room sleeping soundly. I had good reason. The day began at the early morning hour of 2:15 a.m., when I got ready for the Southwest Airline flight out of Raleigh, a city two-and-a-half hours away. Once in Houston, I did what any marathoner would do before race day. I went to the mall and walked and walked and walked.

I also stopped by Minute Maid Park where I saw landscapers sprucing up the grounds outside the Astro's ballpark. Days later, the team spruced up its chance to claim a pennant by persuading Roger Clemens to come out of retirement. Also on the sightseeing list was the Astrodome or as it was called upon its completion in 1965, *The Eighth Wonder of the World*. The former home of the Astros and Oilers, the Astrodome is probably better known as the site of the *"Battle of the Sexes,"* when in 1974, Billie Jean King quieted Bobby Riggs in their much hyped tennis match.

If "hype" is going to be mentioned, you have to only look right next door. Reliant Stadium was getting ready for Super Bowl XXXVIII, but was America going to be ready for Janet Jackson? Her infamous "wardrobe malfunction" during halftime had people forgetting one of the most exciting games in Super Bowl history, as New England fought back Carolina, 31-29.

There was no hype in Kingwood. Kingwood wasn't even humble. That name belonged to a town to its south, 20 minutes north of Houston. However, on January 1st, 2004, many would come to Kingwood to run four loops around its greenbelts. The runners came from all over the Lone Star State. They hailed from League City and Lake Jackson, Pearland and Pflugerville, Bullard and Boerne, Allen and Alvin. Some were running their first marathon, while many others were adding to their list. Race Director and co-founder of the "50 States Marathon Club," Steve Boone, ran. Boone had completed the 50 state circuit twice. When a reporter asked him, "What's your goal after you run marathon # 200?" Steve's reply was, "To do marathon # 201." In December of 2009, Steve completed his fourth time around as having run a marathon in every state.

Brent Weigner also began the year with a marathon run. However, the Cheyenne, Wyoming school teacher would have to dismantle his globe to show his students two of his most spectacular runs. The metal rod goes through the North and South Poles. Weigner is also one of the few runners to have run a marathon on each continent, a feat he's accomplished five times.

The saying, "If it were a snake it would have bitten me," applied to the starting line at the Texas Marathon. The day before, I made a dry run to the corner of Falling Brook and Brook Shadows, smack-dab in the middle of a beautiful neighborhood. It looked nothing like a marathon start. However, when I saw the basketball court and playground equipment, I knew I was in the right place. I had seen pictures on the Internet of past races. That green slide was in all the photos. Okay, it starts and ends here, but what's in between?

The next day the playground was full of people, but none of them looked under seven and no one was going headfirst down the green slide. I stood in line at the packet pick-up table, but the man in front never moved. It wasn't his fault. He was giving out the shirts. Realizing my mix-up, I quickly moved to the other side of the table.

Like the Rocket City Marathon, the bib numbers were personalized with the runner's first name printed in bold letters. The names made for a friendlier race. No matter if you were fast or last, you saw runners coming or going all morning long, and you could call them by name.

The runners, waiting for the 8 a.m. start, were lined up on the narrow concrete trail like stock cars on the Daytona track. Up front, the 16 fastest runners took up the first eight rows. The trail meandered through wooded sections, around lakes and behind very expensive homes. It was a popular course for runners, bikers, and walkers, but on this drizzly, New Year's Day morning, it was the runners who took the lead.

Starting behind the fence from the Greentree Pool, the course made four loops. We would cross the finish line three times before making it official on the fourth. The Texas Marathon was purely a neighborhood run. It was one of the few marathons that had no police presence directing traffic or cordoning off streets. There were no cheerleaders, no bands, and no straggler bus to pick up tiring runners, but the distance was just as long as the New York City Marathon and just as tough.

Texas had many marathons from which to choose from. Each year, thousands run in Austin, Houston, Dallas, and in San Antonio. Kingwood had something the others didn't have: Shade. Ninety-eight percent of the course was shielded from the sun. And yes, that drizzle did give way to sunshine, but it hardly touched my face. Kingwood also had other amenities big city races lack. The runners had personal trees.

On my first return trip back to the finish area, I said "hello" to co-director, Paula Boone. Although she wasn't running, Paula is no slouch. She has run in well over 200 marathons. In 2007, she completed her second time around as having run a marathon in every state. As I ran by her on this day, I was a bit puzzled. Why was she holding a staple gun? I hoped she wasn't looking for her husband. Coming back from the turnaround, I had my answer. She

and a friend were tacking up motivational messages on trees runners. For a half mile, the forest was dressed in pink, 8½ x 11" signs. *"Go David"* ... *"Super Job Mindy"* ... and my personal favorite, *"Lots of Marathons Paul M."* Vicky had a sign, Ray had his message, and I'm sure Eric appreciated his sign too. There was even an *"I Love You"* for Steve Boone. The Texas Staple Gun was no Texas Chainsaw.

I said "hello" to Cindy, said "good job" to Brian, and gave a thumbs up to Ryan. It was as if we all knew each other. From the runners to the volunteers doling out refreshments, we all saw a lot of each other that day. Every now and then I was passed by faster runners. It was no secret. They were the leaders and I was being looped. It was a bit frustrating coming into the finish area with another runner knowing he was about to finish, when I had one more loop to go, but hey, he deserved it.

I was handed water from Kayla six times. However, the pretty little girl, who stood with her father at the aid station, opted to play in the nearby sandbox on my last two trips through. It was just as well. Seeing a runner throw up would probably end her volunteerism for years to come.

I never knew what mile I was on, because the course wasn't marked. It wasn't until I was at Kayla's station for the last time that I was told I had one-mile to go. All I knew was I should follow the trail for a few miles, turn around at the X, veer off to the right, circle the lake, and then head back to the start/finish area. Do that four times and you're done. I liked it that way. Four times sounded better than 26, but I couldn't fool my body.

I was running for the last time around the manmade lake, behind the expensive homes, when my arms said to my legs, *If you're not moving, why should I?* I was feeling nauseous and welcomed the

Porta John around the corner. I threw up shortly after sipping water. I had two miles to go. I walked and slowly ran, feeling sick the entire time. Often, I pulled off to the side of the trail, put my hands on my knees, and stared into the ground in a position as if I were looking for a lost contact lens.

The race that began at 8 a.m. ended at 1:15 p.m. With a finisher's medal around my neck, I sat on the top step of the green slide and could take only a couple of sips of Coke. I was still nauseated. I walked backed to the car and sat by the curb and threw up again. Twenty minutes down Highway 59, I pulled off the side of the road and threw up again. I felt sick for the rest of the day and into the early morning of the next, vomiting several more times.

I met wonderful people during my visit and visited wonderful sights, but if someone were to ask, "Where's a good place to run?" I'd think long and hard and say, "Iowa, South Carolina, Connecticut, or Arizona. Just don't mess with Texas."

New Year's Day run in Texas

A Run to Remember
in
OKLAHOMA CITY, OKLAHOMA

Oklahoma City Memorial Marathon / OK

Sunday, April 25, 2004
Age 45

Starting out like any other day in Oklahoma City was Wednesday, April 19th, 1995. Parents rushed to get their kids ready for school, traffic backed up on Interstate 40, and merchants unlocked their doors for another day of sales. The people of Oklahoma City were doing what they had always done; educating their children, putting in a hard day's work, and carrying out their business. Little did they know at 9:02 a.m. their lives would change forever and 168 lives would be eternally remembered.

On that fateful morning, the two-ton explosives cut not only into the Alfred P. Murrah Federal Building, but also into the hearts of all Americans. It was the worst terrorist attack on American soil when Timothy McVeigh ran away from his explosive packed Ryder truck, after parking it in front of the nine-story federal building.

The sound was heard for miles. The help was there in minutes. The healing continues today.

Minnesota's John Taylor reflects at the Memorial

The slogan for the Oklahoma City Memorial Marathon was right on target. Runners from around the country came to this city, not so much to race, but to remember. *A Run to Remember* was manifested eloquently by Frank Shorter, who spoke during the prerace pasta dinner. The 1972 Olympic Gold Medal marathoner sat quietly in a chair addressing the large gathering on the pavilion of the memorial. His message was not about his moments at Munich, but about his moments at the Memorial. The site was spiritual and special, and Shorter felt somewhat reluctant talking about running to his audience of runners. But all his message did was to take the pain and soreness away from every participant who toed the line the following day. In this city, running 26.2 miles was going to be easy.

The connecting flight from Kansas City to Oklahoma City gave me a sense as to what to expect after meeting Kathy Thomas and Ted Wilson. Kathy, a psychologist, and Ted, a fire chaplain, were returning home from a Washington, D.C. conference where they presented a class on dealing with victim's grief. The two were well qualified. They counseled hundreds after the bombing and worked with officials in New York after the 9/11 attacks. Kathy told me about what she had seen on that April morning, and prepared me as to what I would see at the site. She couldn't have prepared me for the pasta dinner though.

The hands that served me lasagna, potatoes, and salad, were from those who survived the attack. Standing on the site where they once narrowly escaped death, the servers greeted everyone with a smile and a spoonful. They were appreciative we chose to run in Oklahoma City.

After the remarks and Q & A session from three of America's greatest marathoners in Shorter, Bill Rodgers, and Dick Beardsley, I walked around the corner to the Memorial. Flanked on both sides by a long reflecting pool, stood two tall monumental gates. Above the entrance on the East Gate read, "*9:01,*" representing the innocence of the city before the attack. Above the entrance to the West Gate read, "*9:03,*" representing the moment we were changed forever.

Reaching into the information box, I pulled out an extra brochure to give to the person coming up from behind. He recognized me instantly, saying, "You ran in Huntsville. You had that long trip ahead of you." John Taylor of Minneapolis came to Oklahoma for the same reason I did. Opening the pamphlet, we could see where the Murrah building

. A guide approached. Pointing his finger to the row of trees down the far right-hand side, he said, "The third tree from the end is where McVeigh parked the truck." All I could say was, "Wow."

Along the south side of the pool were the bronze chairs, 168 of them, representing one for each victim. The smaller chairs were for the 19 children. The chairs were aligned in nine rows signifying the floors where they were killed. It was easy to see the daycare was on the second floor. John and I stood by the West Gate and talked for well over an hour. As the day turned into darkness, the Memorial lit up. The translucent bases to the chairs illuminated, as well as the times on the gates. It was getting late. We both had to run a marathon the next day.

The next morning, in the predawn darkness, the Memorial was still illuminated. I walked the perimeter of the field before making my way to the start. At that moment, the chatter from thousands of runners became quiet. We stood with our heads bowed for a moment of silence for 168 seconds. Afterward, we raised our heads for the playing of the National Anthem.

Stretched across Robinson Street the banner read, "*A Run to Remember*." And it was. Throughout the marathon course, banners hung from lamp posts with names of each victim. There was a banner for Ethel Griffin, Cheryl Hammon, Randolph Guzman, Jaci Coyne, Gilberto Martinez, and names of 163 others. Many runners dedicated their run to one who had been killed. I saw a name almost each time I was passed. I read a lot of them.

The course took us through downtown streets, past the AAA baseball park of the Oklahoma Redhawks, and past the Oklahoma Capitol, the only

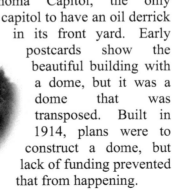

capitol to have an oil derrick in its front yard. Early postcards show the beautiful building with a dome, but it was a dome that was transposed. Built in 1914, plans were to construct a dome, but lack of funding prevented that from happening.

In 2002, the wait was over when the dome was finally erected. Now, the dome and the derrick each touch the sky.

Reading the names on the banners, and knowing what this race stood for, took my mind off running 26 miles. My legs never ached as the miles went on. The race continued as we ran along the shoreline of Lake Hefner. The huge, man-made lake is an oasis for boating and swimming enthusiasts during the summer. If I hadn't known better, I would have sworn I was running in Wisconsin, Illinois, or Michigan. It looked like one of the Great Lakes.

From the bike path along the lake, we turned and headed back downtown. In the early stages of the race, I ran very slowly, but later picked up my pace and passed several runners. The day was clear and sunny with temperatures right where they should be in late April, in the low 70's.

I felt no discomfort with the finish line in sight. I had just run 26.2 miles in 4:12:39. I could have comfortably run more, but when they told me to stop, I obliged. No sense in overdoing it. After showering at the hotel and meeting up with John, we headed back to the Memorial. This was our chance to tour the Memorial Center Museum, which we hadn't visited the day before. We were part of a tour led through double doors. The room was empty, except for the black recorder resting on the table behind the glass enclosure. While others sat at the back wall, I stood and listened. The voices on the tape recorder came from a room across the street from the Murrah Building. We listened to the court hearing that began at 9 a.m., April 19th, 1995.

Two minutes into the tape came the explosion. A voice was heard asking, "What was that?" Suddenly, on the wall across from us flashed pictures of the 168 people who perished. The doors to our right opened and it was instant chaos. Sirens and screams filled the room. Television monitors, hanging from the ceiling, showed breaking news reports of the disaster. Exhibits, along the walls and all in front of us, showed car keys, shoes, and broken computers, sitting in a pile of rubble. There was shattered glass, ripped clothing, and personal belongings among the debris. It was a room full of mortar, madness, and mayhem.

I started getting sick. I couldn't escape it. The noise, the confusion, the feeling of *"how do I get out of here?"* made me nauseated. The next several rooms we entered were quieter, but the pictures on the wall were anything but. There were newspaper accounts from all over the world, information on the capture and the trial of the terrorist, and a large screen showing individuals giving their accounts of the tragedy. One of the people speaking was Ted Wilson.

After touring the museum, John and I stepped backed into the sunshine and walked across the Memorial grounds one more time. We walked up to the Freedom Tree, which miraculously survived the explosion, looked across the reflecting pool to the 168 chairs, and then exited by the East Gate. We each had a plane to catch.

It's been said, running a marathon can have a dramatic effect on your life.

I should have saved my energy. I just had to visit The Oklahoma City National Memorial.

Marathoners at the Memorial

3 of the Best

Frank Shorter, Bill Rodgers, Dick Beardsley

26 on 27
in
CARRABASSETT VALLEY, MAINE

Sugarloaf Marathon / ME

Sunday, May 16, 2004
Age 45

Fumbling for my Kodak disposable camera, I hurried to rip open the box, but struggled when tearing open the plastic bag that delayed me from taking the ultimate picture. "Why didn't I open this earlier?" I muttered to myself. Fortunately, my subject was patient. He just stood there staring at me, while I stared at him. Finally, the camera was out and I snapped away.

I didn't assume the sign to be so accurate when I drove up Route 27 into Carrabassett Valley. What did they mean by, *"From here on your life will never be the same?"* A few miles later I found out. When I turned left down the dirt road to the site of the packet pick-up for the Sugarloaf Marathon, I heard the leaves rattle up ahead. Moments later, a moose emerged posing for the perfect portrait. It looked like we would stay fixed indefinitely, until a car barreled around the corner up ahead. The driver never slowed, acting as if this magnificent animal were only a squirrel, with apologies to squirrel lovers. The moose scrambled into the woods. I resumed my drive and scowled at the passing car.

I walked into the small wooden building and told the lady from behind the registration desk I had seen my first Maine Moose. She said he'd been out on the road all day. I thought, the way that car came by, he may not resurface again.

I came to Maine without securing a hotel, but after a quick telephone call from that small wooden building, I had a room at a much larger building just down the road. The hotel was the Grand Summit Resort Hotel at the base of the ski lift at Sugarloaf Mountain. I'm sure all the guests had obeyed the sign posted near the elevator that day. No one I saw was wearing skis. Once inside my spacious room, I swung the curtains open. The vista represented another sign posted on Maine highways: *The Way Life Ought To Be.*" An hour later, I drove back down the mountain and returned to the small wooden building for the pasta dinner. My four-legged friend was still in hiding, and so were my two-legged ones who owned "50 State Marathon" shirts. Most of the runners were New Englanders. I reached back into my Rhode Island accent and sat.

After telling my moose story, a runner from New Hampshire told his that had happened hours earlier. He and his wife were staying nearby at a campground. He decided to take a picture of the life-sized wire sculpture of a moose near his truck. Seconds after he retrieved his camera, the life-sized moose was joined by another life-sized moose. This one came without wires. In Maine, the moose were on the loose. No telling how many I'd see during the 26 miles I'd run the next day.

Rain was falling steadily outside the resort when I checked out at 5 a.m. I hurried to my car and drove 12 miles down Highway 27 to downtown Kingfield. The only business I noticed was the place I needed to go. I parked a short distance from Jordan Lumber Company and boarded the school bus for the ride back up Highway 27 to the start. Huddled in the front seat, attired in the blue rain gear and looking cold and tired, was Shelly Kaufmann. "Shelly, is that you?" I asked. I met Shelly two months earlier at the Oklahoma City airport. She had good reason to be tired. She was a few hours away from checking off her 48th marathon state.

The first of three busloads of runners moved back up Highway 27. I paid more attention to the hills, knowing I'd be running up and down them soon. The brochure listed the first 5 miles as flat, miles 5 through 10 rolling, with a steady two-mile climb at 8. The last 16 would prove to be downhill. Of course, the only thing I remembered reading in the brochure was that the race started at 7 a.m. The morning was rainy and chilly. I had already been on the highway three times. Why do I have to see it again? Can't I go home?

There was still 40 minutes to go when the bus came to a stop at Cathedral Pines Campground, north of Stratton. I stepped out of the bus and quickly decided the tall pines could stand without me. I headed back inside. Shelly hadn't moved. I'm 26 miles from my car. Forget about the marathon. I'm running to drive home.

I was laughed at the night before when I asked if there'd be orange cones on the route protecting us from traffic. "You're not going to see traffic," was the reply. Okay, but what about that 18-wheeler that looks like it's coming straight at me? Essentially, he was right. There wasn't much traffic on this stretch of highway in Western Maine. The route didn't need any painted arrows in the road either. Quite simply, it was 26 on 27. The route was a two-lane highway surrounded by pines all the way to Kingfield. The people at Jordan's didn't have to go too far to stock up on inventory.

The morning started out gray and rainy. For marathon runners, it was the perfect day. For the most part, the rain fell gently and there were many periods when it held off. Similar to other marathons, I started off very slowly. I was in no hurry to finish. It had only been three weeks since I had run the last 26-miler. I wanted to make sure I could go the distance.

The crowd of runners quickly spread out. There were times I looked down the highway in both directions and saw no one. Not a creature was stirring, not even a moose.

I was in dire need of a bathroom near the halfway point. The tall pines weren't going to help me on this one. Up ahead I spotted a convenience store. I had no choice. I veered off the road and headed straight toward the front door. It felt strange to have this number pinned onto my race garb when I walked inside the store. It was then I realized I was not going to win the race. I think it also became apparent to the customers. The proprietor was quick to tell me the restrooms were next door at the gas station. "The gas station I just passed, you mean?"

I returned the key to the mechanic and I was on my way. I made sure I ran to the same spot I left off on. As I ran down the entrance to the gas station, the woman in the blue rain gear sped by. "Hi Shelly." The delay gave me fresh legs and I played a game with myself. I was going to start passing people and keep count of

everyone I caught. Shelly was number 1. I caught the next runner for number 2. There wasn't another person in sight. I continued running hard, yet comfortable and saw a pack way up the road. I passed 3, 4, 5, 6, 7, and 8. Up ahead I blitzed by 9, 10, and 11. I sped on and passed 21, 22, 23, 24, and 25. I was running a negative split and my car was getting closer, as I passed 35, 36, and 37. I ran and kept passing people. Here was the group that passed me long before I took the bathroom break, as I moved by 44, 45, and 46. Here are the runners who passed me when I was going so slowly, as I mentally counted 66, 67, 68, 69, and 70.

I had made up considerable time and pressed on, but the last mile my numbers went backwards. I began to tire, but still finished with a negative split. My 4:17:14 time could have easily been a 4:50 time. I was satisfied with my efforts and slowly walked back to my car. After showering at the nearby high school gym, I got back on Highway 27. This time I drove south. At 5 p.m., under sunny skies, I pulled into the driveway of my parent's house in Cranston, Rhode Island. They were happy to see me. I arrived back safely and their car was vacuumed, washed, and full of petro.

At the dinner table, I showed my parent's my finisher's medal. The colors matched my mother's shirt. She draped the medal around her neck. It was the last time I touched it. It was the least I could do for all she had done for me.

Turn Off the Wind
in
LARAMIE, WYOMING

Wyoming Marathon / WY

Sunday, May 30, 2004
Age 45

O f all the exits to take on Interstate 80, why did it have to be 323 between Cheyenne and Laramie? It wasn't that I didn't like the scenery, the area was beautiful. It wasn't that I didn't like the rest stop, the mammoth bust of Abe Lincoln was impressive. What I didn't like was that small sign posted by the exit on a road that stretched from New Jersey to California.

Highest Point on I-80
8640 feet.

And this is where the marathon starts? Well, not exactly. See that big hill? It begins up there. That's at 8,739 feet.

If the Wyoming Marathon were a bear, it would have been a Grizzly. The course was rated as one of the most difficult in the country. *The Ultimate Guide to Marathons* ranked it number 12. From what I was looking at, I contemplated giving up the sport. After Wyoming, my next two events were ranked as the 9th and 11th toughest in the country.

The view out the window looked more like Denton than Denver. The plane was making its final approach and there wasn't a mountain in sight. If this was the Mile High City, then someone's measuring tape was off. Denver International Airport is a long way from Denver. From a distance, the airport, which sits by itself topped by a white canopy, resembles a site for an enormous party given by the rich and famous. Like an uninvited guest, I drove away as quickly as I could. On the trip north on I-25, the skyline of Denver appeared. The mountains towered beyond the city.

I was a long way from home, but it wasn't until I crossed into that next state I felt even farther away. Wyoming had Yellowstone, the Tetons, and Devil's Tower. It had fresh air, free roaming horses,

265

and a feeling you were "Out West." Wyoming also had a marathon. I knew that race, like the people who lived there, was going to be tough. I had a hunch the marathon was going to resemble the state's license plate. The picture depicts a cowboy about to be thrown from a bucking bronco. Whether the cowboy got bucked, I'll never know. Although their goal is to stay upright for eight seconds, my goal was five hours and not be kicked in the process.

The first person I saw when I walked through the door to the Little America Hotel was Cathy Troisi. The Seneca Falls, New York, resident, whom I first met in Arizona, was on a marathoning threshold. By crossing the finish line the next day, Cathy would join the ranks as having run a marathon in every state. At the registration and pasta dinner, I talked with Art Walker from Oregon, Marv Bradley from Colorado, Ira Robinson from Texas, Betsy Terry from Alabama, and my friends, Susan Sinclair and Carolyn Krumrey from Houston. On this night, no one was shy in Cheyenne.

After dinner I drove 50 miles west on I-80, just minutes past exit 323, to my hotel in Laramie. The cowboy pictures and artifacts hanging from the wall confirmed I truly was "Out West." On race morning, I stretched in front of the television while watching highlights from the previous day's dedication of the WWII Memorial in Washington. Hours before the dedication, I was a few miles away at Reagan National boarding my airplane. Two days later, I would be back, but first, I'd have to run 26.2 miles.

It was chilly at the Lincoln rest area, but I was content in my shorts and long sleeve shirt. It was Memorial Day weekend. Wasn't it supposed to warm up? The race was as pure as you would find. The only thing left behind would be our footprints. The starting line and mile markers consisted of white flour. Officials made sure nothing was going to disrupt the environment. We were told to carry our own water bottles and no paper cups would be distributed on the course. Roving refreshment stands on the back of pickup trucks would supply all the food and drink we needed. With our shoelaces tied and our numbers pinned, there was nothing more to do. It was 6 a.m. It was time to run.

Knowing it was an "out and back" course, the long downhill run from the start would turn uphill at the end of the race, but let's not think about that now. I'm feeling strong, I'm in Wyoming, and the elevation is dropping. It was a shame that motorists speeding across I-80 didn't stop at Exit 323. It was spectacular. We were in the wilderness running down a dirt road. The trees were green, the mountains were alive, and the day was perfect. It was sunny and cool. There was no better sport than the Marathon.

We entered Medicine Bow National Forest, part of the Curt Gowdy State Park, named after its native son. When the State Legislature passed the resolution, the broadcaster and outdoorsman said they couldn't do anything nicer for a fellow than do that. 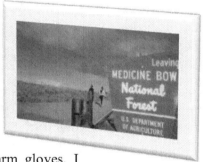 If someone had given me warm gloves, I would have said the same.

My hands were numb. It started early and the short time they warmed up didn't last long. They were cold for most of the race. Past the 12-mile mark, I stopped to untie my shoe to remove pebbles that found their way inside. I had great difficulty retying my laces. As the miles wore on, I would have continued, even if broken glass got inside. There was no way I could have gotten my shoe back on. My hands were that numb.

Far in the distance, I could see the top of trucks traveling along the crest of the mountain. With Interstate 80 hidden from view, I saw no cars and no black top. Farther in the race, our course went under the interstate and then ran parallel to it. On the other side of the

267

interstate the wind was whipping. The billboard for the Little America Hotel, advertising its swimming pool, would have persuaded motorists to pull up to its rival, the Hitching Post Inn instead. It was cold and very windy.

The only spectators throughout the day were those speeding at 80-plus mph down the highway. I know one passenger noticed us. A dog, leaning out the window of an 18-wheeler, barked instructions for us to go faster.

Crossing back under the interstate, the course continued for another four miles, before we'd turn around to retrace our steps. The beauty of the course got more breathtaking when we entered the rock formation area called Vedauwoo, a haven for climbers. Hopefully, they were well tied to their ropes. The wind didn't let up. A couple of miles from crossing back under the interstate, the wind had become as intense as I had ever experienced. We were out in the open and there was no protection from it. Any runner under 105 lbs. would have gone backwards. My hands were cold, my face was raw and windburned, and I was having the time

of my life. If my friends could see me now. We were running into a direct headwind that refused to give in. Turning right, after crossing under I-80, the wind battered us on our side. It would not turn off.

From the pavement, we got back onto the dirt and reentered Medicine Bow Forest. As we moved down the valley, the wind

started to lose its power, but that was no victory. It started to snow. At first, I thought it was white blossoms falling from trees, but the flurries kept coming. I was extremely cold. More importantly, my noon checkout was fast approaching, yet the finish was two miles away.

The hotel clerk told me she wouldn't be able to extend my checkout an additional half hour. I was in no mood to pay extra for my impending delay.

My run became a walk with a little over a mile to go. The walk didn't last long. I started to jog, as a handful of runners came toward

me. These hearty souls were in the middle of their ultra run. To them, 26.2 was halfway. God Bless 'Em.

That hill seemed a lot steeper running up it, but I did it and finished the race. I never stopped running and continued to my car. I opened the door, buckled up, and started the engine. I raced down the highway to the Laramie exit. I could see the hotel in the distance. It was the same time I noticed the car's digital clock flash "11:59." I was going to make it, until I spotted another flash. My rearview mirror was flashing blue.

Telling my story, while handing my driver's license over, did no good. The cop showed no mercy. At 12:15 p.m. he presented a $127 ticket to me. A minute later I pulled into the hotel. "12:30 check-out? No problem," she said. That's just great. Why didn't you tell me yesterday?

269

Goddess of Fire
in
VOLCANOES NAT'L PARK, HAWAII

Kilauea Volcano Marathon / HI

Saturday, July 31, 2004
Age 45

Getting farther away from New York, Allentown, and South Bend, the red line kept going. Growing, as time retreated, it caught up with Davenport, Des Moines, and Denver. It passed under the Great Salt Lake, the Great Nevada Basin, and through Yosemite. Coming face to face with San Francisco, the city didn't have a chance. The red line crossed out everything in its path. It was now over a blue background, and would continue effortlessly for miles upon miles, but a glance to the television monitor showed a formidable foe was waiting.

After 4,958 miles and nine-and-a-half hours of travel, the red line, led by the little white plane, had stopped. Honolulu had won out. Aloha! Welcome to Hawaii. It was hard for me to believe I was actually in Hawaii. I was so far from home, so far out in the Pacific Ocean, and so far so good. The sun was out, the mountains were up, and the waves were crashing in.

My stop in the state capital didn't last for long. Less than an hour after I landed, I was jetting to Hilo when the feeling of being in Hawaii started settling in. Businessmen working on their laptops sported Hawaiian shirts, flight attendants wore flowers in their hair and served Hawaiian drinks, and the writing across the airplane read, "*Aloha*." Meanwhile, I was flying "by the seat of my pants." I had made no hotel reservation. I was going to Hawaii and didn't plan on spending any of it inside.

Upon receiving my keys at the rental car counter, I inquired about campsites in the area. "Try Arnott's Lodge," the woman said. I found it less than two miles from the airport. Under the big white tent above the patio were washing machines and dryers, computers and televisions, and a lot of college kids spending part of their summer in paradise. For $14 you could sleep inside and get a bunk. For $9 you could sleep outside and possibly get a "*bonk*." I settled for the latter, but made sure I positioned my tent away from the coconut trees.

It was wonderful. I was nestled in my green tent sleeping under the Hawaiian sky. At 6 a.m., I was up and out ready to explore the island. I swam at numerous places along the coast, including one

271

spot where I wedged myself between a rock and a hard place, as the waves crashed over me. My legs got scratched and my toe was cut, but it was a lot of fun, as the surf tried to push me off my resting place and onto my final one. The sun and the wind dried me quickly and I was off in my car again. Behind every turn were spectacular views of mountains, rock, and water.

At 6 p.m., I made my way to Volcanoes National Park, which was about three quarters of the way around the island. From the entrance, I drove 45 minutes to find the "Greatest Lightshow on Earth." At the end of the road, past all the parked cars, I joined the many onlookers and walked about two miles over the lava fields to the end of the rope. Sitting in the dark, with a flashlight in my hand, I looked across the beach, as the red fire spilled into the ocean. It was a perfect ending to a long day. The red line I watched on a television screen was coming alive right in front of me. It was beautiful. It was magical. It was Hawaii.

If being near the lava made me feel like I was a long way from home, then being at the packet pick-up area made me feel like I was back at home. I saw Jim Lovell, Art Walker, and met a woman from Richmond, Virginia. A month earlier, I volunteered as a timer at a triathlon event in Richmond. My boss was Jim Lovell. The man was so skilled at multitasking, that if he desired, could balance plates at a circus. Instead, he travels the globe making sure races go off without a hitch and all finishing times are accurate. The Kona resident was also the race director for that city's marathon each June.

Sitting by Jim as he was doling out bib numbers and checking off names, I spotted Art Walker. I sat with the Portland, Oregon, chiropractor at the pasta dinner in Cheyenne. Art would also be at my next race in Oregon. And then there was Mary Ann. She accompanied a friend to the registration area and heard Jim say we had met in Richmond. "Richmond? That's where I'm from," said Mary Ann. Now living in Hawaii, she would make the trip back to her native city the following month. I came to Hawaii alone, but you'd never have guessed it on this night. I talked with everyone.

The next day, I moved my tent from Arnott's in Hilo to a campsite near the National Park. Sleeping on the ground the night before running 26.2 miles is not recommended in the marathon books, but what do they know? I slept soundly. Plus, I didn't have a long way to go to reach for the alarm. And, the price was free.

The race was considered the toughest measured marathon in the world, but at the start, it looked anything but. We were on a paved street and going downhill. Many runners wore bicycle gloves, since several miles were to be run across sharp lava fields. A fall was like landing on broken glass.

At the marathon dinner the night before, Tanya Refshauge of Minnesota, had a nice little wound on her knee she received from walking out on the lava fields. She was bleeding and limping, but undaunted. Nothing was going to get in her way from running the marathon. Billy Conner, who had run the course many times, told me there would be a 50% chance I'd fall during the race. "You better wear gloves," he said. I've run 53 marathons covering over 1,300 miles and have never fallen. My bicycling gloves were home on my bike. I had no regrets. However, I did regret not bringing sunblock.

The downhill didn't last long. The pavement quickly pointed to the sky. Soon, we would leave the roads and enter the parking lot to the observatory. On our left was the vast lava field, punctuated by the enormous caldera. I had visited the area the day before, but hadn't noticed the narrow trail at the edge of the lot. On this day I followed the feet in front and carefully side stepped and climbed up and over the rocks. The seven miles we ran on the Ka'u Desert Trail, a combination of black sand and rock, was no day at the beach. After stumbling and catching myself three or four times, I thought a lot about those biking gloves, knowing more difficult terrain was up ahead.

The lava on the Mauna Iki Trail looked like chocolate cake mix that had spilled from the bowl. This was the glass I had been warned about. I stopped and put my hand on the surface feeling the tiny crystals. Each step produced a sound as if I were running on Captain Crunch cereal. Near the eight-mile mark, runners carefully crossed a narrow path beside a crater that could have fit a Volkswagen. My toes were taking a beating, but at least I was staying upright. The panoramic view was like nothing I had ever seen, except for pictures I had seen of the moon. If this wasn't Hawaii, it had to be another planet. Nothing on planet Earth looked like this.

Red ribbons, tied on sticks, kept us on course. The markers were spaced about every 50 feet. At one point, I followed a few runners up onto a ridge, until I noticed the person in front had her arms extended. The next runner repeated her move. It was easy to see we didn't know where to go. There were neither runners, nor ribbons up ahead. Instantly, we were lost. However, off to my right I spotted a ribbon and life was good. It was now a 26.3 mile race.

Not only did it take sweat to run this course, but also to volunteer on it. Water and sports drinks were carried out a long distance the night before by those who spent the night in tents. It was amazing to see the enthusiastic volunteers who had waited all night for you to show up. Being prepared was serious business. You couldn't take on this challenge halfheartedly. For any runner who couldn't go on, only a helicopter or a mule could rescue you. You were out in "nowhere land". You certainly couldn't depend on Madam Pele to get you out.

Hawaiians refer to her as the *Goddess of Fire*, born of the female spirit Haumea. She is both the creator and the destroyer. She throws molten fountains into the air, directs the flows of lava, and sometimes shows herself in the fires of Kilauea. The myth says she is protective of her territory, and has been known to punish those who steal or trespass on her sacred land. Don't believe me? Ask those who had visited Hawaii if they ever brought back lava, and if bad luck soon followed. Knowing about The Goddess, I was a bit reluctant to relieve myself during the long run. I had no choice. As I hid behind a shrub, I asked Pele for forgiveness, hoping she wouldn't discipline me for my disrespectful act. So far so good. I continued running without any discomfort. Maybe the Goddess of Fire wasn't looking.

The race was halfway over when we left the lava fields and ran back onto the pavement. It was a welcome sight. After trekking on the chocolate-like cake mix, the pavement was a piece of cake. The route climbed steadily, but I didn't care. I no longer had to hop, jump, or side step. That was a big relief. I felt strong  going up the hills and started passing people. Although I was running slowly, I kept moving. After a long steady climb, we turned right onto a two-lane highway that cut through 30-year-old lava flows. It was the easiest part of the course. We were on pavement and running downhill, but I wasn't overly enthused. I knew the finish was in the opposite direction, at a higher elevation.

From pavement we ventured onto grass, as the course made its way to Escape Road. The makeshift thoroughfare is used in case Pele

gets in the mood to trap you. As we entered the road, it began to rain, but that was the only relief we got. The course marched up and up and up for four miles. The grassy trail reminded me of the stretch I ran in Northern Minnesota. We ran between lush trees and stepped on green grass. I ran in and out of the tire tracks trying to find the perfect footing. Bring back the lava. This was tough. Finally, it ended, but the race was still on.

Through the parking lot of Thurston Lava Tube and up on the rim trail I ran. Down below on my left was the caldera I had seen earlier in the day, but now I was right on top of it. A hiccup or small misstep would have sent me barreling over the edge. I felt as if I were on top of the world. Soon, civilization came into view when the course passed behind the Volcano House. Running by the picture window of the hotel's restaurant, I noticed people eating lunch and sipping wine. I got a nice smile and applause when I snapped a photo of two women enjoying their cuisine, but another woman was scowling. Madam Pele wasn't finished with me yet.

Less than two miles from the finish, the route took us by the steam vents produced by the Goddess of Fire. I felt badly for the volunteer at the aid station enduring this. I lowered my head and held my breath through the smoke. One final climb and I was across the street, on my way to the finish behind the military compound. I could hear the announcer call out Art Walker's name. My turn was a minute and 16 seconds later. Running into the clearing, a large gathering cheered me in. There was Mary Ann, Lisa, and others I had spoken to the night before. As I turned for the finish I heard,

"From Richmond, Virginia, Paul Mellor, who is on his way to running a marathon in every state. He's at 44 and we're pleased he chose Kilauea for his Hawaii run."

Immediately after crossing the line, Jim Lovell hustled from the scorer's table, handed me my finisher's card and said, "How's this for service?" It was a nice gesture thanking me for helping him during the Richmond triathlon. As Jim was congratulating me, Lisa was giving me a big hug, and Mary Ann presented me with beautiful Hawaiian flowers she had picked from her yard. Art and his wife C.J. congratulated me too.

I was so happy and elated. My biggest hurdle to completing the 50

states was over. I had made a tremendous sacrifice to make the long trip to Hawaii, but as I was hugged and supported by my new friends, I felt as if I had never left home.

Bluer Than Blue
in
CRATER LAKE, OREGON

Crater Lake Marathon / OR

Saturday, August 14, 2004
Age 45

Waking up to a beautiful day, after an evening of violent weather, is what it seemed like. Listening to the angry skies and seeing all its destruction, one would hardly imagine beauty would ever return. It was a night that seemed to go on forever. But in order to appreciate the calm after the storm, you'd have to be patient. You would have to be very, very patient. Beauty was taking its time. No need to look out the window. Go back to bed. This storm would last a half-a-million years.

When Mount Mazama blew its top over 7,000 years ago, it produced 150 times as much ash as did the Mount St. Helens eruption in 1980. The mountain's magma chamber was emptied and the volcano collapsed, leaving a huge bowl-shaped caldera. Over time, snow and rain filled the cavity. Today, that once hollowed hole, at 1,943 feet, is the deepest lake in the United States and seventh deepest in the world. The wait was worth it. Crater Lake is nothing short of spectacular. The lake is pristine, the water is bluer than blue, and the road that rings it is part of the marathon course. Any wonder why I chose my *Oregon* run at the nation's fifth oldest national park?

I arrived in Portland two days before the national spotlight. In a political first, President Bush and Senator Kerry both planned campaign swings in the same city, on the same day. I hurried out of town, as I listened to talk radio describe how Portland was going to be in a gridlock beginning Friday. Like a seasoned politician, I also made campaign stops. I drove to the jagged coastline and pitched my tent in a campground in Newport. The next night I entered California, not because of all those electoral votes, but because of all those elevated trees. I slept under the stars in Redwood National Park, then bid farewell to my neighbor, Jason. He was on his own little marathon. The bike he rode from Seattle was leaning on the nearby picnic table. His finish line was San Francisco.

As I had done 10 days earlier, I spent the first few days looking out over the Pacific. The only difference was this time I was looking west. I looked down from high cliffs, watched water crash upon rock, and saw well over 100 sea lions lying out on their coastal condo. All that was wonderful, but the star of the show was coming up next. It's time to see Crater Lake. Located about 100 miles inland and about 60 miles north of California, I was anxiously waiting to see this beauty. In the meantime, I'd have to settle for looking at it on the Oregon license plate. Could it be as wondrous as people say? The sign up ahead showed two arrows. To the left was Diamond Lake, to the right was Crater Lake. It was 5 p.m. I'd have to wait and see it the next day.

Art and C. J. Walker graciously invited me to stay with them at their campsite in Diamond Lake. Art and I were spending the summer running the same courses in Wyoming and Hawaii. We couldn't get rid of each other, neither could the Pacific. We both landed safely in Oregon. They welcomed me like one of their own. I met family and friends and joined them for a top-of-the-line pasta dinner prepared by C.J. Afterwards, we gathered by the fire near the edge of dazzling Diamond Lake, as I questioned how Crater Lake could top this. I was going to find out the next morning.

When the mountain erupted, it covered over 5,000 square miles of Mazama's ash. I saw evidence as I drove through the vast Pumice Desert, with ash lying 50 feet below. Later I'd get my first glimpse of Crater Lake. The air temperature was slightly cooler and the skies were partly cloudy, but the lake was gorgeous, even with the fog that lay atop it. Nestled inside a rocky ring, the lake was being gawked at by several marathoners. Among the onlookers was Cathy Troisi, my friend from New York, whom I had run with in Arizona and Wyoming. There was also Brenton Floyd, whom I had run with in Georgia, Tennessee, and Mississippi. And then there was Cyndie Merten of Oregon and Tom Adair of Georgia. It was a reunion on the rim. With the 7 a.m. start moments away, I walked down from the viewing area and onto the street. Don't let the snow on the bank fool you. Although it was cool, the day was going to be hot.

With the lake hidden from view, we ran down the paved highway. On our left was the Pumice Desert, with mountains in the distance. Up ahead I sensed why the Crater Lake Rim Run was ranked as one of the most difficult races. Many runners were already walking. I passed several of them and easily made my way up the steep grade. The day was already getting warmer, and the blue had returned to the sky when my head began to turn to the right. Crater Lake was back in view. The water appeared to be a lot bluer than when I had seen it earlier in the day. I could see pockets of snow along the shoreline and on the cliffs above.

The marathon route brought out two prominent colors. On my left was the color green from the hemlocks, firs, pines, and spruce trees. On my right was the color blue from Crater Lake. The architects of the highway would have been great builders of baseball fields. They left no room for foul territory. There were stretches when the road went as  close to the lake as it could get without dropping off. For several miles, the lake was in and out of view. Shielded from trees or the twists of the road, the lake was too big to ignore. Each time it appeared, I snapped a picture and looked across the six-mile body of water, gauging how far I had already run. The lake gave me a new look every time it showed itself.

Knowing the tough reputation of this course, I continued to run slowly waiting for its bite. My legs felt strong and my breathing was normal, but my watch said otherwise. I was well behind a five-hour pace. I attributed it to all the pictures I had taken. I looked more like a tourist than a trotter, but I wasn't the only one. Many runners stopped their cadence with cameras.

Running near the nine-mile mark, I heard a runner saying to his partner, "We have to go up there." I looked up to see where *up* was. You have to be kidding me, I thought. High, high, up in the mountain I saw movement. I would have never guessed those people were in this race. How in the world did they get up there? I had a feeling I was going to find out. I would have to be patient. It was going to take at least an hour to get there.

During this climb I met Stewart Buck, one of the volunteers for the Baton Rouge Beach Marathon. He said it was going to be a great event. We'll have plenty of food and drink at the pasta dinner, including gumbo. He also said he would arrange for me to get bib number 50 for my achievement as having run a marathon in every state. Thanks Stewart, but first, how do I put Oregon behind me?

With each turn of the road, the views got more spectacular. When I made it to the top, I could see tiny runners below and wondered how they were going to get up here. Probably the same way I did. For several runners this was the end of the race. The 13.1 segment of the Rim Run was complete. For marathoners the race was just beginning. And yes, I wasn't at the top yet. Around the next corner was a little more climbing. The turnaround came at Hillman Peak. Thank goodness. The lake was directly in front of me and there was nowhere to go. Soon, Mount Scott was in front of me and a half marathon was behind. Plus, at an elevation of 8,151 feet, the highest point on the rim, I was ready to run downhill.

The course dropped in elevation for the next several miles, but in the back of my mind, I kept waiting for 22. I kept hearing about the stretch from 22 through 24 as being very tough. So far, I wasn't feeling much discomfort from this course. At the 19-mile mark, the sign read, *"Lost Creek Campground - 3 miles."* Okay, I'm starting to get tired. It was hot, and as far as I could see, the road didn't quit.

I noticed a lot of activity when I got to the campground. The finish was on the other side of the trees. Runners, with smiles on their faces, were coming home, as I was pointed down the dirt road. I might have been pointed *down* the dirt road, but I was running *up* it.

I was moving very slowly, until finally, for the first time, I started walking. I was out of breath. This was no hill. This was a %&*#@ mountain. It didn't end. Just when I turned a corner expecting to see the crest, it went up and up and up. Runners were flying past me in the opposite direction, while I was doing everything possible to keep moving. I was walking and huffing and puffing. How could this be? I hadn't huffed and puffed all day. Welcome to the 22nd mile. I had heard so much about you, but I never expected this. The trek was a grim reminder of climbing Pikes Peak. It felt just as steep. However, at Pikes Peak, the climbing was in the first half of the race. It became apparent a non-runner designed the last few miles of this race.

Feeling nauseous, I stopped to put my hands on my knees. After I lifted my head, I got sick a second time when I saw the climb was still in progress. I moved to the side of the road and sprawled out. A race volunteer stood by me. Most runners were covered in sweat. I was covered in dirt. I tried to vomit, but nothing came. I was trying desperately to eliminate the thought I'd have to return to Oregon another year.

Cathy Troisi, a veteran of over 100 marathons, moved by me saying this was the toughest course she had ever run. I hear you, Cathy, I hear you. I stood and walked with the volunteer. My head was down as he gave me a play-by-play to the turnaround. "You're at 100 yards. A football field away." I put one foot in front of the other while thinking, 5, 10, 15 yards. He said he could see people up ahead and that I was almost there. Still, I never looked up. I just focused on my feet. I got to the turnaround and then sat on the ground one more time. I was sick to my stomach. I sipped Coke and then got back on my feet. I started running and started feeling better. I moved down the mountain going faster than I had all day. Up ahead Art's daughter, Alexe Bellingham, was waiting for me. She had already run the half marathon when she joined me for the trip down. She encouraged me down the mountain, as we continued to run a quick pace. I passed Cathy and a couple of other runners. I turned into the campground for the finish, in a time of 5:45:15.

It was a great feeling, until my sickness returned. My body started shutting down and I felt nauseous again. Art and C. J. stayed with me and suggested I get medical attention. After looking at my bib number, I should have known I was destined for an IV. My number was 4. With the bag tied to a tree, med student, Grover Shipman put a needle in my vein until I was no longer bluer than blue.

It was a long day for my friends, the Walkers. They had run the half marathon and stayed with me well into the afternoon. When Grover finished up, I tossed my car keys to Art and he drove us back to the campsite. With storm clouds hovering, Alexe's husband, Greg, prepared steak, potatoes, and vegetables on the grill. With ice pellets coming down hard and fast, we cheered *Hail to the Chef* as Greg got pounded, while the rest of us watched from under an awning. After the storm, we sat by the warm fire and watched the sun go down over Diamond Lake. It was an end to a magnificent day with friends, food, and fellowship.

It's amazing where a pair of running shoes can take you.

Is that snow up there?

Runners who are Walkers
and Givers ...
A 10 (& 11) in my book.
Portland's C.J. & Art Walker

A Powwow
in
BISMARCK, NORTH DAKOTA

Bismarck Marathon / ND

Saturday, September 11, 2004
Age 45

Strolling by gate C20 at Minneapolis - St. Paul International Airport, one could easily think passengers were off to a T-shirt convention. Many of the people boarding flight 5627 were wearing colorful shirts that rivaled those at the airport's gift shop. The only difference was none of the shirts had the word *Minnesota* on them. Instead, the words were *California*, *Florida*, *Iowa*, and *New York*. It was easy to see why everyone was going to North Dakota. They wanted another shirt. It was also easy to see what they had to do to get it. They had to run 26 miles, 385 yards.

Idaho's famous potatoes, Montana's Big Sky, Tennessee's Smoky Mountains, Georgia's peach, Carolina's beach, and North Dakota ... well, that's a reach. What is North Dakota known for? The State Legislature questioned that too. There was talk the state had an identity problem and the word *North* be dropped. *"I'm from Dakota. How 'bout you?"*

The trip to Bismarck was slow to get off the ground. It wasn't encouraging when the Northwest agent suggested my small carry-on bag was too big to be carried on. She said, "You won't believe how small this plane is. Last week we had to check a man's briefcase."

The plane never moved for several minutes. I began to think someone had smuggled on a large purse, or worse yet, the Sunday edition of the *New York Times*. Finally, the declaration was made. Instead of North Dakota going to the dogs, the dogs were going to North Dakota. The higher ups in the cockpit would have none of this. The size of the aircraft prohibited more than one dog from being transported. Now, with two dogs aboard the belly of the airplane, we weren't going anywhere. Shortly, both dogs were removed. It was learned the owners tried to sneak their pets onto this earlier flight. Later, they would join their four-legged friends in the doghouse.

Even with all the runners, I was happy to sit next to non- runner John Huten. The professional sports photographer wasn't going to be at the Bismarck Marathon. He was on his way to Dickinson for another assignment. John shared with me interesting stories about the Olympic venues he had worked. At the Winter Olympics in Salt Lake City, he told me how he saw Gold Medal winners Sarah Hughes and Jamie Salé of Canada sign each other's posters. The young skaters gave John a strange look when he asked if they wanted him to sign the posters too. It was Huten who took the picture.

It wasn't long before the lakes of Minnesota gave way to the plains of North Dakota. I spotted haystacks, cows, and miles of straight roads that cut through farmland. Minutes after driving away from the Bismarck airport, I found Sibley's Campground off Washington Street. In a field across from RV's and campers, my tent was the only one around. Once the tent was up, I was out. It was time to explore my new city.

I didn't need a map to locate the capitol building. I just looked for the "Skyscraper on the Prairie." The building looked more like an office building than a capitol. In the lobby, I studied portraits of famous North Dakotans. There was Fargo's Roger Maris, Jamestown's Peggy Lee, Kulm's Angie Dickinson, Velva's Eric Sevareid, and Strasburg's Lawrence Welk, to name a few. Also in the lobby, but not on a wall, was Kauai's Kamika Smith. That's Kauai, Hawaii. A quick look at Kamika told me why he was here. The marathon shirt gives it away every time. Kamika and I talked and walked, while checking out both the House and Senate Chambers of the country's 39th state. Meanwhile, a few blocks over at the YMCA, preparations were being made for the marathon pasta dinner.

At the dinner, I sat with Beth Davenport of Santa Fe, New Mexico. Later, we were joined by teenagers Krista and Nicole. The two girls helped serve the pasta and were genuinely interested in the running exploits of these two out-of-staters. Nicole told me how her swim team was raising money by selling candy bars. I told her I'd buy one from her before I left town.

The day's temperatures were well into the 80's. However, the thin blankets were no match for the night. I was cold and was never able to get comfortable. At 3 a.m. when I got out of the tent to scamper to the bathroom, I thought things couldn't get much worse. The only comfort I had was knowing the sun was coming back for another day. I was well awake before my alarm sounded and I was ready to run, but a more important issue was pressing. On my way to the marathon start, I stopped at Walmart and bought a sleeping bag. I should have bought an umbrella too.

It started to rain when I got out of my car at Pioneer Park. What a difference a day makes. Unlike the day before, with warm temperatures, it was apparent this day was going to be cooler. It was a great day to run. Fortunately, the 161 runners had more endurance than the rain. The precipitation didn't last long. The route took us south on Riverside Park Road and by Keelboat Park. On our right, was a 55-foot, full scale keelboat resembling the one Lewis and Clark traveled on along the Missouri River. The state was celebrating the 200th anniversary of their journey. The city had posted several signs showing that we were running on parts of the famous trail. We were the lucky ones. I doubt Meriwether Lewis and William Clark had the benefits of mile markers and aid stations.

After recently running three difficult marathons in succession, North Dakota was a welcome relief. Unlike Wyoming, Hawaii, and Oregon, this race had no hills, no mountains, no lava, and no snow to deal with. Still, I ran very slowly, knowing I had another marathon the following week. I met several runners whom I had known from other races. Up ahead was Paul Piplani, whom I had met in Idaho. On my right was Carl Hunt, whom I had met in Wyoming. Farther back was Don Lang, Sharon Mordorski, and Tom Adair. At the six-mile mark, I heard a familiar voice from behind when I was taking out my camera. *"Paul, do you want me to take your picture with the HA-SES."* You have to love that Maine accent. "No thanks, Mike. I'm just going to get a shot of this horse with a runner in the background. *"*

Mike Brooks is a tough-looking Mainer with a heart of gold. Through his running, Mike has helped raise thousands of dollars for charities, including *Camp Sunshine*; a Maine oasis for children with life threatening diseases. I wondered how many times during the course of his runs, including a 10-day 500-mile jaunt, he was seen by drivers as only a jogger. Little would they know he was a lifesaver.

As Mike and I veered left on Burleigh Avenue, it started to rain, but the rain didn't last long. If it had, there was a big umbrella up ahead to hide under. The tree in the middle of the road separated the runners who were coming and going on this "out and back" course.

The course took us to the outskirts of the city, as we moved down Washington and Sibley Drive. At the turnaround in the Briarwood subdivision, I passed a family dining out on their lawn and cheering the runners. As I moved closer to take a picture, I recognized a familiar face. "Hi Krista."

I was running a comfortable pace by the time I hit 13 miles; 2 hours and 15 minutes into the race. Knowing exactly where I needed to go, I wasn't concerned with mile markers. I treated it like a training run because I knew the route and knew where I'd stop. I also knew it was a long way off. Far in the distance I could see the "Skyscraper on the Prairie."

While running through the tunnel, under the Expressway Bridge, I realized I didn't know the course as well as I thought. I turned to the left on the bike/run path, until a runner behind me pointed me to the other fork. The 15 seconds I was off course made no difference. I pushed a little harder and continued to run. Up ahead, was the narrowest part of the course with runners occupying the sidewalk on busy and congested Washington Street. Here, many runners had been known to hit the wall, but another tragedy was about to happen.

Moments before the crash

Behind me I heard the screech of tires, and cringed as I was hoping a collision wasn't to follow. I was wrong. I heard the crash and turned to my right when I saw two motorcycle riders airborne. It was no match for the car they hit. Volunteers from the aid station ran toward them, as I continued to run away. Traffic had come to a stop when I turned left on Arbor Avenue. The softball players on my left were oblivious to what had happened, but that didn't last long. The sirens filled the air, as help was on its way to the accident scene. I had only a few miles left, but my thoughts were back on Washington. I could still hear the sirens as I pushed forward onto Sertoma Park and then to Riverside Park Road.

I had passed several runners during my return trip, but couldn't catch up with 54-year-old, Un Ha Lee of Olympia, Washington, who was 30 seconds ahead of me. Instead, I spotted the man with the WWII hat walking toward me on the trail in Pioneer Park. I stopped and shook his hand. He appreciated my gesture, but then said, "Keep running." I followed his advice and two minutes later I was done. My finishing time of 4:10:47 wasn't fast, but it was the fastest I had run all year. The first person to congratulate me was Larry Harding of Arvada, Colorado. Like many others who had come to North Dakota, Larry's goal was to run a marathon in every state, but Larry doesn't dilly-dally. He runs them hard. On this day his 3:25:35 run tied him for 20th, earning him an age division award.

After the awards ceremony at the YMCA, I returned to the campsite to shower. At 5:30 p.m. I would meet up with Lonnie Smith, Albert Shum, Elisha Huricks, and the other runner who tied for 20th, Bernadette Samson, to attend the big Indian Powwow. But first, I had to find Mustang Drive.

I had promised Nicole Johnson I'd buy a candy bar from her. With less than an hour to spare, I had to find her house and then find Kelly Inn to meet up with the gang. My eyes followed my finger on the Bismarck map in search of *Mustang*. I found it a minute later. I drove to the northwest part of town and pulled into the driveway of Nicole's house. When the woman answered the door, her first words were, "You're the guy who doesn't like garlic." It was Nicole's mother who served the breadsticks at the pasta dinner.

Nicole wasn't home, but Brenda invited me in and gave me a tour of their beautiful home. After a nice visit, I drove away toward the hotel and started eating the first of two candy bars.

At 5:45 p.m. we all piled into Elisha's car and headed off to the Powwow. We saw drummers, dancers, and hundreds of colorful costumes. The event brought competitors from all over the West. It was a beautiful and festive night. Afterward, we went to the Peacock Alley and Grill to celebrate our productive day. It was the five of us; Elisha from Maryland, Lonnie from Indiana, Bernadette from Missouri, Albert from California, and me from Virginia, sitting in a North Dakota restaurant sharing good food and a lot of laughs. To top it off, we were joined by the race director who bought us dessert. "Thanks, Mark."

I left Bismarck the next morning, but returned a week later after finishing up a 10-day excursion that included two marathons and a speaking engagement. Strangely, my memories of the city weren't focused on the reason I came here. Instead of thinking about the marathon, I thought about all the friends I had met in Dakota. If all their portraits were hung in the "Skyscraper on the Prairie" a wing would need to be added.

Look at those fools

Larry Harding (CO) and
Kamika Smith (HI)

Finding the Way Back
in
BILLINGS, MONTANA

Montana Marathon / MT

Sunday, September 19, 2004
Age 45

Traveling from one place to another was my routine for the first seven days. From the time I left Bismarck, I'd driven over a thousand miles, toured some of the country's best landmarks, and slept in a tent for many nights. Aside from presenting a seminar to the Wyoming Health Care Association in Casper, I had spent all these days alone. Add to that, my cell phone didn't work.

I struck up conversations with people at Mount Rushmore, chatted with people in Deadwood, and befriended folks at Old Faithful. Everyone I met was nice, but they weren't my kind of people. To them, hitting the wall was about climbing Devils Tower. Getting a negative split was about a photograph that didn't develop. Taking water on the run was about hustling back to a car during an afternoon storm. I was overdue for a runner's "hi."

In Grand Tetons National Park, I saw deer on both sides of the road. In Yellowstone, I saw buffalo walking down the center of the street. Near Mammoth Hot Springs, I watched a herd of elk grazing outside shops and restaurants. But it was in Billings, Montana, when I spotted the strangest sight of all. Across the street, on the other side of the bank parking lot, I saw it. The gentleman walking down the street was wearing a Richmond Marathon T-shirt. I quickly turned the car around, raced through the parking lot, and stopped on the other side of the street. I had found a friend.

The man wearing the Richmond shirt wasn't from Richmond. He was from South Carolina and he had come to Montana to put another notch on his state-by-state marathon list. For Jim Browder, it would be a difficult task. A) Jim is a minister. B) Most marathons are run on Sunday. C) Jim had an injured foot. But Jim's determination, and the power of prayer, was all he needed to succeed. I was in search of that power too.

The Montana Marathon was eight days after my marathon in Bismarck. It would be my closest span of running 26.2 miles. Could I do it? I was hoping in a town called Billings, I wasn't going to be paying a heavy price.

In 1976, I had come to Billings on a family trip. I remembered Cobb Field and finding two baseballs on the other side of the fence. Twenty-eight years later, here I was again, driving by the same minor league ballpark reminiscing about finding those souvenirs.

I was so far from home, but the streets looked like any other you'd find across America. There's a Wendy's, a Burger King, and a KFC restaurant. There's a Walmart, a Target, and a Home Depot. There's a tremendous amount of familiarity in Billings, as there are in other cities across the country. You can pull up to a drive-through window at McDonald's in Hilo or Hartford and order the # 3, knowing a Quarter Pounder with cheese, fries, and a Coke would await you at the next window.

If you needed money 30 years earlier, the cash had to be wired to you. Today, you just have to pull up to a bank, slide a card into a slot, and your name appears on the screen with the words, "How much do you want?" Thomas Wolfe might have said "You can't go home again," but take it from me, you can get awfully close.

Richmond's Rodney Johnson

Familiarity was also in store at the prerace pasta dinner. The venue, similar to Bismarck, was held at the YMCA. Also, the guy wearing the L.A. Marathon shirt looked very familiar. Rodney Johnson, whom I had met in Iowa, lives in my hometown. The next day, these two Richmonders would get more familiar with Montana's largest city. After dinner I drove back to my room. It looked a lot like the one I stayed at during the week, but this time, I pitched my tent behind the truck stop along the fence. In the middle of the night, when I heard the train whistle blow, I was hoping I wasn't on the wrong side of that fence.

The next morning I drove back to the Y and waited for the doors to open. While sitting in my car, I looked at the three school buses parked across the street and wondered, where in the world are they going to take us? On the bus ride out of town, I sat with Martha Corazzini of Henderson, Nevada. It might not have been the first time we sat on a bus together. We had both been bused out of Pocatello, Idaho and Midtown Manhattan, en route to a starting line. We always managed to find our way back. On this day in Billings, we were going to be tested again.

Although many of the bus riders weren't novice runners, one of the bus drivers was a novice driver. The bus stopped after a few miles. It appeared as if the driver thought we were running a 5K. The flashing lights in front of us said otherwise. The police pulled us over because the bus behind us had no lights. As it was, our driver had to show the other driver where the lights were. At this hour of the day, the bus lights were the only things shining.

The bus continued for mile upon mile as the sun met up with  Montana's big sky. Then the bus rolled to a stop and we stepped out. The driver didn't have to look for the start line. The rows of Porta Johns gave it away that this was the place to release all passengers. It was a beautiful setting. In every direction there wasn't a structure, a billboard, or a plow in sight. It was sky meeting field or vice versa. They both were enormous.

I felt no soreness from my marathon a week earlier. I stayed near the rear of the pack, negotiating the gravel road, while snapping pictures of the runners and the open field before me. The buses and race vehicles had pulled away, kicking up dust as we made our way back to town. The last vehicle that passed was an ambulance. Talk about pressure.

After a few miles, the gravel gave way to hardtop. Civilization was getting closer. We started passing some homes, silos, and cows. As I passed a barn, the mooing was almost deafening. I thought the cows were being slaughtered, but I was told by a local it was a "happy sound" they were making. Okay, I'll buy that. Kind of like the sound a mouse makes when he sees cheese in a trap behind the refrigerator.

A local also told me the course was flat. It might have been on  paper, but on the roads it was a different story. There were long, gradual hills throughout the 26 miles. I continued to run slowly, yet felt no discomfort. At the halfway mark, I looked behind me and saw no one. With 13 miles to go, I started to pick up the pace and began to pass people. The first runner I passed was Jim Browder.

He was hobbling and said his foot was giving him a lot of problems. He was grimacing, but not quitting. Years later, I learned Jim's injured foot was actually dystonia, a neurological movement disorder in which muscle contractions cause twisting and repetitive movements. Not only did Jim finish this race, but in June of 2009, Jim had joined the elite group as having run a marathon in all 50 states.

Up ahead, I kept my eyes on the runners and slowly reeled them in. I passed runners on the downhill, uphill and on curves. I wasn't focused on mile markers, but on the next runner in front. At the steep hill beginning near mile 17, I kept my pace as I passed even more runners. At mile 22 on Poly Drive, they started passing me.

The biggest pain I suffered wasn't coming from my legs, but from my neck. The back of my neck felt like it was on fire, even though the day was cloudy. I sustained a burn from previous marathons from not applying sunblock. On this day I learned a lesson. Any slight movement of raising my arms, the pain was intense. I was sure my back was blistered. Surprisingly, it wasn't, but the pain lingered for weeks.

A right on Virginia Lane, a left on Parkhill, and a right on Third brought me 385 yards from the finish. Up ahead was the high school

stadium, as well as the finish, just ¾ of a mile around the track. Like an Olympic champion, I entered the track, but did something no Olympian had ever done. I stopped and took a picture of the finishing banner. The time on the clock read, "4:19:39." Slowly, but surely, I saw more of my friends whom I had met the night before. Some finished before me, others I watched enter the stadium. We had made it, but our trip wasn't over yet. I asked a race volunteer to point me back to the YMCA. There were still a few blocks to go.

At 6 a.m. in front of the YMCA, I shared a seat on the bus with Martha Corazzini. Now, over six hours later, we met up at the stadium and walked back to where our day began. Like two unwanted pets dropped off in the country, we found our way back. It's the life of a marathoner.

Familiar Faces
in
RAPID CITY, SOUTH DAKOTA

Mount Rushmore Marathon / SD

Sunday, October 10, 2004
Age 45

"Wait a minute, I know that guy. " I had to do a double take when I spotted the man sitting in the chair on the corner of 5th and St. Joe's, as I drove through downtown Rapid City. "That's Richard Nixon. What's he doing in South Dakota?" At the next block, I asked myself the same question when I saw Ronald Reagan standing outside the restaurant, and Dwight Eisenhower waiting to cross the street.

On every block there they were, Presidents of the United States, disguised as ordinary citizens, frozen in time in Rapid City. Later in the month, more presidential visits would follow with the unveiling of five more. Yes, this city was onto something. If you build it, they will come. That's something Gutzon Borglum had already known about over 70 years earlier.

In 1927, Borglum and his men came to the Black Hills to begin work on the sculpture of George Washington, Thomas Jefferson, Theodore Roosevelt, and Abraham Lincoln. The site was chosen because Borglum said it was this type of granite that could handle the carving of the four faces. Don't despair if you didn't make it to Rushmore this summer. With Washington's nose measuring 20 feet, his eyes 11 feet, and his forehead to chin 60 feet, they'll still be there next August. Geologists believe the faces will erode 1/10 per inch every one thousand years.

After visiting Rushmore a few times almost 30 years earlier, this trip would be my second in three weeks. The faces I saw in the Black Hills were beginning to look familiar. However, most of them weren't here because of their run to the White House, but instead their run to the finish line. Outside the Journey Museum in Rapid City, I boarded the big bus that would take runners to the pasta dinner at Mount Rushmore. The 30-minute drive gave everybody an opportunity to see four familiar faces. I saw them

A few rows behind me was Rodney Johnson of Richmond. In front of him was Albert Shum, whom I had dinner with in Bismarck. Across from him was Deo Jaravata, whom I've run with in three states. Sandy Harting was also here. I met her in Billings. There was constant chatter all the way to Rushmore.

What a contrast from the last time I came to Rapid City. I was alone. I toured the museum and then sat on a bench looking up to the Presidents. However, on this trip, the familiar faces weren't just in stone, they were here in person. They were wearing T-shirts from races I've run, wearing shoes from brands I own, and wearing smiles from people I know. With Deo and Albert from Los Angeles, Rodney and me from Richmond, we sat with Caroline Philson from Atlanta, Barb Wnek from St. Louis, and Don Huston from Ohio. On this night, there was a rush on Rushmore.

As the bus pulled away after our dinner from the Rushmore parking lot, I looked up to the illuminated faces one last time. Even with their large eyes, the Presidents weren't going to be able to see any runners during the following day's Mt. Rushmore Marathon. The route would be a few miles away.

It was sunny and a bit chilly when I stepped out of my car at Sioux Park. The 26.2 mile bus ride to the marathon start would trace our run. Sitting next to me was Gary Perusse. "Where are you from, Gary?" I asked. "Virginia," he replied. There are some days you just can't meet a stranger.

The marathon distance is grueling. You never know how it will treat you. There are times when it throws all types of weather at you, such as wind, rain, heat, or snow. Sometimes, the Marathon Monster will give you hills, mountains, or rough terrain. In South Dakota, the welcoming sign didn't look promising. The area was dotted with names that were bleak. This area was known for its *Black Hills*, *Badlands* and towns like *Lead* and *Deadwood*, which weren't too far from *Needles Highway*. How would you like to run on a road named that? You couldn't escape it. Right over the border was another fearful place called *Devil's Tower*. I found nothing upbeat about any of those names. Rapid City was the only positive name I knew. But this race was 26.2 miles and *Rapid* doesn't apply to me.

In the middle of Highway 385, twenty miles from Deadwood where Wild Bill Hickok was shot in the back, the bus reached its destination. Most of the runners donned sweatshirts and pants for the hour-long wait to run. I stayed in my singlet and shorts. Larry

Harding twice offered me a plastic bag to put on, but I declined each time. It was cool, but not uncomfortable. All indications showed the day was going to be hot. I could tolerate the low 50-degree feeling a few more minutes. With the music of Gloria Estefan playing, runners were stretching, talking, or visiting one of the many Porta Johns set up by the side of the road. The cows didn't know what to think.

A few minutes after the 9 a.m. start, I stopped to take a picture of one of the best posters I had ever seen. At the registration site the day earlier, I met Kristen Skidmore of Chesapeake, Virginia, who had come out to run and to visit her sister and mother. I asked the two to cheer for me. They did not disappoint. Michelle and her mom were holding a colorful poster that read, *"Go Paul. # 157. Richmond, VA."* Yes, there are days when you just can't meet a stranger.

It was a beautiful sunny day in South Dakota with fall colors beginning to show. The temperature was just about ideal, especially for mid October. That time of year, there was no telling what the weather could be like. For 10 miles we ran down the highway, with steep terrain on our left and golden fields across the street to the right. It was a beautiful setting, but the cars kept coming.

While running on a main highway, we were careful not to become "*deadwood*" on the main drag that went through there. Even with the country setting, there weren't a lot of secluded spots to go to if nature had to call. On average, I generally head for the woods on one or two occasions. I value my privacy, and in South Dakota, I veered across the street and down the embankment. I felt better, but I lost a lot of time. My buddy, Rodney, didn't lose half as much time. Up ahead I spotted my friend running, and then saw him take two steps to the left and stop. When you have to go, you have to go. He couldn't have cared less. That's so wonderful about this sport. We get away with so much. We stop traffic, we spit, we litter, and we pee right off the main highway.

At the 10-mile mark we turned left onto Highway 44. I stopped here too, but only to take a picture. Michelle and her mom were still holding my sign. I saw a lot of other signs too, but the names on those signs weren't represented by runners. In less than a month, South Dakotans would go to the polls. There were signs for Senate candidate John Thune and incumbent Tom Daschle. There were also signs for Bush/Cheney and Kerry/Edwards. Politicians and runners were both anxious for the race to end.

The course was easy on the legs, until shortly after the 17th mile. Runners who had covered the distance said this area was a quad killer. The sign up ahead, depicting a truck pointing straight down, indicated it was. The 11% grade was ideal for those on skateboards or bicycles. Still, I'd take *down* versus *up* any day. The course descended 1,150 feet over the next five miles. My energy was descending too.

The last two miles, I was moving as swiftly as the residents at the nearby convalescent home. I was feeling dizzy and ready to drop, but the course wouldn't let me. I had to press on. I was doing everything possible to keep moving. Coming into the park, with the finish around the bend, Larry Harding was cheering me on. He was holding his digital camera and asked if I wanted a still picture or a moving picture. It was a wonderful compliment. I didn't think I was moving. I crossed the finish line and immediately sprawled onto the ground, as other runners squeezed by.

My head was spinning and I was out of breath. I felt awful. The rest I needed most of all I couldn't get. It was 1:30 in the afternoon and my flight was in 90 minutes. I had to shower and get to the airport. I grabbed a couple of things off the food table, sprawled on the ground again, and then headed directly to the Porta John. I was huffing and puffing as if I had run a sprint. I started feeling better when I walked with Larry the couple of hundred yards to my car. I loosened my shoes and gave Larry some pictures from the Bismarck race we had run a month earlier.

With just a few minutes to spare, I boarded the small airplane for my flight to Minneapolis. On board were several runners who had finished much earlier than me. While sitting next to Jennifer, a woman whom I had just met, I told her she was on my mind when I went to the YMCA 30 minutes earlier. She appreciated my actions after I told her I paid $10 for a five-minute shower.

157 feeling like # 1

The benefits of running 26.2

Kids and Cups across America

South Dakota

Move over George!

Familiar faces at Mount Rushmore

Football and Flowers
in
HUNTINGTON, WEST VIRGINIA

Healthy Huntington Marathon / WV

Sunday, November 14, 2004
Age 46

It's in the back of the mind of every marathoner. It's called, *Hitting the Wall*. It's the point in the race when your body has gone beyond its capacity to function, when your legs are screaming at you to stop, and your head is screaming at you for signing up to run this thing. Sometimes *The Wall* hits you at 20 miles or 24 miles or even 100 yards from the finish. Every race is different with that invisible wall standing somewhere along the course waiting for you to hit it. For an inaugural event, organizers of the Healthy Heart Marathon knew something long established marathons did not. Ronald Reagan would have been proud. The wall was coming down.

No matter how tired you must have felt from the hours upon hours of pounding the pavement, one simple gesture, made by a young college girl, took it all away. After receiving the carnation, the thought of running 25 miles had instantly vanished.

I remembered hearing about the tragedy 34 years earlier. The folks at Marshall University didn't want you to forget it. On November 14th, 1970, a plane carrying 75 people, including players, coaches, and staff members of the Marshall football team, crashed into a Wayne County, West Virginia hillside. There were no survivors. Lost were the dreams of lives cut short. I clutched my carnation and instantly felt a surge of strength that had come over me from young men and women whom I did not know. I followed the courses' maze through the beautiful campus, until I placed my flower in a box with others at the edge of a fountain. Pain from running a marathon? We should be so lucky.

On the anniversary of this tragic day, I felt connected to this school and a little ashamed on how I looked at Marshall University years earlier. I, along with my fellow students at Western Carolina University, didn't exactly embrace the Thundering Herd of Marshall. The two schools, over 300 miles away from one another, battled in the Southern Conference on playing fields and courts. When I came to Huntington, all I could think about was how Jay Kilgo, my sidekick at WWCU Radio, referred to the school across the airwaves. Jay had a habit of replacing the *H* with a *T* when the Thundering Herd came to town. Western Carolina students no longer hear such a thing. The team in the green and white moved up to a better division.

Excitement was in the air at the inaugural run of the Healthy Huntington Marathon. Marathoners, relay runners, and those registered in the half marathon walk, stood and stretched outside the Cam Henderson building on 3rd Street. Among the racers was Boonsom Hartman wearing number 100. The Chicago resident had run a marathon in every state and had run more marathons than the number on her shirt. Featured in *Runner's World* magazine, for not only her running accomplishments, but also for her ritual of applying lipstick between the 25 and 26-mile mark. Her notoriety has cosmetic companies sending her lipstick to sample and rank.

After a moment of silence in remembrance for those who died, and after the singing of the National Anthem, the running of the Healthy Huntington Marathon began. While most runners were settling in, trying to find the right pace, I was trying to find the right moment to take a picture. As I'm running, I take a quick glance from behind, waiting for a sizable gap so I can turn and snap a picture of runners coming toward me. I may not be very quick with my feet, but I'm quick with my fingers. No one has run over me yet.

At the first aid station, it was easy to tell this was the inaugural event. The table of drinks was a couple of feet from the curb, the drinks were toward the back of the table, and the water was in large plastic cups. Plastic cups are perfect for parties and picnics, but not for drinking on the run. I ran up on the curb, grabbed a cup, and put more on my shirt than in my mouth, as I continued down the road. Runners prefer paper cups so they can funnel it. It's also easier on the feet if you're stepping on them. Other aid stations in Huntington used cups that were just as bad - *Styrofoam*. However, on this day there wasn't much to complain about. On a day when they could be spending with their family or simply staying home, hundreds of volunteers cheerfully applauded our efforts and encouraged us along the way. There were the two young teenage girls holding colorful posters that read, *"Good Luck"* and *"You Can Do It."* There was the woman who tossed me a bagel, the man who got out of his car to cheer on the runners, and the one who played the music from *Rocky* that helped power us on.

The course weaved through all of Huntington. We passed big, beautiful homes by Ritter Park and not so big homes near an industrial park. Regardless of size, many of the homes had porches that told a story of the people who lived there. I saw flowers, pumpkins, and one house with two bowling pins standing on the porch railing. I thought it odd, but then figured, it's probably where they kept their *"spare"* key.

The day was perfect. Temperatures were in the low 50's, and the sun followed us throughout our trek. I ran very slowly in the beginning miles talking to Andy Sangray of Helena, Montana, and Steffen Schneider of Las Vegas. Andy and I were on a threshold. West Virginia was our 49th state to run a marathon. Steffen had run more marathons, but fewer states. The two would, most likely, converse again the following month on the streets of Honolulu. The 50th state would be Andy's 50th state.

On the "out and back" course, I passed Martha Corazzini, Boonsom Hartman, and Merrie Guyton. I shouted "hello" to the first, high-fived the second, and hugged the third. There was good reason for the latter. She was holding my car keys. At the halfway point, my time was 2 hours, 15 minutes. I was running slowly but felt no pain. The morning run was like a jog around town. I told myself once the 18-mile mark appeared, I would step up the pace. I started passing people while continuing to feel comfortable.

Up ahead I spotted a runner in a familiar red cap. It was Martha. The first thing she said was, "What are you doing here?" She thought I was miles ahead, but it was the other way around. She was feeling dizzy and very light-headed. Most people would have drastically reduced their speed or bowed out, but Martha never slowed. What my friend needed wasn't at an aid station, it was at a drug store. To see Martha at a coffee shop or around town, you'd never guess this lovely woman was a *Marathon Maniac*. On New Year's Day in 2007, she finished her 50th state. It was also her 100th marathon.

At the 20-mile mark I caught up with George Stump. "Hello, George, remember me? We met in Huntsville last year." The Cincinnati resident was wearing a 50 State Marathon shirt. I'd own one in three weeks.

The finish was coming soon. I felt like it had to. On the left was the huge Marshall University football stadium. We took a left, then another left, and then another left. Finally, the race marshal from Marshall pointed her finger down the ramp to the opening of the field. At the bottom of the ramp, I had my hands open to catch the pass. Yes, this marathon was different. A flower at 25, a football at 26. I stepped onto the green synthetic turf, which was softer than the mattress at the Holiday Inn, and ran the final 100 yards. I felt more energized than I had at the start, as I rushed down the field with the football tucked under my right arm. Forty yards to go, 30 yards to go, 25, 20, 15, 10, 5, TOUCHDOWN! What a thrill!

The issue of those plastic cups seemed secondary. The organizers of the inaugural running of this event, along with the residents and students of Marshall University, made this entire experience a spectacular one. Shame on you, Jay Kilgo.

Along the Ohio in West Virginia

All signs lead to a successful run

The $20,000 T-Shirt
in
BATON ROUGE, LOUISIANA

Baton Rouge Beach Marathon / LA

Saturday, December 4, 2004
Age 46

Of the hundreds of race numbers prepared for the Baton Rouge Beach Marathon, none was more visible than number 50. It was the number race director, Craig Watson, hung in his office for months. Every day there it was, the red digit five and zero waiting for its rightful owner to pick it up. *"Mr. Watson, come here. I want you. The race is about to begin."*

I had anticipated this moment for 17 years, but it wasn't until the previous year when I knew which city where this moment would happen.

The distance from Kingwood, Texas, to Baton Rouge, Louisiana, is 285 miles. However, the scenic route from my first marathon of the year to my last would be 19,294 miles. It would be this route I'd need to take. From the Houston suburb of Kingwood, my AAA TripTik would take me north to Oklahoma City, then east to Maine, west to Wyoming, and farther west to Hawaii. From Hawaii, it was back to the mainland to Oregon, and then I'd bounce around the Dakotas with a stop in between in Montana. Farther on from Big Sky, it's Almost Heaven in West Virginia, and then if my wide body planes are on time and my thin body health holds up, it's down to the Bayou. Me, oh, my, it's going to be a lot of big fun.

Baton Rouge was more than just 26.2. Baton Rouge was 50, my 50th state to run a marathon. Craig Watson was waiting for me. It seemed appropriate Louisiana should be my 50th state. The state begins and is shaped like the Roman Numeral 50. Baton Rouge is located on the Mississippi River, the dividing line of all my marathons. Louisiana is home to New Orleans, America's number one party city. What better place to celebrate.

Louisiana is unique. The state has parishes, not counties, with several of those parishes below sea level. The state has a language all its own, a brand of cooking all its own, and a way of life all its own. Bayous and Bourbon Street, critters and Creole, pelicans and parishes, Louisiana, here I come.

After spending a couple of days in the New Orleans French Quarter, I was ready to drive the 80-mile trip north up I-10 to Baton Rouge. Louisiana's capital city had been on my mind for over a year. I was anxious to get there. Each time I read a sign with the words *Baton Rouge* on it, a feeling of emotion came over me with the thought, I can't believe this day has come.

Like the majority of my other marathon trips, I traveled to my 50th alone, but I had friends waiting for me. Cathy McCarty and Cynthia Christen of Tallahassee, Florida, specifically came to Baton Rouge to see me finish. Cathy, who finished her 50th state two months earlier in Maine, signed up to run the half marathon. Cynthia signed up to run the full. For Cynthia, this race would be a tune-up for her marathon in March, when she and her husband Ron would check off Hawaii as their 50th state. Richard Friedrichsen also came to Baton Rouge, but the 62-year-old Nebraska marathoner didn't come to see me. Baton Rouge would be his 50th state too. Yes, turning 50 never felt so good.

I made sure I wasn't going to cut it close to get to the starting line, as I had for far too many other events. I awoke at 5:15 a.m. and was out the hotel door within the hour. My first hurdle was done. I parked my car and found the start. As I walked across Stanford Avenue to the starting area, I was clutching a large envelope that was mailed to me days earlier. Inside was my *50 State and DC Finisher's* shirt. I paid $15 to order it, but in a few short hours it would cost me $20,000 to wear it. I handed the package to a race volunteer, and asked Cathy if she would have it ready for me once I crossed the line. She said she was happy to do it.

As I had done in 49 other states, I stood in the sea of runners with my finger on my watch timer waiting for the word to run. At 7 a.m. I pressed the button. The route got picturesque in a hurry. We ran through beautiful neighborhoods, under huge oaks, along a mammoth lake, and through a sprawling university campus. For any runner who missed all that, they had another chance on this double-loop course. Quite simply, Baton Rouge was one of the nicest courses I had ever run on.

In a city of over 200,000, organizers did a terrific job of keeping us away from busy streets. Thankfully, this race day wasn't game day. Baton Rouge is home to the LSU Tigers, the defending national football champs. On this day the football stadium was empty. On Nicholson Drive we passed the LSU baseball field on our left, with the football stadium and basketball arena across the street. We turned right onto the campus and by the banners that read, *"Geaux Tigers."*

My mind was ready for this event, but my body wasn't. I felt sluggish and weighted down. Could it have been from the prerace gumbo the night before? Could it have been from the cheeseburgers and fries the day before that? Could it have been from the walking I did throughout the French Quarter? My last marathon was three weeks earlier, and I hadn't run much since. With 10 marathons already in the books for the year, I knew I could go the distance, but on this day in Baton Rouge, I wasn't able to *"Geaux"* very fast.

The finishing banner was up ahead. I was beginning to realize the feeling of running a marathon in every state, but the orange cones wouldn't let me get that sensation yet. Marathoners were instructed to stay to the left, while half marathoners were finishing up.

With my timer reading "2:25," I was confident I could run a faster second half. I immediately picked up my pace. I knew exactly where I needed to go and I knew how to get there. I ran by one runner after another while constantly thinking about the threshold I was about to cross. With seven miles to go, I was looking directly at the finishing area, but a narrow body of water stood in between. The course turned left, under I-10, and by the part of the lake where I had seen hundreds of pelicans on my first loop.

The 26-mile marker was up ahead. I stopped to take a picture with only 385 yards to go. I turned right onto Stanford Avenue and saw the banner I assisted in setting up five hours earlier. From across the street, I heard my name called and a congratulatory remark. On my right, was Cathy McCarty who held the magical package. In front of me the banner was getting closer, and then ... I finished. I sliced 30 minutes off my second loop finishing in 4:22:30. Cathy handed me the bag and I tore into it. I put on my $20,000 shirt.

At the awards ceremony, Craig Watson, whispers to me saying, "You're up first." He presents me with a beautiful plaque, as having run my 50th state in Baton Rouge. Craig also honors Richard Friedrichsen, who finished six minutes in front of me. Unbeknownst to me, Craig Watson, himself, had already conquered the same feat a year earlier.

As the race winners are being announced, I sat on the cooler of drinks, holding my prize and feeling proud of what I had accomplished. Hours later, I'm treated to a wonderful dinner by Cynthia and Cathy, as they remind me, "Today was my day." They didn't disappoint.

That evening, as I drove back to New Orleans, the emotion came out as I called my parents informing them, "I had done it." My journey began in 1987 in Richmond, Virginia. On this night, it ended in *The Big Easy*, but after 17 years, 50 states, and 60 marathons, it was anything but.

Cathy McCarty welcomes two more members into her elite club (with Richard Friedrichsen)

The $20,000 T-Shirt

319

THE ROAD TO BOSTON

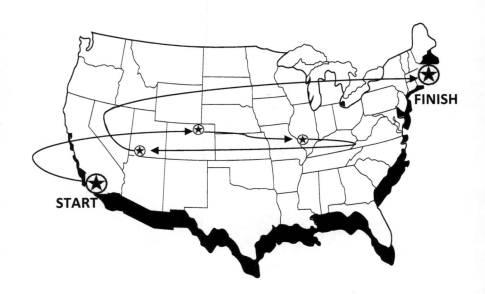

I had already run 60 marathons. I had the medals, certificates, and photos to prove it, as well as the 50 state names printed on T-shirts neatly folded on shelves in my closet. Although I ran on some of America's most beautiful avenues, trails, and byways, I knew something was missing. It wasn't running a marathon 6,000 miles from home; I had already run in Hawaii. It wasn't running to the top of the world; I had already run Pikes Peak. It wasn't running in America's largest city; I had already run in New York. The marathon I was missing was right in my home state's backyard. It was *Boston*. I believed my marathon journey would not be complete without it. I had to experience *Boston*.

You had to qualify to run the Boston Marathon. Other marathons had qualifying standards as well, but those were: A) be of a certain age and B) have the necessary funds to back up your registration check. Boston had that too, but they also had another little requirement. You had to have already run an official measured 26-mile, 385-yard marathon within a certain time. For a 46-year-old male, such as me, the time would have to be 3:30:00 or less. I hadn't pulled one of those off in 10 years. In fact, I had only run that fast in 5% of my races. Still, I had decided 2005 would be my year to pull it off again.

LOS ANGELES, CALIFORNIA

In March I ran the Los Angeles Marathon. Amazingly, I finished the race. I hardly slept the night before and I had hardly trained since my last marathon three months earlier. During that time, I had run a total of two hours. That's it! Which proves there's something to be said about running 11 marathons the year before: you do, in fact, have a little in reserve after long layoffs.

If there was a motto to the L.A. Marathon, it would have been *"Celebrations and Cell Phones."* The celebration began at the start when Muhammad Ali waved to me, but he could have been waving to the 19,984 other runners who waved at him. I still wondered how I got bib number *21158*. Needless to say, I was deep in the pack, while single digit bib number wearers, with names such as Kipkemboi, Kimutai, and Mbithi, were farther up front.

I doubt the runners up front were witnessing what I was seeing. I saw many jovial runners talking on their cell phones. There was even a cell phone station set up during the race, where you could call a friend for free. Perhaps some of those calls were to get tickets for that evening's Academy Awards presentation. Most likely, marathon spectator, Halle Berry, was on her cellphone. The Academy Award winning actress would have preferred a carpet that was magic, instead of red. Blocked streets caused delays for many Hollywood Stars. It would be the last day when both events would be held on the same day.

It was an interesting experience running in La-La Land. I passed the Beverly Hills sign, saw the Hollywood sign, and passed several stop signs when I wanted to do just that. I struggled badly. Finishing near the Staples Center, home of basketball's Lakers and hockey's Kings, in a time of 5:21:66, I was glad my game was over. Proper training, I had learned, had its merits. I promised myself I would do better the next time.

FORT COLLINS, COLORADO

Two months after running L.A., I headed back to the state where I recorded my slowest marathon. I was headed to Colorado. However, this time I drove in the opposite direction of Pikes Peak and settled for Fort Collins. The beautiful "point to point" course was run along the Cache La Poudre River Canyon in the Roosevelt National Forest.

My running was slow, yet steady, with my fastest surge coming after the 12-mile mark. There was good reason. I looked across the river and saw a bear. The animal started to run. I immediately thought back to the lesson I had learned on how to outrun a bear, by making sure I outran the person next to me. Although the bear would have had to cross the river to get to us, I never looked back. I also never looked back to that runner, not knowing if he ever finished the race ... or survived it. However, after the bear incident, it made me wonder why the race was dedicated to "Wiley," America's #1 Running Canine, but perhaps, not the fastest.

My award in finishing the race was a beautiful medal and a souvenir drinking glass, as well as the nifty nylon shirt I received the night before. It was all worth my Colorado adventure and my 5:10:56 time. Although it was 11 minutes faster than L.A.'s, it was still a long way off to get me to Boston. So, I decided to head farther east to get a better view. Remembering St. Louis had that big arch with an observation deck, I decided to go there.

ST. CHARLES, MISSOURI

Beginning the first quarter of the year, with very low training miles, I had made considerable gains by the time September's race had surfaced. I was praying for a much faster time in Missouri. I was praying for St. Charles. Would it matter I wasn't Catholic? Located 30 miles from St. Louis, the Lewis and Clark Marathon was held in St. Charles, Missouri. It would be my first visit to St. Charles, but not to Lewis and Clark. Their presence had been with me in a couple of races the previous year in Bismarck and Billings. I was counting on "three time's the charm."

The course stayed close to the Missouri River and I stayed close to my water. I carried my water bottle the entire time, running relatively hard throughout the race. In prior events, I'd conserve energy in the early miles, so I wouldn't feel flat at the end. However, during the previous few years not only did I start slowly, I ended slower. I was a little nervous with the "start fast" approach, but stuck to the game plan. I kept me head up and focused on finishing with a much better time than I had demonstrated in L.A. and Fort Collins. The course consisted of pavement and dirt trails and one steep hill, to be run twice on this double-loop course. When I came to water stations, I made the liquid transfer from cup to bottle, and then ran on. I also carried the energy gel, *GU*. Yes, in St. Charles, I had my hands full.

After the race, I got my postrace goodies of Cokes and hot dogs in the lobby of the multipurpose, Family Arena. I settled in Section 102 to enjoy them. Coincidently, the section number also marked my finishing place amongst the 453 runners. I was pleased, especially with my time of 3:50:11. Still too slow for Boston, but I was pleased I was getting closer.

After finishing the race in St. Charles, Missouri, on Sunday, September 18th, I was thinking about the next marathon on my calendar to another Saint city to the west. It would be another opportunity to qualify for Boston. My training had definitely shown improvement during the past few months, but how much could I improve by the next race, especially when that next race was only 14 days away? Regardless, I was determined to press on.

ST. GEORGE, UTAH

From the glitz of the Las Vegas Strip, you have to travel 120 miles north on Interstate 15, until you get to Exit 6. Next, you turn left on Bluff Street and go for about three miles. Now, make this left-hand turn, up that steep hill, until you get to the Rococo Motel, right by the airport. Get out of your car and walk over to the edge of the cliff and look. It's a view of one of the most beautiful cities in America, a jewel of a place in the southwest corner of Utah. Welcome to St. George.

The pace of this Utah town of 70,000 isn't as fast as that Nevada metropolis you came from. You'll find no casino, no bright lights, and if it's Sunday night, you may not find many people. When it comes to competing with Las Vegas, only the clock is faster. It's always one hour ahead. Speed comes in another form here as well. The St. George Marathon is rated as one of the fastest marathons in the country. On October 1st, 2005, I was going to find out.

The start of the St. George Marathon began at the finish. Beginning at 4 a.m. from Worthen Park in central St. George, yellow school buses transported runners 26.2 miles away. The good news was the bus climbed over 2,500 feet in elevation. The buses' engines might not have liked that, but knowing I would be running back down would please my engine.

The scene at the start reminded me of what I had seen at the Lost Dutchman Marathon in Arizona, as fire logs warmed the waiting runners. This time, however, I didn't hover. Instead, I paced and concentrated on the miles ahead of me. This race would be my best chance to qualify for Boston. Martha Corazzini, who had run the course many times, told me my St. George finish time would be about 20 minutes faster than my average marathon time. After running a 3:50 marathon two weeks earlier, twenty minutes was all I needed.

As I stood waiting for the start, I truly believed I had the training behind me to qualify for Boston, but was I trained mentally? Moments before the race, I decided I would not concentrate on the miles, but on the Mellors. I would dedicate each mile to members of my family.

From the start to mile 10, I dedicated the time to my young sons, Ben and Max. I thought only of them, their smiles and the wonderful times we share together. From miles 10 to 15, I brought my father on the run. For a man who had always been with me throughout my life, taking him with me for 5 short miles was easy. From 15 to 20 miles, I mentally ran with my mother. Her positive attitude and energy helped power me through some of those tough miles.

Like clockwork, I was constantly running 8-minute miles. I held packets of *GU* in my left hand, with more packets inside my pack strapped around my waist. In my right hand was my water bottle. St. George wasn't all downhill, as I learned from running miles 7 through 11, but my pace wasn't compromised.

After mentally escorting my mother to the viewing stand after her 5-mile run, I took my older brother, Duke, along. The sound of his name shows how tough he is. As a young boy, he heard the name associated with a tough guy on television. Afterward, he told our mother, "I want to be called Duke." The name stuck, which eliminated any confusion when his son, David, was called for dinner.

After dedicating a mile to Duke, I dedicated the next mile to my brother, Tom. Perhaps my older brother should have taken his name. He was tough too. Tom battled through arthritis as a young teen, yet at age 22, the Boston College, All American hockey player, won a silver medal in the 1972 Winter Olympic Games in Sapporo, Japan. On this day he was helping me get my medal.

Picking up mile 23, I dedicated the next 8 minutes to my brother, Don. Oh how he would have enjoyed this breathtaking beauty of sheer rock, but he knew all about it. His book, *American Rock*, found in bookstores throughout the country, explores the region, rock, and culture in American climbing. No wonder I had always looked up to him.

At mile 24, I thought only of my older sister, Joan. Just an age difference of a year-and-a-half, she had maturity that widened the gap. Always hardworking and responsible, Joan knew about payroll taxes long before I did. Although I was enjoying my moments in Utah, Joan already had them. She graduated from Utah State University, even met her future husband there.

At mile 25, still on an 8-minute per mile pace, I dedicated that stretch to my sister, Jackie. There are some people who just light up a room with their presence. Mile 25 was nothing but sunshine. If you'd want someone to be a ham or cook one, you'd want my sister involved. This could be the reason my parents stopped having children. You couldn't get much better than her.

At mile 26, I turned the St. George Marathon into a family affair. I mentally ran with Max, Ben, my Mom and Dad, Duke, Tom, Don, Joan, and Jackie. They pushed when my legs needed it most.

To qualify for the Boston Marathon, I needed a run of 3:30:00 or less. I was cutting it close when I turned down the final straightaway. I could see the finishing area far down the road, as I moved by one city block after another.

In 63 prior marathons, I had always thought about myself, constantly gauging how I felt, constantly thinking, "C'mon Paul, do it." On this day my thoughts focused only on others. In return, they helped me. The time on the clock proved it: **3:29:29**. Boston Marathon here I come.

BOSTON, MASSACHUSETTS

It was *THE* marathon of all marathons. It was the Granddaddy of them all. First run in 1897 with a field of 15, (a third of them dropped out), the Boston Marathon had become a showcase for the elite, with thousands more all part of the show. It was a privilege for me to be invited.

I had often wondered what it would have been like to stand in the outfield with the great Willie Mays or to be in the huddle with Tom Brady, or to be on the court with Michael Jordan. I knew the closest I would ever come to living those dreams was just a box seat away. The ushers wouldn't let me get any closer. The sport of marathoning was different. The Boston Marathon gave me an opportunity to share the same arena with world class athletes. I would experience, as they would, a Boston Marathon bib number pinned on my shirt, and hear the shouts of support from thousands of fans along the way on a playing field we'd all share.

If history was going to repeat itself, I hoped it would come from the 1905 race. That year, with 42 runners, the first one to cross the line was Sammy Mellor. Although his name was never on my family tree, it would be Mellor's leading the way on the morning of the marathon. With son in the back seat, Mom and Dad occupied the front, steering the way toward the start in Hopkinton. Having family nearby, including a brother who lived 12 miles from the start, made this event extra special for me.

The start of the 2006 Boston Marathon resembled a scene from the Fort Worth Stockyards. That's bad news for occupants of the latter, good news for occupants of the former. Runners were corralled according to their expected finishing time, while elite runners didn't have to put up with such a thing. They got a 10-minute head start. I slipped in with thousands of runners on this chilly, gray Massachusetts Monday, better known as Patriot's Day, a state holiday commemorating the anniversary of the Battles of Lexington and Concord.

Each direction I turned, I saw runners who looked serious and fit. I'm sure to them, Monday, April 17th, 2006, had long been circled on their calendars. Unfortunately, for one runner a serious look turned into sadness. I saw him come up lame after stepping on debris minutes into the race. From a downhill in Hopkinton, the course went through Ashland, Framingham, Natick, and onto Wellesley. The girls of Wellesley College were out in force, screaming and yelling, as if *The Beatles* had rolled through town. Many of them had signs that read, "*Kiss Me.*" I reluctantly continued running.

The Boston Red Sox, playing their annual Patriots Day game near the 25-mile mark, were losing to the Seattle Mariners. Runners were kept up-to-date with the score posted on chalkboards at many points along the course. My running was strong throughout most of the race, until I started to cool off near Coolidge Corner, with only a few miles to go. I felt dizzy and nauseous. Spectators were very enthusiastic, but I ignored them, while thinking, this isn't fun anymore. To my right I could see Fenway Park. I was feeling as badly as when I had walked there from Cranston with my brother over 30 years earlier.

The crowds got thicker while I got sicker. I pressed on, but my steps were far from Sammy Mellor's steps over 100 years earlier. I turned onto Boylston Street, a street I've walked on numerous times during my many visits to Boston so long ago. I could see the banner up ahead. Strangely, my pace got a tad quicker and I finished. I had done it. I had run the Boston Marathon in 3:57:39.

After getting my finisher's medal, refreshment, and a Boston Marathon Heatsheet Blanket, I got the best prize of all, my father's embrace. I felt a lot better, and so did Boston. The Red Sox came back to win in the 9th inning.

A father's embrace after running the 2006 Boston Marathon

Max Mellor, 11 (July 2010)

Ben Mellor, 11 (July 2010)

Standing tall in 2018
(James River High School graduation)

Front l to r, Duke, Dad (Don) back row with Don and Tom (2008)

Mom (Helen) and sister, Joan Allison

sister, Jackie Sidle

In my high school yearbook there's a picture of my friend, Bernie McLaughlin. His determined look indicates he's about to win a race. Bernie is outdoors, wearing shorts, on a trail, and looking lean. On another page there's a picture of me. I'm indoors, wearing over 40 pounds of padding, and positioned in front of a goal. What's the matter, Bernie? Don't you know how to have fun?

Why would anyone want to sign up for Track and Field? It's boring, laborious, and every day it's the same, today we run. Hockey was different. I strapped on elbow and leg pads, a chest protector, a mask, and a pair of skates. I traveled to play in cold buildings, had pucks flying at me in different directions, and glanced over to the cheerleaders when the play was at the other end of the rink. Lucky for me I chose hockey. You miss so much when you run. Unfortunately, I learned something after the games were over, another team or another group would occupy your sheet of ice. Hockey had its limits. Running was pure and simple.

Bernie McLaughlin was smart, maybe that's why he got accepted to Harvard. Running was a sport you could do anytime, anywhere. It was an activity you could participate in, in any part of the country, and in any part of the world. And yes, you could have fun doing it.

Sadly, for Bernie McLaughlin the finish line came too soon. On December 21st, 1988, after boarding a Pan Am flight from London to New York, his plane exploded over Lockerbie, Scotland. My parents sent to me newspaper clippings of the terrorist attack. I studied Bernie's picture and thought about this remarkable person, who had already accomplished so much, yet whose innocent life was tragically taken.

I remembered in high school how badly Bernie felt when he accidentally sprained my ankle when we wrestled in gym class. The injury caused me to miss a few hockey games. It was more painful for me standing behind the Plexiglass watching my teammates. A handicapped goalie doesn't play.

In the sport of marathoning, almost everyone is handicapped in one way or another. Those who stand on the starting line in Newport or

New York, Greenville or Greensboro, or Salt Lake or Storm Lake, had overcome something. Everybody had a story. Everybody had made a sacrifice. Everybody had endured. If not, the marathon would do it for you.

There were participants with artificial legs, in wheelchairs, visually impaired, and those with brand new knees. I've met people who had beaten cancer, had open heart surgery, were diabetic, and those who had eaten too many sweets. There were runners who were healthy, but handicapped, without a chance of winning. They ran too much, ran too little, or ran too often. They were young, they were old, they were tall, they were short, they were male, they were female. Some pushed strollers, some held flags, and some carried cameras. I've seen runners wearing boots, runners wearing sandals, and one runner who jumped rope for 26.2 miles. One thing they all had in common was they loved life.

When I signed up to run my first race, I never expected what the marathon would give me. Granted, each race put up a wall, but each race gave me a new view once I climbed over it. The marathon distance was always the same, but over 17 years I treated the marathon differently. In my first few races, my goal was to just finish. Twenty-six miles almost seemed impossible to walk, yet alone run, and then it's another 385 yards to the end. What's up with that? Later, my goal was to run fast enough to enter the granddaddy of them all, the Boston Marathon. Approaching the 100th running of the event, I tried hard to qualify. In Delaware, my time of 3:21:20 was six minutes too slow. Suddenly, my plan shifted once I signed up to run Big Sur in California. I brought a camera. It was the best thing I could have ever done. My focus was on capturing moments.

The marathon is a grueling event that slows your pace, no matter how swiftly you're going. You can't help but notice the beauty of nature. You can't help but notice the beauty in people. You can't help but appreciate life. How was the marathon able to do this? It brought me to a Utah mountain at 4 o'clock on a cool, summer morning, to be awestruck by thousands of bright stars illuminating the dark sky. At this hour, who else would have experienced such a splendid site, than only the fools who had signed up to run the Deseret News Marathon.

Do you know what beauty is? It's sitting by a flickering fire on an Arizona mountaintop, looking at a full moon behind a giant Saguaro Cactus. Why would anyone come to this place hours before the sun? Not many would, except those who were running the Lost Dutchman Marathon.

Have you ever felt mesmerized by an artist's canvas? I have. It came from the Hand of God when I ran the rim around Crater Lake in Oregon. I had never seen anything more stunning.

In Northern Minnesota there's a winding trail cutting through a thick green forest. The scenic route goes on for miles, but unless you're standing on a track behind Walker High School, I'd have trouble telling you how to get there.

On Ocean Drive in Newport the wind whips at you from the Atlantic and you can almost taste the salt. But to experience this, you had to get out of your car, or better yet, run the Rhode Island Marathon.

The lava fields of Hawaii are so vast one could easily get lost. Civilization seemed as if it were half a world away. I never would have ventured out without a compass, a companion, or a complimentary meal. Running in the Kilauea Volcano Marathon I got all three.

There are autumn leaves and then there are autumn leaves. I saw the difference while running on New Hampshire's country roads during a crisp September morning. Seeing them zigzag to the ground, while I exited a covered bridge, gave me another appreciation to this wondrous season.

The marathon gave me emotions of every kind. I felt tall when I stood atop Pikes Peak in Colorado but felt tiny when I stood under Montana's big sky. I felt patriotic when I raised my head before seeing the four faces in South Dakota but felt sadness when I lowered it after seeing the 168 chairs in Oklahoma. I felt a sense of gratitude to the Iowa farmer when I ran past the field that he was plowing. I felt a sense of bravery to Civil War soldiers when I ran past the Georgia fields where they once fought.

The marathon gave me a peek of America which I could have never gotten from a car, a train, a bike, or a book. I had covered America on asphalt, concrete, dirt, cobblestone, gravel, grass, lava, synthetic turf, and the stuff high school tracks are made of. I saw the best of America on all types of terrain.

Running marathons was like a political campaign. Candidates who run for President feel privileged to have traveled the country meeting so many wonderful people. The long campaign affords them to see the best of America in coffee shops, town halls, and auditoriums. Those who run for Congress or County Commissioner can only wonder. My campaign was a landslide. I won in every state.

When asked, "Where are the nicest people?" I answer, "Everywhere." I had strangers handing me bananas, bagels, and drinks in every state. I was applauded for my efforts when it rained in Maine, when it was hot in Hawaii, and when it was windy in Wyoming. In every state, in every town, I witnessed cheerful volunteers who gave me a cup of water, clapped their hands, and shouted support to me. Often, they did it without ever knowing my name.

Each marathon I registered to run, I never knew what I was getting myself into. I knew only one thing: The marathon would be stretched out for 26 miles, 385 yards. The sites I'd see and the people I'd meet were the unknowns.

I never would have imagined a South Dakota woman would personally prepare a sign for me reading, "*Go Paul.*" Who would have guessed a Kentucky couple would give me keys to their log cabin home when I had no other place to stay? Can you imagine the joy it brought to my father when I told him I visited his WWII Navy buddy in Sartell, Minnesota?

It was my father and mother, both WWII veterans in the Navy and Coast Guard, respectively, who gave me an appreciation of being an American. Who would have imagined just by putting a map on a wall would be the beginnings to so much this country has to offer?

I hope I can do the same for my two sons. I don't know whether they'll want to run marathons. At their age, it's too early to tell. But recently, I noticed something while they were eating their cereal. The eyes of both Ben and Max were fixed to the map on the kitchen wall. Could it be, I wondered, they were counting the states that border Missouri?

<u>Running Facts</u>

Years to run a marathon in every state
17 years, October, 1987 - December, 2004

Age from 1st to 50th state
28 - 46 years old

Longest layoff between marathons
1 year, 8 months. October, 1999 - June, 2001

Shortest time between marathons
8 days - September 11 - September 19, 2004

Most marathons run in one year
11 in 2004

Least marathons run in one year
0 in 1990 and **2000**

Total marathons run
66

Multiple states
**VA (7), MD (4), MA (2), CA (2), UT (2),
CO (2), MO (2)**

Fastest marathon
3:21:20 - Delaware. December 10, 1995

Slowest marathon
9:49:49 - Colorado. August 19, 2002

Coldest temperature
15° - Delaware

Warmest temperature
80° - Arizona

Earliest start
5:00 a.m. - Kansas, Utah, Arizona, Mississippi

Latest start
7:00 p.m. - Massachusetts

Largest field
29,345 - New York

Smallest field
35 - Washington

Plane trips
(30) Maine, Arkansas, Louisiana, Indiana, Arizona, Oklahoma, North Dakota, Minnesota, Iowa, Illinois, Missouri, Nebraska, Kansas, Colorado, Mississippi, Wyoming, New Mexico, Nevada, California, Hawaii, Oregon, Washington, Alaska, South Dakota, Texas, Wisconsin, Massachusetts, Montana, Idaho, Utah

Car trips
(19) New Hampshire, Alabama, Rhode Island, Ohio, Connecticut, New Jersey, Delaware, Virginia, West Virginia, Pennsylvania, Maryland, North Carolina, District of Columbia, South Carolina, Georgia, Florida, Tennessee, Kentucky, Michigan

Car/Boat trips
Vermont

Train trips
New York

338

Marathons run while wearing running tights
(2) Pennsylvania and Delaware

Sick and vomited on course
(3) Colorado, Texas, Oregon

Indoor finishes
(3) Shamrock Marathon (VA Beach), Nebraska

Track finishes
(5) North Carolina, Alaska, New Jersey, Minnesota, Florida, Montana

State Capitols seen while on course
(5) Virginia, Oklahoma, Utah, North Dakota, Ohio

Most scenic
California

Windiest
Wyoming

Most unusual sighting
Frozen turkey on side of road in Nebraska

Best pasta dinner
Hawaii

Best food at finish
Utah

Heavy downpour
Massachusetts

Snow falling
(2) Pennsylvania and Wyoming

Course goes in National Forest/Monument and/or Park
(6) New Mexico, Oregon, Hawaii, Wyoming, Georgia, Washington D.C.

Crosses border
Delaware into Maryland**, Kentucky** in and out of West Virginia, **Michigan** into Canada

Best mile markers
Nevada - helium balloons

Best aid station
Maine - Water and Gatorade signs on volunteers

Best medal
Arizona

Best shirt
West Virginia

Marathon months
January, **3**
February, **3**
March, **6**
April, **4**
May, **6**
June, **4**
July, **3**
August, **4**
September, **8**
October, **9**
November, **10**
December, **6**

Marathon days
> Monday, **1**
> Tuesday, **1**
> Thursday, **1**
> Friday, **1**
> Saturday, **25**
> Sunday, **37**

Longest drives after race stopping only for fuel
> **646 miles   Huntsville - Richmond**
> **614 miles   Detroit - Richmond**
> **477 miles   Columbus - Richmond**

Miles driven to and from marathons
> **23,000**

Air miles to and from marathons
> **100,000**

Plane tickets, rental cars, gasoline, hotel accommodations, new shoes, registration fees, speeding tickets, sleeping bag
> **$20,000**

Having run a marathon in every state
> **Priceless**

Marathon Schedule

1987
Richmond Newspapers Marathon   Richmond, VA
Marine Corps Marathon   Washington, DC

1988
Shamrock Marathon   Virginia Beach, VA
Tour Baltimore Marathon   Baltimore, MD
Richmond Newspapers Marathon   Richmond, VA

1989
Pittsburgh Marathon   Pittsburgh, PA
Greensboro Marathon   Greensboro, NC

1990
Las Vegas Marathon   Las Vegas, NV
Washington's Birthday Marathon   Greenbelt, MD
Rhode Island Marathon   Newport, RI

1991
Washington's Birthday Marathon   Greenbelt, MD
Shamrock Marathon   Virginia Beach, VA
Chicago Marathon   Chicago, IL
Upstate Marathon   Greenville, SC

1993
Jacksonville Marathon   Jacksonville, FL
Shamrock Marathon   Virginia Beach, VA

1994
Lake Geneva Marathon   Lake Geneva, WI
Richmond Newspapers Marathon   Richmond, VA
New York City Marathon   New York, NY

1995

Vermont City Marathon	Burlington, VT
Columbus Marathon	Columbus, OH
Delaware Marathon	Middletown, DE
Last Train to Boston Marathon	Aberdeen, MD

1996

Big Sur International Marathon	Carmel, CA
Mayor's Midnight Sun Marathon	Anchorage, AK
White Sands/Alamogordo Marathon	Alamogordo, NM

1997

Jersey Shore McMarathon	Long Branch, NJ
East Lyme Marathon	East Lyme, CT
Omaha Riverfront Marathon	Omaha, NE

1999

Detroit International Marathon	Detroit, MI

2001

High Plains Marathon	Goodland, KS
Deseret News Marathon	Salt Lake City, UT
Puget Sound Marathon	Elma, WA
Clarence DeMar Marathon	Keene, NH
Spirit of St. Louis Marathon	St. Louis, MO
Chickamauga Battlefield Marathon	Chickamauga, GA

2002

Smoky Mountain Marathon	Townsend, TN
Hatfield and McCoy Marathon	Goody, KY
Pikes Peak Marathon	Manitou Springs, CO
Pocatello Marathon	Pocatello, ID
SunTrust Richmond Marathon	Richmond, VA

2003

Lost Dutchman Marathon	Apache Junction, AZ
Hogeye Marathon	Fayetteville, AR
Marathon to Marathon	Marathon, IA
Run Around the Lake Marathon	Wakefield, MA
Tupelo Marathon	Tupelo, MS
Walker North Country Marathon	Walker, MN
Indianapolis Marathon	Lawrence, IN
Rocket City Marathon	Huntsville, AL

2004

Texas Marathon	Kingwood, TX
Oklahoma City Memorial Marathon	Oklahoma City, OK
Sugarloaf Marathon	Eustis, ME
Wyoming Marathon	Laramie, WY
Kilauea Volcanoes Marathon	Volcanoes National Park, HI
Crater Lake Marathon	Crater Lake National Park, OR
Bismarck Marathon	Bismarck, ND
Montana Marathon	Billings, MT
Mount Rushmore Marathon	Rapid City, SD
Healthy Huntington Marathon	Huntington, WV
Baton Rouge Beach Marathon	Baton Rouge, LA

2005

Los Angeles Marathon	Los Angeles, CA
Fort Collins Old Town Marathon	Fort Collins, CO
Lewis and Clark Marathon	St. Charles, MO
St. George Marathon	St. George, UT

2006

Boston Marathon	Boston, MA

2014

Anthem Richmond Marathon	Richmond, VA